The Twentieth-Century
American West

The Twentieth-Century American West

A Potpourri

Gene M. Gressley

University of Missouri Press
Columbia & London, 1977

For Earl Pomeroy

Copyright © 1977 by
The Curators of the University of Missouri
University of Missouri Press, Columbia, Missouri 65201
Library of Congress Catalog Card Number 76–56903
Printed and bound in the United States of America

Library of Congress Cataloging In Publication Data

Gressley, Gene M   1931–
    Essays on the twentieth-century West.

    CONTENTS: Colonialism and the American West.—The
French, Belgians, and Dutch come to Salt Creek.—
Arthur Powell Davis, reclamation, and the West. [etc.]
    1.   The West—History—1848—1950—Addresses, essays,
lectures. 2. The West—History—1951—   —Addresses,
essays, lectures. I. Title.
F595.G828   978'.03   76–56903
ISBN 0–8262–0218–7

Foreword and Acknowledgments

These essays are not proffered as a tightly structured, unified volume on the history of the twentieth-century West. They are submitted as a collection of essays illustrating ideas and themes that have impressed the writer and numerous other historians as possessing validity in the restless quest for a *leitmotif* of the contemporary West.

These essays are intended to be evocative; the historicist will find little of comfort in the following pages. Many of the motifs in the individual essays could be magnified into full-length tomes. From the over-all increase in quality, as well as quantity, in the historiography of the West in the recent past, there is every indication that our chosen field of historical investigation is, at last, at the "take-off" point in the Rostow sense.

Over the years, the writer has increasingly fallen in arrears in acknowledging the *pourboire* that he owes other historians. Through their communication, criticism, and undefinable transference, perhaps best described as *osmosis*, their impact on the writer's thought will be self-evident.

Though the list would be lengthy, it would be a pleasure and a privilege to acknowledge each historian individually. To do so might perhaps result in a modicum of embarrassment to those recognized, but inevitably it would result in omission. Therefore, though I express my gratitude, those historians who should have appeared here will recognize their contributions on the following pages.

One historian-teacher-friend, whose impact on the writer is beyond calculation, has been registered on the dedication page. It would be impossible for me to assess or comprehend the debt that I owe him.

My appreciation to Mrs. Esther Kelley, Archives Assistant, who has not only typed several drafts of this manuscript, but who manages to keep the "shop" running while the undersigned broods about the unknown, and travels to the known.

Finally, to Joyce, Deborah Ellyn, and David Randolph, who have allowed their husband and father to unmercifully exploit their time; and have permitted dozens of historical personages at the dinner table—my thanks. As the years pass, the debt grows enormously, never to be erased.

Gene M. Gressley
Laramie, Wyoming
5 January 1977
Windy, clear, and 29°

Contents

These two eastern gentlemen on the Sturgis-Goodell Ranch of eastern Wyoming in the 1880s banished cultural colonialism when they introduced Oriental prints, china, and portraits as decorative items for their ranch living room. Perhaps the only occasion on which they were aware of economic colonialism was in the autumn when they marketed their cattle.

An early "gusher" in the Salt Creek field of central Wyoming (circa 1910). Oil field sights such as this provoked efficiency-conservation sermons from George Otis Smith and Henry L. Doherty. Both gentlemen lived long enough to see the federal and state governments and the petroleum industry take their first tentative steps toward unitization, proration, and other conservation policies that Smith and Doherty had enthusiastically advocated since the early 1920s. What many observers, including early conservationists, failed to realize or at least concede was that the early federal legislation favored the "first in time, first in right" concept of rampant, unregulated mineral resource development. Promoters and developers of the domain had little empathy for those who urged rational and slow growth of the West's economic wealth when they realized that if they did not quickly exploit their opportunities others would.

Henry Blackmer in full dress! "This man of the hour," as one of Blackmer's closest associates recalled, "could be a suave, congenial gentleman, a cold, hardboiled banker, a friendly, story-telling host, as the occasion required." Blackmer was all of that and more. An indefatigable negotiator, Blackmer, through persistence and entrepreneurial genius, molded the industrial chaos that was the Salt Creek scene into one integrated company—the Midwest Refining Company.

This sparkling vehicle represented the very latest in bulk station equipment. The filling station with mock tile roof and a shiny truck were daily evidence of the progressive, affluent, and aggressive marketing structure devised by the Midwest Refining Company in the 1920s.

Arthur Powell Davis soon after "enlisting" in the Reclamation Service. A distinguished engineer, Davis emphasized a creed that included Henry George's single-tax banner, the high value of efficiency, and the sanctity of private property. In essence, Davis brought to the reclamation program those Progressive tenets he had heard so often as a child.

A portion of the unfinished Salt River Project in Arizona in 1910, one of the earliest reclamation-irrigation projects with which Arthur Powell Davis was associated. For Davis the Salt River Project embodied many of the components of his reclamation policy: a sizable project with enormous potential for irrigation and hydroelectric power; a reverence for the private rights and initiatives to be included in a water resource program; and a long-range outlook for substantial profit and economic independence of the project.

A senator from Wyoming for almost thirty-five years, Francis E. Warren was first and foremost a political realist. Although few senators have ever excelled Warren in "wresting" funds from that well-guarded public treasury, few also have worried as much about federal encroachment on states' rights. In this attitude Warren reflected the views of his constituents.

This cartoonist's view of George Otis Smith—with geologic pick in hand and a far-off gaze in his eye—represents how many friends and associates remember this long-tenured director of the United States Geological Survey. In common with his friend and fellow bureau chief, Arthur Powell Davis, George Otis Smith found the canons of progressivism an appropriate guide for the Geological Survey. Along with a scientific appreciation for efficiency and a strong emphasis on the Benthamite philosophy of the greatest good for the greatest number, Smith strongly advocated a decentralized approach to the bureaucracy—especially in regard to those bureaucrats who managed conservation projects. Smith also reflected the tone and approach of his era by stressing cooperation with the natural resource industry.

The two antiadministration strategists of the famous 1937 "Court fight"—Senators Joseph C. O'Mahoney (*left*) and William E. Borah. Although a staunch and unrelenting Democrat, and a strongly partisan supporter of FDR, O'Mahoney's independent inclinations and his Progressive heritage triumphed on the Supreme Court packing plan with the inevitable break with President Roosevelt. While O'Mahoney might have occupied the national political doghouse for his opposition to the most popular figure of his age, in Wyoming O'Mahoney was never stronger than after his contretemps with Roosevelt on the Supreme Court issue.

Thurman Arnold looking his iconoclastic best. A western Progressive first and foremost, like his fellow Wyomingite and friend Senator O'Mahoney, Arnold discerned America's future in terms of less economic concentration, which he was convinced would insure America's democratic way of life. For he agreed with Dorothy Thompson's testimony before the Temporary National Economic Commission that economic concentration was the breeding ground for totalitarian regimes. In a remarkable letter to William Allen White, Arnold prophesied, "Liberalism in this country is going to change from faith in Government bureaucracy to the sort of thing that you have represented for so many years."

An American "original," Thurman Arnold's irreverent ways and speech were always good copy for journalists and cartoonists. One of Arnold's most enigmatic traits to both his backers and enemies was his propensity for attacking economic restraints wherever he uncovered them. As the result, Big Labor, Big Business, and Big Government all found themselves at one time or another under investigation by the Department of Justice. Arnold simply could perceive no reason for playing favorites among labor, industry, or government. While no one could quarrel with the judicial fairness of such a strategy, this approach assured Arnold's political demise.

Preface

A reporter and a politician boarded together a United Air Lines plane at the Los Angeles International Airport for a flight to San Francisco. The reporter welcomed the opportunity to have the former vice-president, recent presidential aspirant, and then-current California gubernatorial candidate to himself for a couple of hours. In turn, Richard Nixon appears to have looked forward to a relaxed informal conversation as they flew north. After a half hour or so of discussing the issues in the California campaign, Nixon began an analysis of Californians and their way of life. On the one hand, he saw his fellow citizens as hard-driving, forceful, "go-ahead people." He found much in their pattern of living that he could approve, even applaud. On the other hand, he discerned an erosion of the Puritan ethic. Life was almost too good: too much sun and leisure, a place where one could play golf every day under sunny skies; the result, the former vice-president put it quite bluntly, was simply that "some of our more creative people are not creating as much as they should." As another indication of the mañana malaise, he found a go-as-you-wish pace in the intellectual atmosphere. As he listened to his fellow Californians he heard a basic intellectual shallowness. He confided to Neil Morgan, his journalist seatmate, that after returning to Los Angeles from years in the East, he and Mrs. Nixon had been shocked to hear the banality of subjects under discussion at dinner parties and other social occasions. How really terribly "unsophisticated the conversational pace and the intellectual pace" seemed to the Nixons.[1]

1. Interview with Richard M. Nixon, Neil Morgan Collection, Western History Research Center, University of Wyoming, Laramie.

That Richard Nixon peered at the Westerner and saw a paradox should not be surprising. For years Easterners, foreign visitors, expatriate Westerners, and the "natives" themselves have been practicing amateur depth psychology on the West in a confused attempt to reveal the character of the West to themselves and to others. Much of their analysis has culminated in merely clouding the definition of the West beyond recognition. The West as myth has long been the subject of debate. Yet so successful have the mythologizers been in inventing their personalized West, that their creation has been engraved on the national consciousness. Nor can this distorted state be blamed entirely on the "manufacturers of blood and thunder," the Zane Greys or the Max Brands, who contrived to leave their readers with the impression that the Wests of old were one series after another of gunfights at the O.K. Corral, or fast fadeouts into the Hole-in-the-Wall. Far more sophisticated practitioners, such as Charles Dickens or Isabella Bird, have perpetuated the mythology of the West. For instance, traditionalists would have us believe that individualism, à la James Bridger, has always held sway and still hangs on as the dominant hallmark of life in the West; even though—as the Mormons demonstrated, and those proponents of reclamation, Francis Newlands and Arthur Powell Davis, repeatedly told succeeding generations of Westerners —an organized society was essential to anyone wresting a livelihood from an arid land.

Knight-errant Westerners have tenaciously defended the myth of individualism even if they did not believe in it, or were only self-conscious. The popularity of John Wayne's West with the debunking young was not entirely due to superciliousness as they moved through theatres' turnstiles to view *Rio Bravo* or *True Grit*. For the Westerner who had faith in the folklore, it more often meant failure than success. If he could have brought perspective to his life, the Westerner should not have felt as betrayed as he often did. After all, that same folklore that he found so appealing had, more often than not, been imported from the East by his neighbors! Nor could the Westerner take much consolation in the fact that it took a certain courage to start a life in a new land, for it also took a certain amount of foolhardiness—more than he liked to admit.

Yet one cannot deny that the West translated into opportunity for enough people to make it seem a success for all. As the western society and economy stabilized, if not matured, moving from the nineteenth to the twentieth century, the speculative possibility of affluence appeared increasingly feasible. Decade by decade the twentieth-century West became more and more symbolic of an attractive way of life for refugees from eastern urbanism. In this flow of population, each immigrant discovered his own western experience, whether transitory or long lasting.

One educator, who had recently moved from Long Island to Santa Fe, gushed to the writer about the freshness, the newness, the exuberance of the West, where, as he said, "one can still experiment." We did not interrupt his preoccupied state to point out that many fellow residents of the New Mexico capital had journeyed there for precisely the opposite reason, the "old-world" charm, leisurely life, and perhaps most of all the fact that taxes on half a city block, six blocks from the storied Plaza, remain at the 1920 level of less than four hundred dollars! The motives for emigration from the East are almost as numerous as the emigrants. Climate always ranks high on individualized lists. On a Sunday morning in Tucson, one constantly hears testimonials to nature and God—both seem close by to a high proportion of the residents. For many Arizonians, their state is truly God's waiting room, for sufferers from arthritis, allergies, and emphysema.

For the young entrepreneur just three months removed from Chicago, the West is an exciting land of opportunity, to put it in the cliché-ridden language of the chambers of commerce. The less stratified society that he finds is not an illusion. He does not have to make it at the Greenwich Round Hill Country Club before he ponders his economic future. The twentieth-century West, then, for some individuals, is a composite of anticipation, dreams, and reality as it has always been.

If you ask a Westerner, recent or past, how he interprets the West, usually a puzzled look will cross his face and he will begin enumerating what he likes about his life. His definition will be expressed in terms of appreciation, not understanding. Much of the problem centers on how he circumscribes—intellectually, geographically, and culturally —the West as a region.

Not having endured a holocaust such as the Civil War, the Westerner has difficulty finding a common unifying bond that will lend meaning to his region. He may come closest to giving his region identity when he describes it on the basis of economic indicators. With relative ease and accuracy, the Westerner can note that the West's economy is fragmented into intraregional fiefdoms. The metropolises of Billings, Spokane, Denver, and Albuquerque all rule over their immediate hinterlands. In so doing, he has, whether he recognizes it or not, pointed to one of the most singular characteristics of his region's economy, namely, that it is largely a distributive economy, not a productive one. Although the Denver resident, with justifiable pride in the products of Gates Rubber or Shawyder Brothers, may not like to admit it, his region's exports are primarily natural resources rather than manufactured products. True, a change is going on; more and more plants are locating west of the Mississippi; but until resources such as skilled labor and water are available in abundance, to name just two factors, the industrial scene is not likely to alter very rapidly.

Yet the common western colonial condition rests not merely on geography—on physical limitations and resources that predispose the West to depend on other regions for markets, manufactures, and services—but on arrangements made elsewhere for the western economy. Patent monopolies and the basing-point system dictate, to a large extent, which products Westerners buy and sell, so that Easterners and foreigners have given the West its apparent unity in diversity.

The difficulty of defining western regionalism precisely also appears in the political sphere. If a Balkanization has occurred in the western economy, there has also been a Byzantine-like fracturing of the western political scene. On national issues there has been a remarkable divergence, with mixtures of strong isolationist, internationalist, liberal, and conservative sentiments all coming out of disparate sections of the West. The recent senior ex-senator from Wyoming, Gale McGee, a former professor of history at the University of Wyoming, gained national prominence from his "hawkish" stand on Vietnam, while the surrounding states of Idaho, Montana, and South Dakota had Senators Frank Church, Mike Mansfield, and George McGovern, all highly vociferous advocates of the "dove" position on Southeast Asia.

Perhaps these discordant positions on foreign policy are merely a reflection of the personalization and individual political leadership that have historically surfaced in the West. For if one discounts the myth of individualism, the western electorate has demonstrated a proclivity for the nonconformist personality in the political sphere. The Burton K. Wheelers, the Glenn Taylors, and the Henry Ashursts received the blessing of the western electorate in part because they were simply more interesting and colorful than their opponents.

On the domestic side, it is worth noting that when it comes to a federal subsidy for a post office, a reclamation project, or a highway, the western congressional delegations quickly discover interests remarkably similar to those of their eastern cohorts; for in elemental language, the pork-barrel slogan becomes "What is good for Ohio is also good for New Mexico." Sen. Francis E. Warren of Wyoming, who was unrivaled in his talent for draining the federal treasury on behalf of his Cowboy State, advised a friend that he should merge his interests "as soon as possible with those of other states, if you want to help yourself and your friends."[2]

Much of the present tone and character of western politics is, in reality, a legacy from the western progressivism of the early twentieth century. In effect, western Progressives bequeathed a political creed that was ambivalent and one that has tended to lend a schizophrenic style to western politics. The Progressive had a strong commitment to economic collectivism in the West; at the same time he could be constantly

2. Francis E. Warren to Thomas H. Carter, 12 December 1906, Warren Letterbooks, Western History Research Center.

worried about economic monopoly. An Edward Costigan or a Hiram Johnson could be emotionally dedicated to individualism and worry about federal political encroachment and at the same time be frantically trying to secure a governmental handout for a federal building in their home states.

As a result of this political heritage, today western audiences may hear the most conservative, states' rights stands being orated from a political platform on a Tuesday evening, followed by speakers proclaiming a rampant liberal speech on Friday night in the same auditorium, even to similar audiences. It was this stand on states' rights that inspired Barry Goldwater to rely on a natural empathy between the South and West so heavily in the early stages of his presidential bid in 1964. Ironically, it was the myopia of his western campaign council that cost him heavily in the election. For there appears to have been a remarkable underassessment of the sectional, as well as national, political drawing power of their native Texan opponent. That Lyndon Johnson would have appealed equally to the South and West should have hardly been news to political pundits (as Kirkpatrick Sale has observed), especially after the lessons of the presidential race of 1960, in addition to the fact that Texas and Texans have never been able to decide whether they are Southerners or Westerners.

In spite of Goldwater's defeat there are those who argue that the West is becoming more and more potent politically, for no other reason than the westward movement of population. The fact that Goldwater hailed from Arizona was not as impressive as the tremendous financial underwriting that he received from southwestern financial czars such as Henry Salvatori. Seldom if ever have any West Coast politicos been able (without smiling or trembling) to tell East Coast rivals that not only did they intend running a candidate for president, but they would finance (which of course is one and the same) the effort as well.

That these southwestern kingmakers could swagger so in the 1964 election was due as much as anything else to heavy post-World-War-II migration of both human and financial resources, particularly their concentration in urban centers. If cities were the spearheads of reform, culture, and financing in the nineteenth-century West, they are increasingly playing a more dominant role (as Gerald Nash has noted) in the last half of the twentieth century. Of the seven million or more service men and attached military personnel who saw the West for the first time during the Second World War, by far the largest number who decided to return came back to Denver, Albuquerque, Los Angeles, or other metropolitan centers. This rapid population influx caught the urban leadership in the West unprepared. Young real-estate promoters, many of them only two or three years separated from the East themselves, hastily threw up acres of tract houses, encircling the city limits. The rows of domino-erected structures, precut and prefab construction, were often distinguished by tasteless design, an absence of intelligent zoning, and a slipshodness in workmanship that promised to make them the suburban slums of a decade later. These drab, grid subdivisions filled a need for low-cost housing for the masses, a need the public sector only partially attempted to remedy. Unfortunately city planners all too often abdicated or at best only half-heartedly tried to meet the challenges endemic in burgeoning growth.

Ten years after he first arrived in Denver, the late William Zeckendorf, the urban promoter who built the realty concern of Webb and Knapp with more dreams than cash, told the writer, "Hell, I built Denver and that was why I came West —to get that town moving!"[3] Zeckendorf had uttered these same sentiments with a few less expletives when he first landed at Stapleton Airport in Denver in 1955. Such blatant pronouncements did little to soothe the first families of the Mile High City, the descendants of those noble "thirty-six" whose exploits have been memorialized in *The Unsinkable Molly Brown*. Nevertheless, Zeckendorf was only saying what many Denverites were already thinking—they had done very little in the way of responding to the urban problems that were now on their doorstep. Not only had they accomplished little in the way of urban design, but they soon showed Zeck-

3. Interview with William Zeckendorf, New York, 5 November 1968.

endorf they resented Easterners who told them they were unenlightened. For four years, the Denver financial kingdom that was lined up along Seventeenth Street fought this son of a former Arizona merchant-capitalist, only to yield him the field in the end.[4] Today the visitor to Denver can see the monuments that Bill Zeckendorf built in a bank-office building complex, a Hilton hotel, and a May Company department store. Zeckendorf's influence has been more concrete than these edifices; much of the present building boom in Denver comes as a result of his shaking loose the Denver financial leadership. As one enlightened Denver banker said, "If we do not build this town, others will." This sentiment received reenforcement when the Texas petroleum magnates, the Murchisons, followed quickly on the heels of Zeckendorf by constructing the Denver Club skyscraper, an office building.

Quite evidently real-estate development by Easterners is only part of the dilemma facing the urban West. A far greater Gordian knot to slice is simply that when Easterners go West, they migrate with the intense conviction that they are escaping the metropolitan vexations of the East. They believe with the fervency of a convert that they are exchanging the gray, dirt-laden atmosphere for clean, fresh air, the jarring, unsettling rides on the New Haven for shorter commuting time, the crime-filled streets for safe nocturnal walks with their dogs. What they consistently fail to realize, or brainwash themselves into forgetting, is that they are only bringing these same urban problems—high population density, crowded transportation, and industrialization—with them. Anyone who has recently visited Denver or Missoula can dimly see that the only difference between Eastern smog and Western smog is a matter of degree—and that difference is decreasing.

Unless western cities can imaginatively solve the problems of environment, the answers to which have so far eluded the East, there may come a day when western urban planners will insist that the place quotas on immigration. After all, the

4. In his autobiography Zeckendorf has told part of the story behind the roller coaster ride he received from and gave to Denver's financial community. Zeckendorf (New York, 1970).

superintendent of Yellowstone Park suggested as early as 1970 that visitor permits would probably reduce the influx of the summer tourists. The energy crisis may accomplish what national park policy failed to do.[5] (One can visualize "lotteries for western holidays.") It is difficult today to imagine the entrance highways to Alburquerque blocked off by immigration police. However, the West's limited available water reserves are a key restriction to population increase. And unless the West finds more water, immigration offices at the edge of community borders may be part of the West's future.

While the West is threatened with a lack of water, there has been no dearth of proposals to remedy aridity. In the late nineteen fifties and early sixties, the governor of Colorado, Steve McNichols, argued that the West should finance its reclamation projects through revenue bonds. McNichols maintained that going the usual route of (1) defining a prospective project, (2) doing a survey, (3) finding out the cost-benefit ratio, (4) requesting authorization to make a study, and finally, (5) seeking appropriations was simply too tortuous a process to be effective. McNichols contended that entire cities would be placed in peril while their water redemption was trapped in congressional committees.[6] As an answer, he proposed that since reclamation projects had long demonstrated that the cost-benefit ratio was better than one-to-one, in essence, projects did pay themselves off. Therefore, contending that reclamation did have a proven profit basis, McNichols's idea was simply to finance all future reclamation through revenue bonds. Whether the governor realized it or not, his proposal harked back to the early days of reclamation, when Morris Bien, the solicitor for the Reclamation Service, had lobbied for a similar plan.[7] McNichols was more successful in converting Coloradoans to his plan than Bien had been with Congress more than a half-century previously.

5. Denver *Post*, 12 August 1970.
6. Denver *Post*, 15 January 1961.
7. Morris Bien to Mrs. Morris Bien, 1 March 1906, Morris Bien Collection, Western History Research Center.

In the early 1960s a tremendous amount of publicity poured out in the press pertaining to a grandiose plan conceived in the offices of the Ralph Parsons engineering firm in Los Angeles. Indeed the concept was even more expansive than its breathtaking title: "North American Water and Power Alliance."[8]

The basic idea, if not the politics, was elemental enough. Through a series of reverse river flows, dams, and canals, an enormous interlocking waterway would be constructed from the Hudson Bay to western United States. With the copious water resources of the Arctic and Canada at the West's disposal, theoretically the water problem for the land beyond the one hundredth meridian would be solved. There were transparent hurdles to remove such an enormous design from the drawing board. Canadian politicians, always extremely sensitive to intimations of exploitation from south of their border, responded in predictable fashion. Their oratory ran the gamut from "they will not get a drop of water," to "the price must be high."

The reaction to the NAWPA plan in the nation's capital went from downright boredom with the entire matter, through skepticism, to enthusiastic endorsement. Of more than cursory significance was the fact that the plan's most strenuous advocates came from the western state that had done the most to answer the challenge of regional aridity. Sen. Frank Moss of Utah may have even been the father of the entire scheme in skeletal form, although his parentage has never been widely discussed nor publicized.

Regardless of the ultimate fate of NAWPA, the West's demands for water are obviously going to increase enormously for the foreseeable future. The water will have to be imported, either from freshwater sources or from the ocean, if the technology for desalination is resolved to make it economically feasible. Slowly, ever so slowly, the West has made steady progress on an interstate basis in solving its water disputes. Gov. Pat Brown, with the technical leadership of William Warne, hammered through the California water project. The long-standing and highly emotional suit between

8. Denver *Post*, 1 May 1966.

Arizona and California over the Colorado River finally reached settlement after hearings before the Supreme Court. Whether Westerners like to or not, they are being forced to discard state chauvinism in their search for a solution to a desert existence.

As if a parched land was not enough to plague western psyches, another Delphic warning about the West's future came this time out of the East. Malthusian prophets of doom at the Hudson Institute and elsewhere flatly stated that the nation, East, West, North, or South, was facing an overpopulation crisis. Overpopulation, and what it means for the urban environment, has best been dramatized by a brilliant ethologist, John B. Calhoun, of the National Institutes of Mental Health.

In his laboratory near Poolesville, Maryland, Calhoun built a "futuristic" Orwellian animal farm. Unlike Orwell's, Calhoun's farm was populated by only one species—the mouse. Constructing what he terms a *mousery*, which consists of a series of large steel rectangular boxes, replete with everything a self-respecting mouse could desire: plenty of maze exercise runways, nesting boxes, and unlimited food and water. Under controlled conditions, Calhoun began increasing the mouse population in ratio until he reached approximately twenty-six hundred mice in a nine-foot-square box. Calhoun had now "procreated" a population of about sixteen times as many mice as would normally live in the same amount of space in their natural habitat.

At this juncture, Calhoun had created what he calls *behavioral sink*, a term he defines as a situation in which pathological conditions have been induced in animals or in man by overcrowding due to overpopulation. This psychoneurotic state is easily observable in his mousery with twenty-six hundred squirming bodies. The mice quickly established a pecking order whereby the dominant group ensconsed themselves in the nest closest to food and water, and so on down the social scale until the proles are reached—the most beat up, dejected, rejected, miserable mice imaginable. Physical deterioration in Calhoun's animal colony was the least frightening aspect of his experiment. Tremendous psychological and behavioral aberrations were induced in the mice by creating this enormous density. Cannibalism occurred, all the mice suffered from degrees of a "withdrawal syndrome," homosexuality became rampant, reproduction ceased altogether, and even enzyme and endocrine balance was upset. In sum, Calhoun had created a doomed animal society—a veritable 1984-type existence and worse.[9]

As far as Calhoun is concerned the moral is clear for human society. The same conditions that he produced in his mice, he predicts will result in high-density-population areas of the human race. In fact, Calhoun sees many parts of India in the 1970s as illustrating his theses. While he willingly concedes that cities in the West are at present far from producing a lemming-like future, he does forecast that within fifty years, Homo sapiens, regardless of his refuge, will be in serious trouble because of overpopulation. Calhoun points out that there have been ten doublings of the human race in the last nineteen hundred years, with each successive doubling taking only about half the time of the preceding increase. Most recently it took the world population a mere forty years to increase by twofold. He now believes that it will take only twenty years to double the present population. What does Calhoun see as the answer? To avert this satanic destiny, he insists that population must not cease increasing; it must actually decline. Then, Calhoun argues that man should develop his mental capacities in the style of what he calls "a mental prosthesis." What, in effect, Calhoun is forecasting is an "extension" of the human mind, whereby man will be able to conceptualize and form ideas to enlarge the scope of his

9. Calhoun's theories are offered in a series of papers, some unpublished, but most are available from the author. "Psycho-Ecological Aspects of Population," (manuscript, 21 February 1966); "Population Density and Social Pathology," *Scientific American* 206 (February 1962):139–46; "The Role of Space in Animal Sociology," *Journal of Social Issues* 22:4 (1966):46–58; "A Behavioral Sink," in *Roots of Behavior*, ed. E. Bliss (New York, 1962), pp. 295–315; "Promotion of Man" (manuscript for Unit for Research on Behavioral Systems, 4 June 1969); and "Aggression—Poverty—Dialogue—Legitimacy and Population" (Paper presented at the symposium of the Committee of Preventive Psychiatry, 11 November 1966).

reality beyond his present mental horizons. Calhoun states an analagous process was the wheel in extending the mobility of society. If man can so broaden his mental capacity, he may be able to exchange "conceptual space" for physical space like the academician who possesses less space than the farmer, and so on.

Calhoun's devil world may in 1977 appear to most Westerners only as an exercise in fantasy. A resident of Glasgow, Montana, who gazes across unlimited space, which only the northern lights cut off, finds it difficult at best to focus on the problems of the teeming mass of humanity in South Harlem on an August eve.

Some Westerners, however, are thinking about the unthinkable and the year 2000, and what the demands on the West from an ecological point of view will be. Several years ago an imaginative petroleum entrepreneur in Denver, Sam Gary, in his design concept for the Bell Creek community in southern Montana is considering importing, en bloc, industry and labor from the East. The labor would be recruited from overpopulated and economically depressed metropolitan areas. As first envisioned, the town of Bell Creek was to serve as a housing and distributive center for the Bell Creek oil field—one of the largest discoveries in the Rocky Mountain region in the past thirty years.[10]

Men with the vision of Sam Gary are far from common in the Rockies or elsewhere in the West. Undeniably, western leaders are coming to expect that the West will be called upon to carry some of the overburden of the nation's population. How much of this obligation they will be in a position to accept depends in large measure on how they meet the endemic problems of urbanism and aridity. In addition, the enormous extent of the public land in the West under federal control still shadows all western decisionmaking regarding their land policies and politics.

In spite of an unending stream of pronouncements on multiple use, the national government has been little more creative than the states in long-term planning for optimum utilization of this immense domain. The absence of forecast-

10. Interview with Sam Gary, 21 July 1968.

ing for the future, plus the rampant speculation in private real estate, has led the West into a chaotic state as far as land development goes.[11]

With the all-too-brief exception of a few golden years, such as those before the First World War, ranching has been a marginal operation, with profits highly dependent on extra-industry factors of interest rates, land values, and a diminishing labor supply. Eastern and corporate capital continues to pour into western ranch lands, taking advantage of both tax legislation and the perilous situation in the livestock industry. As land values inflate, most investors are happy whether they show a profit or not.

What is happening to ranching in the West was intuitively revealed in a conversation with a former executive of a large eastern transportation company, who had purchased a sizable acreage in southern Arizona eight years ago. During our visit he conceded that he had yet to see a year when his ledger sheets were not in the red. This did not bother him, though, for his deficits had been moderate. In fact, he related all this personal economic history without a touch of sadness or upset. Then, all of a sudden, he brightened perceptively: "Oh well, the land has inflated so much I could liquidate tomorrow with a substantial profit."

In one sentence, the former Manhattan executive laid bare the contemporary predicament of western agriculture. Sharply rising land prices, the impossibility of securing additional water rights, plus high machinery and labor costs have tolled the death knell for family ranching in the West. When the

11. Promotional literature heralding the glories of a western home-site came in a continual flow into western and eastern mailboxes. Some recent pieces, with titles all too descriptive of their contents, include: "Verde Village Was Created for the Utmost Enjoyment of the Leisure Life," "Western Colorado Cattle Empire, Thunder River Realty," and "Lake Havasau City, Replete with the Real London Bridge." For the reaction of one segment of a ski resort to overspeculation and under-planning, see Peggy Clifford and John M. Smith, *Aspen Dreams & Dilemmas: Love Letter to a Small Town* (Chicago, 1970). Bumping along Aspen streets a visitor sees more than one bumper sticker with the message, "Save Aspen—Ski Vail."

dynamic Lee Moore of Douglas, Wyoming, died in the 1920s, he endowed each of his seven children with a ranch of his own. Today if more than one heir in a ranching family is interested in following the family tradition, he must consider another vocation or at best become a manager for corporate ranching interests. Gates Rubber Company has bought huge sections of land in western Colorado and southern Wyoming. Reynolds Aluminum, Texaco, United States Steel, and Janss Corporation, to name a few, are other concerns that have rapidly spread over the western landscape. Outside corporate capital input in western land abounds everywhere in the West.

One St. Louis financier, Harold L. Oppenheimer, took advantage of what he perceived as the lack of managerial know-how in the cattle industry. In 1953, he molded a group of ex-marine officers and assorted knowledgeable agribusiness graduates into a junior version of Tex Thorton's legendary "Whiz Kids" of the Ford Motor Company.[12] Setting up what amounted to an investment trust, Oppenheimer established himself as a broker between venture capital and the small underfinanced rancher. Investors purchased "shares" in the firm; Oppenheimer then placed this capital in ranching operations where he believed good management would turn an unprofitable operation into a profitable one. Oppenheimer never invested without assuming managerial control—in essence, if a rancher wanted his dollars, he also had to take Oppenheimer's supervisors.

Oppenheimer has been successful in applying this conglomerate approach to agriculture. Part of the reason, he believes, is emotional, "At a club or cocktail party it carries a little more impact to refer to your 500 cows in Wyoming, than to your 500 shares of AT&T." As a close relative of the Music Corporation of America czar Jules Stein, Oppenheimer

12. Oppenheimer's managerial and investing techniques can be found in: *Cowboy Arithmetic: Cattle as an Investment* (Danville, 1971); *Cowboy Economics: Rural Land as an Investment* (Danville, 1971); and *Cowboy Litigation: Cattle and the Income Tax* (Danville, 1972).

has had an unusual opportunity to solicit would-be cattle barons at Beverly Hills cocktail parties.[13] From listening to poolside chatter, the writer has the opinion that there are more self-imagined cattle kings in the backyards of the film colony than anywhere else in the United States.

Leaving this presentist and futurist dash through the West of 1977, what is most striking is how many themes that distinguished the West of 1900 are still apparent today. Indeed most of the questions, problems, and issues that we take up in the following essays remain of vital relevance for the contemporary West. The West, in spite of a dramatic improvement of exports over imports, still has the colonial economy that stirred the protests of Thurman Arnold, Walter P. Webb, and others four decades ago. The West unproudly stands as the classic example of an exploited region. The West has become so accustomed to living (some would say slumming) on borrowed capital that one petroleum executive informed me that when he wanted to buttress his financing he never gave a second thought to local financial firms. A major part of the problem is that some regional banking institutions act as if they like it that way. When Elwood Brooks first arrived in Denver fresh from a small country bank in Kansas to assume control of the Central Bank and Trust Company, he was amazed at the conservativeness in the Denver financial community. Old-line families ran their banks in formal fashion, basically making their major loans to well-established regional companies, concerns that were often con-

---

13. Film society readers of *Daily Variety* have been treated to an advertisement of an Oppenheimer-like enterprise, Ankeny Breeding Systems/1970. In a strange mixture of phraseology, which manages to combine computer terminology, 1870 promotionalism, and clichés, would-be Hollywood riders of the range are told of "The Investment that Stands on Its Own Four Feet. . . . This is to introduce a new offering of 400 units of Limited Partnership Interests in Ankeny Breeding Systems/1970 (ABS/70). The partnership will engage in the breeding and cross breeding of pure-bred and commercial cattle in order to achieve possible capital appreciation. This tax shelter-oriented investment is designed for persons in the upper income tax brackets. The minimum investment is $2,500 every six months for a five year period (a total of $25,000)" (*Daily Variety*, 6 November 1970, p. 9).

trolled or run by their cousins, nephews, or brothers-in-law.

By adapting and adopting the methods of Giannini, in enticing the small depositor to his bank, introducing a pay-as-you-go checking plan, Brooks dramatically increased the Central Bank and Trust Company's assets from $8 million to $150 million in a little over twenty years. Nor did Brooks limit his talents and energy to banking. Almost single-handedly he forced through an urban renewal project that completely changed the facade of Denver's city center.

One of the many mystifying paradoxes of the western economic credo surfaces in the attitudes toward banking. Local financial leaders for years have vociferously lobbied against branch banking, under the premise that once you open the door to branch banking you also let in out-of-state entrepreneurs who will immediately dictate your economic development. Somehow the logic of this position vanishes when these same bankers turn up at major eastern banks and insurance companies for capital reserves, agreeing to terms for loans that amount to as much or far more dictation than they could conceivably receive under "foreign" branch banking. They in this way undermine their own economic growth in a manner that can be classed as neurotic.

Another aberration is that with an economy intimately connected with the national business cycle; regional financiers become unaccountably infected with delusions of grandeur and act as if they were entirely independent of eastern board rooms. That is, they do so until one of their loans is vetoed or the prime rate jumps; then they bewail their sad state of serfdom.

On the other hand these regional businessmen will blat the most wildly sounding economic provincialism, maintaining all the while that their businesses are far superior to those of the rest of the country, all the time denying their words by adamantly refusing to underwrite a new manufacturing company right in their financial backyard. They exude copious sentiments of doctrinal faith in themselves and their region, but their actions belie both. Admittedly, in the twentieth century, as well as the nineteenth, much investment in the West is enormously speculative. The Frenchmen, Netherlanders, and Belgians who stumbled onto the Salt Creek oil field in the nearly 1900s soon learned how risky it was to invest in a land that lacked a sustantial market for their product, or a way for them to reach one. But as Bernard De Voto noted long ago, the Westerner may scream with the eagles about his economic independence, but he will muzzle this indignation when he has a chance to buy stock in a company like Exxon.

Part of the problem of the West's struggle for economic independence is simply that the West does not believe in itself. This skepticism carries over into the promotion the Westerners employ to boom their economy. Interpreting the glories of the West to a would-be investor, the Westerner, more often than not, does not sound convincing. For as a chamber of commerce member in Spokane or Tucson, he is acutely aware of the fallacies in his sunset spiel. Not only does he slide over the problems of skilled labor, water, and market, in spite of what he will frequently argue, the resident of Grand Junction wants only a selected type of industry, Eastman Kodak and IBM plants are coveted, the steel- or coal-using factories are scorned.

A Tucson reporter in the early 1960s undertook a man-in-the-street survey of the attitudes of Tucson's residents toward new industry. His syllogistic questionnaires went along the following lines: first he asked his fellow citizens whether they wanted more industry. The majority replied with an emphatic yes, they avidly desired more industrial payrolls. His next question, did they think that additional industry would result in Tucson being a less pleasant place to live. The interviewees quickly conceded that life in Tucson would deteriorate. Then came the third and obvious query, "Why do you want industry?" "Because," they unanimously replied, "industry means progress."[14] For those second-generation residents of Arizona, their affirmation of "progress" may merely have been reflecting the faith of their fathers.

A boomer has long been a watchword in western society. That is, until very recently, when more and more Westerners have begun to view their chambers of commerce as disguised

14. Tucson Interviews, Neil Morgan Collection.

chambers of horrors. Caught up in the environmental crisis as much as their eastern relatives, western urban dwellers are becoming increasingly sensitive over that indefinable quality of life. Meccas of leisure, such as Aspen, Colorado, are becoming the source of battlecrys in the environmental crusade. It is only slowly dawning on Westerners, as on Americans in general, that there is a built-in poverty in economic abundance. And if the Aspenite appears slow to grasp the value of his natural surroundings, conservation organizations are quick to point out to him the potential for disaster.

The Westerner, then, is endorsing a fascinating ideological coupling of the century-old protest of eastern economic exploitation and the new shibboleth of environmental cataclysm. Now the Westerner has a new motive for becoming incensed over the rock wool plant on the edge of town spewing forth huge billowing columns of debris. On top of sending their profits east, these companies add insult to injury by polluting the atmosphere at the same time. Increasingly, Westerners are demanding a white-collar West. Whether their demands will be met is another question, because, as John Calhoun has so acutely observed, the West will be under enormous pressure to absorb the excess population and urban problems of the East. It is doubtful, to say the least, that this human migration, enforced or voluntary, will exclude blue-collar industry.

A second *leitmotif* in the history of the West, which, along with colonialism, is omnipresent in the following essays, is the bureaucratic syndrome with its broad impact for and on the West. In varying degrees and on sporadic occasions, western political leaders have alternately decried and paid homage to the federal bureaucracy. That indefatigable, tenacious, tunnel-minded senator from Wyoming, Francis E. Warren, wrote to a political crony in the winter of 1912, "I am gratified with what you say about politics and am feeling sure that you are absolutely right in thinking and reporting that Mr. Pinchot will be in the next cabinet—and high up at that—if Mr. Roosevelt should be elected. There can be no question about this." Letting the appalling consequences of this nerve-shattering possibility sink into his reader's mentality, Warren pounded on, "It is unfortunate that we have never seemed to be able to squelch and blot out the effect of the poison in the Forest Service that was distributed in the early days; and since those fellows go through civil service, we never know whether we are getting Democrats or Republicans."[15]

The poison for which the good senator from Wyoming so ardently desired an antidote was not bureaucracy per se, but only the age-old prerogative to manipulate the allegiances of bureaucrats. For even Senator Warren, for all his passion for office, dimly realized the necessity of the expertise which the bureaucrat contributed to the federal administration.

Perhaps Warren may be at least partially forgiven for his reluctance to perceive the rise and evolution of bureaucracy. After all, many in Washington and out were slow either to divine the significance of the bureaucratic movement or to discern its evolution brought on by the response to technological problems. In the late nineteenth century, much of the bureaucratic function was interpreted solely in terms of political opportunism—in essence, in the light of patronage, as a political ally to represent a metier, a section, or an interest.

Indeed, the surrender to bureaucracy often came in the twentieth century only when the bureaucrat managed to convince the layman constituency of the value of his talent. Even so, the infiltration of the bureaucratic pursuit into nineteenth-century federal government was a creeping creation. As late as 1888, of the 125,000 nonmilitary positions, some 96,000 were in the post office. As the century drew to a close over the next decade or so, it became more and more apparent that if the complexities of governmental regulation were going to be rationalized, a technically qualified bureaucracy with substantial authority and security from political influence was not only essential but inevitable.

In arriving at this conclusion, consciously or unconsciously, the early twentieth-century federalists were only moving in tune with the times. If they were entrapped in an age of excess, trusts, and nationalization, they were also in an age of

15. Francis E. Warren to Elmer Bletz, 29 February 1912, Warren Letterbooks.

organization. For the federal bureaucracy had institutional models and guidelines at hand in several spheres—in the private sector, in the political scene, and in the states. For instance, in spite of considerable testimony to the entrepreneurial genius of James J. Hill or Charles Eliot Perkins, these executives managed systems far less innovative than we have been frequently informed; they founded the successes of the Great Northern and the Burlington on strong organizational structures.

Nor were the political lessons of the Gilded Age lost on that and succeeding generations. If the Republicans proved nothing else, their continued victories established the undebatable point that in the political pit, strategy and organization triumphed over localism, antinationalism, and just plain ineptness. Finally, as has been observed, the states often led the way in the growth of bureaucracy, devising innovations to deal with regulatory problems and multiphasic aspects of economic development that became the laboratories for national administrative departures.

Nothing highlights the role of the bureaucracy more than the fact that between 1850 and 1970 the national government invested more than $300 billion in the trans-Mississippi West.[16] The primary responsibility for administering this enormous cornucopia fell on the national bureaucracy and the western political establishment.

Western congressmen alternately wooed, harassed, and pleaded with the bureaucrats for a voice in the dispersal of these funds. Sen. Clarence D. Clark of Wyoming even went so far as to send a list of "approved" mercantile establishments in southwestern Wyoming where the United States Geological Survey should purchase its supplies.[17] His fellow

16. The estimate of Professor Gerald D. Nash in his stimulating paper, "Bureaucrats and Reform in the West" (presented at the Organization of American Historians meeting in Los Angeles on 17 April 1970). See also Nash's insightful history of the Twentieth Century West, *The American West in the Twentieth Century: A Short History of an Urban Oasis* (Englewood Cliffs, N.J., 1973).

17. C. D. Clark to F. E. Warren, 16 December 1902, Warren Papers, Western History Research Center.

senator from Wyoming, Francis E. Warren, who stood second to none in the successful manipulation of the pork barrel, crowed to a Wyoming crony:

> In the omnibus public building bill just passed, we got one hundred thousand each for Laramie and Evanston public buildings, and although it takes but a few words to write it, and the sound of it creates but little excitement perhaps, yet I want to tell you that it has taken an immense amount of brain and brawn to wrest this much away from a well-guarded treasury, and to impress upon our fellows in the middle country and in the east, that we are of sufficient importance to deserve such generous treatment.[18]

Once he got his hand into that "well-guarded treasury," Senator Warren knew, as did most of his friends who were members of the United States Senate, that his job was far from done. Now he had to make certain that his friends were rewarded for their loyal service. This meant it was necessary to establish an intimate association with the Washington bureaucratic structure.

This leads us to a thesis that we have persistently emphasized, namely, that in the Washington bureaucratic hierarchy, the power resides in the second and third echelons. The assistant secretaries and the bureau chiefs historically have not only administered and implemented departmental policies, but also frequently originated the very policies they have been charged with executing. Arthur Powell Davis, Thurman Arnold, and George Otis Smith are all perfect examples of this thesis. With tenacity and stubbornness, Davis forged a workable reclamation policy along the lines of authority and influence that ran between Washington and the western water users. All the while he was cajoling the water users, he was simultaneously ramming his ideas through the Department of the Interior. Then he selected the men to carry out these policies in the field. Thurman Arnold, employing a mixture of Rabelaisian wit, legal tactics (primarily the

18. F. E. Warren to A. J. Parshall, 27 May 1902, Warren Letterbooks.

consent decree), and public opinion, structured a highly pragmatic antitrust policy, assuredly the most successful anti-monopoly campaign of the century. George Otis Smith, with his unusual flair for friendship mixed with a velvet touch of diplomacy and an incorruptible devotion to science, swayed secretaries and even presidents to his point of view. Taking a vastly unpopular stand on the necessity for coal and petroleum conservation, he jousted with doubting Thomases in both industry and government. True, he received an enormous assist from the public revulsion that followed the exposure of the Teapot Dome and Continental Trading Company scandals; yet had there been no *faire du scandal* it is safe to suggest that Smith still would have won his way.

Though their styles differed strikingly, Smith, Arnold, and Davis all shared an essential trait for survival—tenacity. There exists in the Washington bureaucratic maze a law of natural selection. Only those who can both fight and manipulate the machinery are able to surface, let alone stay on top. Nowhere is the pressure greater than on the level of the bureau chief, who is subject to satisfying the demands of those above him and below him, which seldom coincide.

A third theme, and corollary to the role of the bureaucracy, which recurs again and again in these essays, is the problem of federal-state relations. Thurman Arnold never tired of pointing to the adoption of judicial review in the 1870s as the most significant factor in the ascendancy of the federal government over the states. Further, Arnold insisted that in the Sherman Act, Congress had provided the legislative base for a radical alteration of federal-state relationships, which ended once and for all the states' control over business mergers. Undoubtedly Arnold recognized, but failed to emphasize, other forces behind the rapid development of federal power after the Civil War. Urbanization, growth of national markets and wide transportation networks, massive expansion of industry all are commonly cited raisons d'être behind the burgeoning force of political nationalization.

Less often referred to is the fact that much of the skirmishing over states' rights and federal dynamism in this 1890–

1914 period centered on the bureaucracy, as bureaucrats tried to administer the more and more complex legislation and grant-in-aid programs being molded by Congress. The Newlands Act of 1902, pushed onto a reluctant West, became the anvil on which the Reclamation Service forged a workable program. The way West for the Reclamation official was not easy. In the early years of his tenure as director, Arthur Powell Davis allotted a tremendous amount of time to listening to the tiresome tirades of a seemingly unending flow of delegations of water users. Davis's diaries are crammed with explosive phraseology and references to the "narrow outlook," "the limited mentalities" of western politicians and their constituents. When Davis allowed his intelligence to conquer his emotions, he realized that the harangues of Westerners were as old as the West itself. Westerners had no objection to public endowment, although they did not seek it out in the case of the Newlands Act, but they wanted private control of that investment. Deeply committed to laissez-faire and the status quo, western political and financial leaders fervently held that national control of public monies inevitably was tantamount to treasonous betrayals of western rights.

Westerners airily dismissed the rational broad-scale planning and technological know-how that Davis and his engineering staff brought to reclamation projects as just further evidence of "bureaucratic meddling." Subsequent, though far from total, agreement with the Reclamation Service came only when the water users fell behind in payments on the projects. Until they received relief, their lamentations about the federal dictatorship again rent the air of congressional conference rooms. During his long service as bureau chief, Davis never believed that he convinced more than a handful of western reclamation leaders of the soundness of comprehensive planning.

A fourth motif running through these essays, sometimes subtly implied, is the concept of regionalism. One can pivot indefinitely in search of a definition of regionalism. Years ago in his introduction to the Wisconsin symposium on regionalism, Merrill Jensen stated, "The nature of 'a region' varies with the needs, purposes, and standards of those using the concept."[19] To Turnerians, a region, as much as a geographical entity, has been a state of mind, a process, or a mythical line between forest and prairie.

To debate the nuances in a regional demarcation becomes a game in futility. For the French who came to Salt Creek the meaning of the West, as a region, was all too clear. When Thurman Arnold talked of the economic bondage of the West to the East, the assistant attorney general, along with the Westerners who heard him, had little difficulty in identifying the land he was discussing. When Arthur Powell Davis deliberated on the aridity of the West, he and the dirt farmers on the Montrose Reclamation Project knew the spatial area to which he was referring.

Ira Sharkansky, in an effort to arrive at a more precise regional political methodology, has turned to quantification in anticipation of finding his own regionalism.[20] Starting with the initial premise that regional literature had slighted comparative analysis and that political regionalism remains a viable force, Sharkansky posed a series of questions, which he then attempted to answer on the basis of quantification. How do state politics and public policies conflict? How constant are political configurations within each region? To what degree is political regionalism merely an echoing of economic regionalism? How do other noneconomic factors affect regional characteristics?

After engaging in an elaborate tabulation of empirical data, Sharkansky arrived at answers that were far from startling. For instance, comparing the different regions on voting, political competition, and apportionment, he confirmed that the southeast was clearly less progressive than the trans-Mississippi West or the North. Arranging his statistics on the rationalization of politics and public policies, he found that regions were becoming more alike but that intraregional uniformity had deepened also. Furthermore, economic dif-

19. Ira Sharkansky, *Regionalism in American Politics* (Indianapolis, 1970).

20. Albuquerque has one of the highest crime rates among Standard Metropolitan Statistical Areas in the United States (*Uniform Crime Reports for the United States* [Washington, 1969], p. 74).

ferentiations left most interstate variations unresolved. Sharkansky found more useful long-term regional norms as an exegesis of regional distinctions.

Sharkansky readily admitted that much of his research and conclusions were only tentative and that more precise answers rested on both the refinement of quantitative techniques and more exhaustive examination of regional characteristics. Although many of Sharkansky's insights in regionalism are cogent and valuable, in the final assessment the economic models that have been constructed by Leonard Arrington, Gerald Nash, and Douglass North, among others, may be far more useful in the examination of regionalism.

For example, it is difficult, if not impossible, to ignore the fantastic impact of economic colonialism on the West, or to suggest that colonialism has not had portentous implications for western regionalism. Nor can we shun, except at our peril, the insightful commentary of Earl Pomeroy on the social-cultural traits of the West, most of which have their derivation in the East. This leads us to the banal, if often glossed over, conclusion that western regionalism, like many other problems in historical methodology, will yield to a comprehensive understanding only when we approach it eclectically with a variety of analytical tools.

A fifth chanson running through these essays, repeated time and again, is the idealization of efficiency. If there was one fragile ideological isthmus on which the bureaucrat-technocrat and the western progressive could stand in harmony, that point of agreement would be the necessity of efficiency and long-range resource forecasting.

Waste, corruption, and exploitation became part of the integral rhetoric of Joseph C. O'Mahoney, Thurman Arnold, George Otis Smith, and Arthur Powell Davis. One of the prime tenets in the attack on monopoly by O'Mahoney and Arnold was the inefficiency of monopolistic enterprise. True, the other parts of Arnold's program—the humanization of competition, the championship of the consumer, the use of statutory public policy to compel legal compliance—were all economic goals very much in the forefront of the idealization of the antitrust program that he reiterated in speech after speech as he crisscrossed the nation. Intertwined through his oratory, sometimes strong, sometimes attenuated, was the message that monopoly was inherently evil, if for no other reason than that it was enormously wasteful.

Proof of Arnold's convictions came with his sweeping suits against big labor, legal actions that left both his partisans and detractors mystified concerning his intentions. Some of their clouds of wonderment would have rolled away if they had only paid more attention to Arnold's public pronouncements. As far as Arnold was concerned, the monopolistic power of labor was as dangerous to the country as the cartels of big business. The public, the press, and the politicians found it difficult to believe him; some never did.

The ever-optimistic George Otis Smith developed as sensitive a Promethean spark as Thurman Arnold to inefficiency and the exhaustion of our natural resources. Smith lobbied all through the 1920s on the horrendous consequences of wasting our resources, first to conserve coal and later, and more notably, for petroleum. In this he was buttressed by a plethora of United States Geological Survey studies purporting to show in the foreseeable future total depletion of petroleum reserves at the current level of production. In tandem with a small cadre of leaders of the petroleum industry, most notably Warwick Downing, Henry L. Doherty, James Veasey, and Earl Oliver, Smith managed to win the fight for a moderate conservation program by the twilight of the twenties.

In their war for an effective conservation policy these leaders of government and industry employed two weapons that have been commonly assumed, but underemphasized, by commentators on conservation. First of all, without exception, Arnold, Downing, Smith, Doherty, and Oliver were adept publicists. They unceasingly sought to create favorable public opinion through a continual flow of speeches and books. They were amazingly successful in courting the fourth estate. Arnold and Smith, particularly, found some of their closest friends in the press. By graphically depicting the horrors of waste in rivers of oil running down arroyos in oil fields, and by emphasizing the disastrous economic effects of monopoly, Smith created public pressures that were alleviated by remedial legislation in Congress.

That Davis, Arnold, and Smith utilized the press so effectively is a bit incongruous inasmuch as all three were uncomfortable with the mixture in the press of public morality and sensationalism brought on by the series of scandals from Hetch Hetchy to the Teapot Dome. As technicians and bureaucrats, they had little empathy for do-gooder moralists, even though on occasion they realized that morality campaigns were good politics. But inevitably they felt that wars against evil served only to shift the spotlight away from scientific and natural resource planning. Much of their aversion to politics followed on the political infighting that often went on in their bureaus. The constant bickering in the Reclamation Service so exasperated Davis that he sent long memoranda to his associates deploring political jockeying.

Secondly, all the programs that Arnold, Davis, and Smith pushed through succeeded in part because of an economic depression. The life of the western farmer in the twenties was a continual struggle for subsistence. Sans the subsidy of reclamation projects many more would have fled the farms than did. When petroleum producers in Oklahoma and Texas saw the price per barrel of oil slide to five cents, George Otis Smith's pleas for stopping overproduction suddenly became the essence of wisdom. Arnold's dramatic enforcement of antitrust legislation in the depression of the thirties was a harbinger for many as the answer to economic chaos, especially after the recession of 1937, when everyone lunged at any brass ring that promised prosperity.

For many in the 1970s the West of Thurman Arnold is as remote as or perhaps more distant than the West of 1890 was for the pre-Second World War generation. Yet if the Westerner pauses to consider his present condition, he will realize that much of the cut-off feeling from the past is illusory. As we have outlined above, many of the themes that were evident in 1900 are still present today. The only reminder we need is commonly offered via the news media in one of the urban communities blatting such slogans as, "We must get Denver (or Seattle or Los Angeles) moving again" (or more recently in the 1976 presidential election, where "the nation" was the target demanding propulsion!).

Transposing the issue, many of the perplexing problems facing the West in the 1970s are obviously far different from those of three quarters of a century ago. Earl Pomeroy has observed that the West, with the passing of each year, is transmuting its life-style more and more into that of the East. Our contention is that the pace of this transformation is much faster than most Westerners realize.

Of course the resident of Albuquerque, although he never glances at the Federal Bureau of Investigation's uniform crime statistics,[21] is acutely aware of some of the social crises brought on by unharnessed metropolitanism. His eastern relatives have had more time in which to adjust gradually to the increasing frustration of urban social conditions. For the Albuquerquean all of a sudden, or so it seemed, discovered it literally was not safe to walk to his home in late evening from his office at the University of New Mexico. That sudden shock of recognition of his loss of freedom is a cogent explanation for the western urban dweller's increasing political conservatism during the 1970s.

Still, the Easterners migrating in increasing hordes West are blissfully unaware, as we have noted, that they are only exchanging an old set of problems for a similar array of challenges in a new environment.[22] Indeed the Easterner is often willing to settle for less economic opportunity and a lower standard of living, in the hope of enjoying his dreams of that elusive quality-of-life syndrome symbolized by long skiing weekends, hunting, fishing, and clear skies.

The Westerner of today then is pushing faster and faster into a future in a radically altered civilization, even though

21. One fascinating phase of this western migration is the current California exodus into Arizona. Californians, some only a few years removed from the East, are pushing into Arizona at a rate of four times as many as immigrate into any other state. This phenomenon, known locally in Arizona as the "California bounce," derives from the idea that they are still searching for the way of life that they did not find in the Golden Bear state.

22. Denis Gabor, *Inventing the Future* (New York, 1963).

his institutions and economy are ill-equipped to face the future. Furthermore, his institutional structure faces a serious challenge from the East, for if the Westerner does initiate the planning to solve his water problem, the East will provide an answer whether it is NAWPA or a similar gigantic scheme. Likewise, should the West lack the foresight to diversify its economy to support the nation's population, the leadership and pressure to find the economic solutions will come out of the East.

In a final assessment the West has one resource that the rest of the nation cannot acquire but desperately requires—space. Regardless of how the West may attempt to resist the encroachment of eastern population, the East will demand that the West absorb its surplus population. The process may be full of anguish and lamentations on the part of all regions, but there is little risk in suggesting that it is inevitable. In the final analysis, emigration from the metropolitan East may represent the last great push of eastern colonial exploitation of the West, resulting in the complete amalgamation of the West into the national society.

How should the West meet this eastern *Anschluss?* First of all, its leaders must seek an increasing number of "alternative futures," to use Denis Gabor's simile.[23] The range of predictions regarding the world's future is expanding at an enormous rate; the West must in effect start "inventing" its own future. After all, much of the ideological background of the western movement was a matter of social invention of one sort or another. Consider such shibboleths as the idealization of the homestead, the open-space concept of freedom personified by the range cattleman, and the greatest of all propaganda, manifest destiny.

If the present-day West is going to play a decisive role in its future, it must start immediately to plan for that future, with the realization that its present state is solidly rooted in the West of fifty years ago. Just as assuredly, the West of the year 2000 will come about only in tandem with the East and the rest of the nation.

23. Ibid.

Colonialism
and the
American West

The American West has had a long tradition of protest against economic and cultural exploitation by the East.[1] Populists and Progressives, not to mention the more radical "Wobblies," were perpetually objecting to eastern domination of western resources.[2] Joseph Dixon of Montana, Edward P. Costigan of Colorado, William E. Borah of Idaho, Hiram W. Johnson of California, and Bronson Cutting of New Mexico were volatile spokesmen for these groups.

With the dying out and submerging of the Progressives in the New Deal, a new group of articulate interpreters of western dissent began to echo the old arguments and added a few new ones. Historians, journalists, legal theorists, and assorted intellectuals led the agitation.

Among the intellectuals of this revolt, one of the first to define the old issue of the West as a fief of the East was a history professor from the University of Texas, Walter Prescott Webb. In 1937 Webb published his study *Divided We Stand*, a work in which he outlined in the now-classic form the case of the West's enslavement to the North.[3] Webb lashed out at a whole series of feudal bonds. The attack ranged from a discussion of the tariff as an instrument of the industrial North to the lament that three-fifths (57 per cent) of Americans living in one-fifth of the country had almost

1. The writer takes this opportunity to acknowledge the incisive criticism of this paper by Earl Pomeroy, University of California, San Diego.
2. A good discussion of the Midwest and the "colonial complex" is in Russel B. Nye, *Midwestern Progressive Politics* (East Lansing, Mich., 1951), pp. 1–27.
3. Walter P. Webb, *Divided We Stand* (New York, 1937). *North* was synonymous with *East* in Webb's vocabulary.

four-fifths of the dollars in the nation's checking accounts. Sandwiched in between these complaints was a comparison of the amounts of insurance held in the North, the South, and the West, and a listing of the colleges in the nation with endowments of more than $2 million. Of course, the South and the West were found to be sadly behind the North on all counts.

What was Webb's solution for the serfdom of these two regions? He was certain that the South and the West had "identical" political interests; therefore, he suggested that a new alliance be formed between western and southern senators. Secondly, if this alliance failed, he suggested, with tongue in cheek, that the two regions threaten the North by proposing that internal tariff walls be set up to restrict the importation of northern products into their sections.

While Webb was humorously contemplating the delights of a tariff barrier, an investigation was launched in Congress, which portended to be a concrete blow against the eastern monopolists. In response to an appeal from President Franklin D. Roosevelt, Congress established a Temporary National Economic Commission to study economic concentration in America. Joseph C. O'Mahoney, Democrat of Wyoming, was selected chairman of the Senate investigating committee. The primary purpose of the TNEC was to examine the exclusive control of some basic industries by a few corporations. When the petroleum and steel industries were investigated, O'Mahoney sought the testimony of representative oil and steel companies in the West.

T. A. Loretz, general manager of the Pacific Coast Steel Fabricators Association of San Francisco, went to Washington to testify in behalf of his group. Loretz's chief complaint was against the railroads, which, by perverting the freight-rate structure, favored the eastern industrialist, with the result that eastern firms were not only competing in western states such as Arizona, New Mexico, Utah, and Montana, but they were capturing all but 2 per cent of the business in these states.

Loretz claimed that the rate system of "Fabrication in Transit" was in the main responsible for this competitive advantage. Under "Fabrication in Transit," a Chicago corporation could accept an order from a firm in Kansas City, ship the raw steel to Oklahoma City to be fabricated, and then reship the finished steel to the Kansas City customer, with the Chicago manufacturer paying only the freight charges from Chicago direct to Kansas City, plus a slight additional charge for the stopover in Oklahoma City. This freight-rate system obviously gave an advantage to the larger eastern firm, which shipped raw steel for fabrication in the West.[4]

When the TNEC began inquiring into the petroleum industry, it again invited western businessmen to testify on matters of competition, especially those from the Rocky Mountain region. The first witness, William H. Ferguson, senior vice-president of Continental Oil Company of Denver, was asked to give his views on oil prices in the Rockies. Ferguson was quick to point out that the high cost—and therefore the poor marketability—of Wyoming gasoline did not result from any collusion among the major integrated oil companies, but rather from excessive local costs of production and refining. The higher labor costs, the unusually long, cold winters, and the extravagant royalty payments all forced Wyoming gasoline out of the competitive market.[5]

To provide the viewpoint of an independent producer, Pierre LaFleiche of Casper, Wyoming, was asked to testify at the hearings. He showed little hesitation about disagreeing with Ferguson's arguments. Rather, in contrast to the senior vice-president of Continental Oil, LaFleiche claimed that gasoline prices consistently followed, in kangaroo fashion, the hegemony of the integrated producers. He was of the opinion that many more independent producers were going broke than were succeeding.[6]

Concurrently with the initiation of the TNEC's investigation, President Roosevelt instituted a massive antitrust

4. U.S., Congress, Senate, *Investigation of Concentration of Economic Power*, 76th Cong., 2d sess., 1940, Senate Report 35, pt. 20: 10897–916.

5. Ibid., pt. 17:9376–98.

6. Ibid., pt. 17:9406–24; interview with Pierre LaFleiche, Casper, Wyoming, 17 August 1958.

program under the direction of Assistant Attorney General Thurman Arnold, formerly a professor at Yale. A hard-driving individualist, whom Robert Jackson once described as "a cross between a cowboy and Voltaire, with the cowboy predominating," Arnold set about implementing the antitrust concepts he had outlined in several articles and in his book, *Folklore of Capitalism.*[7] Between the years 1938 and 1941, the assistant attorney general, with the assistance of more than 300 young lawyers in the Antitrust Division, launched 215 investigations into alleged monopolistic practices.

As one phase of his attack on the restraint of trade, Arnold toured the country, speaking to one group after another in an attempt to dramatize for the public the activities of cartels. A favorite theme, whenever his speech-making forays took him into the South or the West, was eastern control of the hinterlands of America. As a native of Laramie, Wyoming, Arnold held strong opinions on this subject; and he was undoubtedly well aware of the popularity of these views with his audiences. Typical of his approach was an address he gave to the Southern Farm Bureau Training School at the Arlington Hotel, Hot Springs National Park, Arkansas. Here he told an enthusiastic audience that a series of investigations was being undertaken to alleviate the plight of the South and the West.

Arnold was particularly disturbed by the basing-point system of freight rates. One of his favorite illustrations of how this scheme worked alluded to the Colorado Fuel and Iron Plant at Pueblo, Colorado. Arnold noted that if a customer in Denver ordered a shipment of steel from Pueblo, the order would be shipped to him directly from Pueblo, but the customer would pay a mythical freight rate from Chicago. All freight rates on steel in the United States, regardless of the location of the plant, were computed on the "base" city of Chicago.[8] Obviously, the West was paying more of this

7. Thurman Arnold, *Folklore of Capitalism* (New Haven, 1937).
8. "Monopoly and the South," address before the Southern Farm Bureau Training School, Hot Springs, Arkansas, 22 August 1941, Thurman Arnold Papers, Western History Research Center, University of Wyoming.

imaginary freight bill than the East. Other industries had base points for computation of freight charges, but Arnold argued that the rate for steel was one that affected the Westerner most viciously.

The patent monopoly of the large eastern industry also nettled the assistant attorney general. In a speech before the Denver Bar Association,[9] the trust buster noted that his listeners were paying an "illegal toll" cost on every milk bottle made in America, in addition to keeping the western manufacturers from competing with the eastern corporations.

Probably the most succinct statement Arnold made on the effect of the eastern economic domination was written in a letter to Joseph R. Sullivan, an attorney in Laramie, Wyoming, and a longtime friend.

> Right now I am impressed and saddened by the fact that no able lawyer has any business settling in Wyoming under present economic conditions. If he has any sense at all, he will move to the Atlantic seaboard. That is not only true of lawyers but of university professors or anyone else who wants either money, intellectual contacts or anything else. Economic disadvantage creates a backward country.[10]

Another voice—direct from the Middle West and more soothing than Arnold's—spoke up to substantiate one aspect of the inferiority of his region. The Sage of Emporia, Kansas, William Allen White, blamed the East for encouraging the abnormally high agricultural prices of the First World War, which lured the western farmer into overproduction. The subsequent market collapse had, White observed, wrecked havoc with the farmer's fortunes. However, the Kansas journalist had indestructible faith in middle-class democracy and was far from blaming the ills of his region on one section or another. If the West could acquire more power (White did not specify how or what type), everything would be all

9. "The Enforcement of the Sherman Act," address before the Denver Bar Association, Denver, Colorado, 13 May 1939, Thurman Arnold Papers.

10. Thurman Arnold to Joseph R. Sullivan, 17 February 1937, Thurman Arnold Papers.

right.[11] After all, what could be wrong with the West if one had a deep trust in the philosophy of agrarianism?

Another journalist, Joseph Kinsey Howard, writing four years later, was not so sanguine about his region's possibilities as was the Kansas editor. Howard, in his book *Montana: High, Wide and Handsome*, adopted the syllogism that copper was Montana, the Anaconda Copper Mining Company controlled copper, and therefore, Anaconda controlled Montana.[12] "The Company" (as Anaconda is referred to in the Treasure State) had "purchased" most of that state's legislatures since 1900, along with the majority of the newspapers. The Company controlled not only the economic life of Montanans, but their thought as well—this was the vilest type of eastern exploitation!

But Howard did not waste all his journalistic salvos on Anaconda. The Federal Reserve System—dominated by the reactionary "treasury administrations of Carter Glass, David Houston, and Andrew Mellon"—came under violent attack by the Great Falls newspaperman. This "quasi-public agency," he asserted, had set out coldly and deliberately to smash the inflated agricultural credit at the end of the First World War.

First of all, the Federal Reserve system deplored the large holdings of Liberty bonds in Montana banks on the basis that as assets the bonds tended to encourage "inflationary borrowing." By restricting credit, the Federal Reserve forced Liberty bonds out of rural institutions at 80 cents on the dollar.

The second phase of this "gigantic shakedown" was the additional collateral "racket." During the First World War, country bankers had been encouraged to lend up to 80 per cent of the value of their agricultural paper; now the Federal Reserve System was asking as much as three times the value of a loan in agricultural paper. The Reserve Board argued that this drastic reduction was necessary since agricultural

11. William Allen White, *The Changing West* (New York, 1939).

12. Joseph Kinsey Howard, *Montana: High, Wide and Handsome* (New Haven, 1943), 83–245.

prices had declined so precipitously. The viciousness of this policy, Howard wrote, forced the farmers to dump more wheat on the market in frantic efforts to pay off their loans. The result was obvious when wheat prices plummeted from $2.43 per bushel in 1919 to 92 cents in 1922. With the Liberty bonds gone and agricultural credit undermined, the Montana farmer and his banker were at the mercy of the eastern exploiter.

At the culmination of the Second World War, a new surge of attacks on the East poured forth. Another free-lance journalist, Avrahm Mezerik, in his book *The Revolt of the South and West*, wondered what would now become of the steel plants at Fontana, California, and Geneva, Utah, which had been born from the demands of the war. Mezerik assured his readers that the continuation of these plants under western ownership would be a significant step toward achieving economic independence for the West. He reiterated the protests of the past half century with his assults on patent monopolies, eastern capital's domination of the West, tariffs favorable to the East, and eastern control of processing of raw materials extracted in the West. Mezerik discarded the work of the Antitrust Division with the flippant comment, "The Sherman Anti-trust Act answered the Western prayer on paper—not in reality" (p. 205).[13]

To his hopes for a steel industry for the West, Mezerik added the vision of the Missouri Valley Authority. The development of the MVA, particularly of its electric power, would go a long way toward stopping the vast exodus of people from the valley and might well prove to be the salvation of the region.

A potent dissent from Mezerik's thoughts on the adequacy of the Sherman Antitrust Act came from Wendell Berge.[14] An assistant to Thurman Arnold, and subsequent head of the Antitrust Division, Berge was confident that the Sherman

13. Avrahm G. Mezerik, *The Revolt of the South and West* (New York, 1946), pp. 50–76, 112–273.

14. Wendell Berge, *Economic Freedom for the West* (Lincoln, 1946).

Act had been and would continue to be an effective brake on the exploitative enthusiasm of the East. Berge set forth his arguments in a book entitled *Economic Freedom for the West*, published in 1946.

It was not that Berge felt that the Antitrust Division had freed the West from its colonial status. Far from it, Berge had discerned in Richard Henry Dana's classic, *Two Years Before the Mast* (published in 1840), the beginnings of eastern domination of the West. The hides in Dana's ship were secured in California and taken around the Horn to Boston to be tanned and made into shoes. These shoes were then worn in pursuit of more hides. The same scheme, Berge maintained, was still in operation in the 1940s.

Berge concurred with Mezerik in the need to develop the steel plants of the West, for unless the West won the public-power fight, the aluminum industry in the West would be directly under the tutelage of the Aluminum Company of America. The railroad basing-point system was also disturbing to Berge. He noted that in 1932 an agreement, which stipulated among other items that all bidding for traffic on a rate basis should cease immediately, had been signed by thirty-five railroads operating in the West. The Department of Justice first learned of this agreement on 9 April 1943, and on 14 April requested a copy, which was promptly sent; on 23 April, the department was informed that the agreement had been canceled.

As a parting warning, Berge stated that it would be a fundamental error for the West to consider itself apart from the nation in this struggle for economic independence. Monopoly was a disease demanding eradication on a national, not a regional, basis.

Following close upon the publication of Berge's study, *Harper's* published in its January 1947 issue an article entitled "The West Against Itself."[15] The author of the article —Bernard De Voto, a displaced Utahan—was well known for his waspish attacks on conservation practices in the West. A decade earlier he had published an article in *Harper's*,

15. Bernard De Voto, "The West Against Itself," *Harper's* 194 (January 1947):1–13.

"The West: A Plundered Province,"[16] which had attracted wide attention. In this earlier disquisition De Voto caustically commented that current theory held that it was perfectly all right for one section of the country to be plundered for the aggrandizement of another section—provided that enough prosperity overflowed on the first section to compensate for being robbed! "In his [the Westerner's] whole country no one has ever been able to borrow money or make a shipment or set a price except at the discretion of a board of directors in the East" (p. 360). Writing in the midst of the dust-bowl era, De Voto suggested that the only solution for the Westerner was to adapt rapidly to the arid land.

In 1947, however, De Voto was not so optimistic about the emancipation of the West, chiefly because it appeared to him that the natives did not want to be freed from their economic bondage. He based his opinions upon observations made while touring the West the previous summer. To prove his point, he recounted a conversation with the manager of a small refinery. Due to the war, the official told his visitor, the company had managed to build up an impressive financial reserve. De Voto envisioned that here at long last was the fulfillment of the western dream of self-sufficiency. So what had been done with this surplus? It had all been safely invested in the stock of Standard Oil of New Jersey! This led to the sarcastic observation by De Voto, "The West does not want to be liberated from the system of exploitation that it has always violently resented. It only wants to buy into it, cumulative preference stock if possible" (p. 2).

This dichotomy in western thinking was apparent in the acceptance of government aid. The West furiously denounced the paternalism of the New Deal, yet it kept a hand outstretched demanding help for a host of irrigation projects. The West had a shakedown platform—get out, but keep giving us more doles. This De Voto saw as a basic split in the western psyche; in sum, the West was committing suicide.

Triggered by De Voto's article, John Caughey, professor of history at the University of California at Los Angeles, re-

16. Bernard De Voto, "The West: A Plundered Province," *Harper's* 169 (August 1934):355–64.

sponded in an editorial in the *Pacific Historical Review*.[17] Caughey, cognizant of the recent flow of protest literature, was convinced that many of the arguments presented were illusory. Certainly the West was in a hazardous position regarding the erosion of its natural resources. But were these problems unique to the West? Every frontier since the colonial age had faced the same difficulties. Much of the federal conservation program was sound and far-seeing, contended Caughey. The average Westerner was much less concerned with domination by the East than the contemporary attacks would imply.

A third study of the economic problems of the West was published in 1947, Rufus Terral's *The Missouri Valley*.[18] Terral saw the deliverance of the West in the hazy guise of a Missouri Valley Authority. He believed that an authority would assist Montana in freeing itself from the grip of the Anaconda Company, and he forecast an immense industrial complex for the valley once the program was completed. Terral observed in the Westerner the same schizophrenic attitude of which De Voto had complained. In the long run, the attitude of "give me and leave me" is an untenable paradox.

At midcentury Morris Garnsey, a University of Colorado professor, published an economic survey of the Rocky Mountain region entitled *America's New Frontier: The Mountain West*.[19] Garnsey was perplexed about the colonial position of the West. The need for industrialization of the region was evident, but how could this be achieved? The Colorado economist saw several difficulties mitigating the possibility of an industrial region: electric power was sadly deficient; industrial sites were few; transportation, with the detrimental freight-rate structure, was a handicap; the small population basis limited the market; and the tax structure in many states

17. John W. Caughey, "Editorial Remarks," *Pacific Historical Review* 16 (1947):228–31.

18. Rufus Terral, *The Missouri Valley: Land of Drouth, Flood, and Promise* (New Haven, 1947), pp. 155–230.

19. Morris Garnsey, *America's New Frontier: The Mountain West* (New York, 1950).

was not conducive to enticing industry. The end result was that the West, in spite of impediments, should aim for a diversified industry. A chief means to this end would be a revision of the railroad rate structure.

A millennium might be expected in the West's future if a liberal political movement combining the farm and labor groups could be developed. Garnsey anticipated the growth of a new regional movement in literature and politics, sparked by the intellectuals of western universities.

From five hundred miles north of the Boulder campus came the next approach to a solution of the West's problems. Carl F. Kraenzel, a sociologist at Montana State College, Bozeman, spent more than twenty years making an intensive study of the problems of the Great Plains. One of the basic assumptions he stated in *The Great Plains in Transition*:[20] "a humid-area type of civilization cannot thrive in the semiarid American Plains without constant subsidy, or, lacking this, without repeated impoverishment of the residents" (p. 4).

The eastern humid area's values, Kraenzel bemoaned, had been superimposed on the West because the civilization east of the hundredth meridian had the powerful support of the federal government. Farmers inexperienced in the agronomy of the West had been allowed to sift onto the Great Plains and had torn up the top soil, thereby bringing bankruptcy both to themselves and to the grazing economy. In a chauvinistic statement Kraenzel argued that the cattlemen and the sheepmen should have been left to wander, for theirs was the life that had been adapted to the physical environment of the Great Plains.

Involved as he was in the problem of colonial status, Kraenzel was perturbed about the exploitation of natural resources; he was especially piqued by the shipment of natural gas and oil to eastern industrial cities. These were the same cities that were holding the West in subjugation by controlling the capital necessary for development, but the Montana professor offered no remedy that approximated Walter Prescott Webb's internal tariff solution. Kraenzel was flatly op-

20. Carl F. Kraenzel, *The Great Plains in Transition* (Norman, 1955).

timistic that the hinterland status of the Great Plains would eventually be corrected. Why? Because a democracy cannot survive if one region is held down by another.

The battle over the "colonial complex" continues. A demonstration of the highly fraught emotions engendered by this subject occurred when Walter Prescott Webb, returning twenty years after *Divided We Stand,* trampled unceremoniously on the outcropped ego of the Rocky Mountain and the Great Plains country in an article published in *Harper's* for May 1957.[21] The Texas historian wrote that the distinct feature of the West was the Great American Desert. In spite of all the attempts of chambers of commerce to ignore their desert, Webb claimed, the aridity of the land dominated the entire region. Compared to the East, the West was a land of deficiencies.

As proof for this concept, Webb enumerated a number of statistics: textbook histories slighted the West, some giving only seven pages out of a hundred to the area that contained one-fifth of the country's population. The bank assets or liabilities of the eight states in the heart of the desert were only $6 billion, contrasted with the assets of $20 billion of Texas and California. The eight states had a population of only eight million inhabitants, while Texas and California announced that twenty million lived within their combined areas. Only 16.7 per cent of the persons listed in *Who's Who in America* were born in the West. In conclusion, Webb stated that dwellers of the Rocky Mountain West were "a normal people trying to create and maintain a normal civilization in an abnormal land."

The reaction to Webb's article from the journalistic and political elements in the West was both prompt and caustic. The Denver *Post,* in a scathing editorial entitled "Us Desert Rats Is Doing Okay," violently dissented from Webb's conclusions.[22] The *Post* announced the tenor of the article with journalistic—and picturesque—comment.

21. Walter P. Webb, "The American West, Perpetual Mirage," *Harper's* 214 (May 1957):25–31.
22. Denver *Post,* 28 April 1957.

It seems to us that a historian without any history to write about ought to put his typewriter away and go out picking Texas blue-bonnets or counting oil wells. But not you, doc. Oh, no. You were determined to write something about the mountain states.

The *Post* editorial went on to contend that nearly everything Webb said was distorted. The rainfall was greater in Colorado than the historian realized. Even if the bank assets were more in Texas and California, so what? Personal income was higher in Colorado than in twenty-eight other states. Perhaps there were not as many people in the Rocky Mountain Empire (the *Post* has a proclivity for this phrase), but one certainly could not argue that the region was being shunned; after all, some of the fastest-growing urban areas in the country were in this empire. As for producing men of distinction, the *Post* reluctantly admitted that this might be true, but there was certainly culture in the Rockies—just note the activity at Taos in New Mexico or at Aspen or Central City in Colorado.

When asked about the *Post* editorial, Webb refused to retract. He still insisted, "When you look at the situation pretty coldly . . . you find the whole West is growing, but it is growing only in the cities and this water problem is staring us in the face."[23]

The politicians, not to be outdone in the defense of their homeland, took up their cudgels on the floor of Congress. Sens. Wallace F. Bennett of Utah and Barry Goldwater of Arizona attacked the article.[24] Bennett termed the implication that the West had not contributed its share to our national development "unwarranted." Senator Goldwater claimed that Arizona was among the leading states in population growth, employment, nonferrous mineral production, and bank capital growth.

Is the West exploited, or is the intellectual protest of the last twenty years only a traumatic manifestation of homesick

23. Ibid., 30 April 1957.
24. Ibid., 6 May 1957.

and displaced Westerners? Many of the intellectual dissenters of the past two decades are now living in Alexandria, Virginia, or in New York City or in Boston. If the average Westerner is upset about the East, why was protest snatched away from the politicians by journalists, historians, and social scientists? The apparent answer is that the Westerner has long since accustomed himself to the phrase "slightly higher west of the Rockies." And he does not write frequently to his congressman, who would—nominally, at least—reflect his views.

The Westerner may even realize that he resides in a colony of the East and that he is being taken advantage of today. Certainly the motorist who stops at Sinclair, Wyoming—where a thirty thousand barrel-per-day oil refinery is located—to fill up the gas tank of his automobile is annoyed to find that the price per gallon is the same as if he were in Boston. The motorist probably will not be aware that the basing-point transportation system is involved in his gasoline price, but he is fully cognizant of the ludicrousness of a situation whereby he must pay the same price for a gallon of gasoline whether his car is two hundred feet or two thousand miles from a refinery.[25]

Aside from the logic or illogic of the basing-point system, if the Westerner sincerely takes time to contemplate his region, it may occur to him to wonder where the capital employed to develop the West would have been found if not in the East? The bankers of Helena, Montana, in 1890 could hardly have financed the Butte copper industry, any more than the Wyoming oil industry could have been developed without the assistance of the New York brokerage house of Carl H. Pforzheimer.

This is not to imply that the Westerner is necessarily content with his lot. He still protests against eastern absentee ownership, especially against the railroad when it comes time to ship his cattle to Omaha or Chicago. Many communities

25. An interesting rebuttal to the basing-point system on gasoline is in Harold Fleming's *Montana Gasoline Prices and Competition* (Helena, 1958). Fleming's study was sponsored by the Continental Oil Company. Another account of the basing-point system can be found in Fritz Machlup's *The Basing-Point System* (Philadelphia, 1949).

loudly oppose federal aid, yet they assiduously woo the federal government for funds to build interstate highways (although even then many become bellicose over the federal regulation stipulating a white line down the center of the road, when "anyone" knows that you can see a yellow line much better in a blizzard).

Another reflection of western ambivalence is the deference paid to eastern culture, an attitude prevalent throughout the arid region. Ranchmen in the Mountain West have for decades been sending their children to eastern finishing schools. Pinedale, Wyoming (population about 650), is renowned for its frigid winters and its Vassar alumnae. Western architecture is replete with examples of classical and Gothic-revival styles taken directly from architectural "pattern books" of the East and Midwest.[26] While the Westerner may resent the current television interpretation of his "frontier" institutions, Earl Pomeroy has shown that the Westerner who is involved in the tourist industry has consistently attempted to cast himself in the image that he believes the Easterner expects to see on his western vacation.[27]

Western chambers of commerce are as eager as any business associations in the United States to attract new industry. They would prefer the antiseptic research labs, federal bureaus, and the relatively clean missile bases to steel plants, but they are by no means above accepting the latter, as is attested by the recent opening of the United States Steel Corporation plant at Lander, Wyoming.

Another reason Westerners may seem more mute than they actually are is the dominance of an ordinary press. There are few genuinely liberal newspapers of national stature west of the hundredth meridian.

The intellectuals of recent years have also failed to express the spirit of western protest. Too much of the intellectual

26. In a suggestive article, Marion Ross shows how until 1890 architecture in Oregon was mainly a carbon of eastern ideas. Marion Ross, "Architecture in Oregon, 1845–1895," *Oregon Historical Quarterly* 57 (March 1956):33–64.

27. Earl Pomeroy, *In Search of the Golden West* (New York, 1957), p. 225.

revolt suffers from irrationality, and their arguments have frequently been ignored by the grass-roots citizens. Carl Kraenzel, for example, offers as one premise the idea that a reduction in population is necessary if the civilization on the Great Plains is to survive. In a later thesis, Kraenzel opposes the exporting of natural gas from the region. Yet what is the West to do with the tremendous natural gas reservoirs when the regional market is limited to a few populous areas such as Seattle or Minneapolis? What advantage would accrue from leaving the gas in the ground and borrowing money from eastern financial institutions to pay for imports from the East? How would a policy such as this help the West gain economic self-sufficiency?

Or how sound is the thesis that eastern institutions were imposed on a recalcitrant West? Western communities have for years attempted to entice the midwestern farmer to settle on the prairie. Even the old enigma of excessive freight charges repeated fervently by Populist, Progressive, and intellectual alike is being contested. E. T. Grether, in his study of the California steel industry,[28] found that the freight-rate structure was a competitive advantage, rather than a liability, for California steel producers marketing as far east as Salt Lake City.

It is this inability of the intellectual to formulate effective issues, plus the schizophrenic attitude of the Westerner toward the East, which has given much of the intellectual revolt a sterile quality. Still, in the final analysis (and barring another depression), Thurman Arnold and Bernard De Voto may represent the last gasp of the voice of western protest.[29] "The New West," symbolized by two hours from Denver to

28. E. T. Grether, *The Steel and Steel-Using Industries of California* (Sacramento, 1946), p. 91.

29. Leonard J. Arrington, in his recent and suggestive monograph, *From Wilderness to Empire* (Salt Lake City, 1961), convincingly argues that Utah is no longer a colony of the East. The increase in manufacturing after the Second World War, accompanied by the startling rise in demand from the California market, combined to decrease radically Utah's economic dependence on the East. Under another title and version this article was published in the *Pacific Northwest Quarterly* 54 (January 1963):1–8.

Chicago via jet, by millions of tourists scrambling over western hills every summer (many of them returning to stay), and by increasing industrialization, may well mitigate the possibility of future protest pressure erupting in the West. The Westerner will find it difficult to talk about eastern exploitation to his new neighbor from Sandusky, Ohio. The only question left to debate may well be whether the East has succumbed to the West!

The French, Belgians, and Dutch Arrive at Salt Creek

Forty miles north of Casper, Wyoming, lies a windswept rolling terrain, approximately twenty-two thousand acres of immensely productive oil-bearing sands. Geologically speaking this oil province is a classic anticlinal dome of remarkable symmetry, easily discernable to the neophyte geologist.[1]

While not as quickly perceivable as its geology, the history of the Salt Creek field, since its first recognition by the prospector, has been the scene of Atlantean corporate struggles, bitter claim disputes, unbelievable fraud, and wild political machinations. During the 1920s the entire nation's attention was riveted in morbid fascination on the daily exposures of the Teapot Dome[2] and Continental Trading Company[3] scandals. From one vista it might be argued that from the first evidence of corporate investment in the Salt Creek field, duplicity was the handmaiden of enterprise, although the first

1. The writer wishes to express his appreciation to S. A. Lane, H. C. Bretschneider, Leslie Parker, and James Donoghue for their reminiscences of the Wyoming oil scene.

2. The Teapot Dome episode has been uncovered in a number of able monographs: J. Leonard Bates, *The Origins of the Teapot Dome* (Urbana, 1963); Gerald Nash, *United States Oil Policy, 1890–1964* (Pittsburgh, 1968); John Ise, *The United States Oil Policy* (New Haven, 1926); Burl Noggle, *Teapot Dome: Oil and Politics in the 1920's* (Baton Rouge, 1962); Morris R. Werner and John Starr, *Teapot Dome* (New York, 1959); David H. Stratton, "Albert B. Fall and the Teapot Dome Affair" (Ph.D. dissertation, University of Colorado, 1955); Robert Waller, "Business and the Initiation of the Teapot Dome Investigation," *The Business History Review* 36 (Autumn 1962): 334–53.

3. One of the more balanced and incisive accounts of the Continental Trading affair is in Paul H. Giddens, *Standard Oil Company (Indiana)* (New York, 1951), pp. 230–34, 362–64.

eastern interest in Wyoming petroleum, while startlingly inept, was not guided by guile—that is, if one ignores the basic land claims.

Throughout the 1880s, central Wyoming had excited the curiosity of a number of would-be prospectors. Indeed, the first recorded claim in the Salt Creek area appears to have been made by the founder of the University of Wyoming, Stephen Downey. Territorial geologists Samuel Aughey and Lewis D. Ricketts, both of whom would have outstanding careers, commented on the rich "petrolcum lands" in the center of the territory.[4] One grizzled old-time forty-niner, Cyrus Iba, kept his faith (although that was about all) in the field from the early 1880s until his demise in 1907. Annually, Cyrus Iba, in company with his sizable family,[5] made pilgrimages to the Salt Creek field, "accomplishing" their one hundred dollar per claim assessment in a couple of days and returning home. Iba's belief in Salt Creek was rewarded after his death, when one of his patented claims, the Iba "80," became the foundation for the family fortune.

Obviously this sporadic local interest did not translate into a systematic development of the field. In 1889, this situation radically altered with the arrival in Wyoming of P. M. Shannon of Bradford, Pennsylvania. "Mark" Shannon had been a highly successful operator-promoter in western Pennsylvania oil country. After looking over the field, Shannon decided to organize the Pennsylvania Oil and Gas Company.[6] Then his

4. Samuel Aughey, *Annual Report of the Territorial Geologist* (Laramie, 1886); Lewis B. Ricketts, *Annual Report of the Territorial Geologist* (Laramie, 1889).

5. If the extraordinary amount of litigation on the Salt Creek field accomplished nothing else, it did provide the historian with rich documentary records of the manifold byways of Salt Creek history. The Iba family migrations and personal history are best revealed in C. W. Iba's testimony in the "Transcript of the Central Wyoming Oil and Development Company vs. William Henshaw, *et al.*" 7:4–429, Midwest Oil Collection, Petroleum History and Research Center, University of Wyoming, Laramie.

6. Pieces of the Pennsylvania Oil and Gas Company history can be put together from "J. W. Gordon Testimony," C. L. Hendershot Affidavits, 7–51; "Minute Book of the Pennsylvania Oil and Gas Company," Midwest Oil Collection; and Wilbur C. Knight, *The Petroleum*

manager, George B. McCalmont, set about securing 105,000 acres of mineral claims. Within a year after the arrival of the Pennsylvania group they drilled the first well in what became known as the Shannon pool on the extreme north slope of the Salt Creek field. At a little over a thousand feet, they struck oil. Within the next two years the Pennsylvania Oil and Gas Company drilled three more wells, all productive.[7] The amazing and enigmatic feature of this activity was, now that Shannon had oil, what would he do with it? Finding a market has been a perpetual problem for the Rocky Mountain oil promoter. Shannon did not bother to solve this dilemma until five years after his arrival in Wyoming, when he erected a "cheese box" refinery at Casper with a skimming capacity of one hundred barrels a day. With a refinery in operation, transportation became Shannon's next challenge. Unable to finance a railroad from Salt Creek to Casper, Shannon organized a series of string teams to laboriously freight the crude from field to refinery. Finally, after considerable maneuvering, he was able to negotiate favorable freight rates from the Fremont, Elkorn and Missouri and the Cheyenne and Northern railroads to sell his crude in Nebraska.

By 1900, it was becoming more and more apparent that the stockholders of the Pennsylvania Oil and Gas Company were finding their investment in central Wyoming as bleak as the scenery. As nearly as can be gleaned from their minute book they had sunk over $600,000 in Wyoming, with the total dividends coming to $37,000 over an eleven-year period, hardly a flourishing enterprise.[8]

At the turn of the century, then, the officers of the Pennsylvania Oil and Gas Company were in a highly receptive mood for any offers that might come their way—especially since they did not expect any! Salvation for the Pennsylvanians arrived

of Salt Creek, Wyoming, Bulletin No. 1, School of Mines, University of Wyoming (Laramie, 1898).

7. C. A. Fisher, "History of the Well Drilling in Salt Creek field in chronological order from 1889 to the Present Time," 1889–1918, (manuscript, Midwest Oil Collection).

8. "Minute Book of the Pennsylvania Oil and Gas Company," 8, 23, Midwest Oil Collection.

in the guise of one of the most contriving charlatans ever to enter the Salt Creek locale—Joseph H. Lobell. Sometime tailor, erstwhile lawyer, all-time promoter, Lobell's personal history is as shadowy as many of his manipulations at Salt Creek.[9] The first trace of Lobell in the United States came when he registered in Chicago as a private detective in 1889; he maintained that profession for the next six years, even though his reputation and competence were questionable in light of his impersonation of a Scotland Yard detective. Although he lacked education in the law, some time between 1895 and 1898, he established a law firm in Chicago in partnership with his son, Frederick J. Lobell. Business must have been slow as they declared bankruptcy on 24 May 1900.

However, the Lobells were obviously not dispirited for long, as they surfaced in London in 1901. Here in camaraderie with four like-minded impresarios they organized the Anglo-Wyoming Oil Fields, Ltd., most commonly referred to as the Wyoming Syndicate. The firm noted that it had an international representation (perhaps even reputation) on its board of directors, which was composed of Henry Walter, London, holding 30 per cent of the stock, Rudi Landeur, Paris, 30 per cent, Joseph H. Lobell, Chicago, 30 per cent, and the Barons Robert and Eugene Oppenheim, Paris, 5 per cent each.[10] Information concerning how the Lobells learned

9. After receiving a flood of inquiries regarding Joseph Lobell, Sen. Francis E. Warren of Wyoming determined to find out all he could about the various Lobell company manipulations. He sent off inquiries to the American consuls in France, Belgium, and Switzerland, besides hiring a special investigator in Chicago. The report that he received from Chicago is an astounding document that graphically outlines the Lobell family biography to 1903. Had Lobell's European investors been privy to this document, it is doubtful whether the Lobells would have been welcome in any of the financial offices in Europe ("Special Report—Class A, on Lobell & Lobell, 67 Clark Street," Chicago, 13 May 1903, F. E. Warren Letterbooks, 2 February 1904—11 July 1904, F. E. Warren Collection, Western History Research Center, University of Wyoming, Laramie).

10. C. W. Burdick, "Organization of the Belgian and American Belgo Companies, Acquisition of Land and Present Status," p. 2, manuscript, Midwest Oil Collection. Harold Roberts, who served as attorney for over forty years for the Midwest Oil and associated

of Wyoming oil, or managed to associate themselves with this group, is beyond our retrieval.

The Wyoming Syndicate had been organized, with its headquarters in Chicago, less than a year before the Lobells decided that more funds were needed to further their expansionist schemes. In Europe, with their Wyoming Syndicate contracts, they organized on 10 April 1902, the Société Belgo Américaine des Pétroles du Wyoming, known to its contemporaries as the Belgian Belgo. The original capitalization was $400,000 but eventually through a domino series of stock issues, it was increased to $6 million. The announced objective of the firm was to absorb the mineral lands of the Anglo-Wyoming Oil Fields, Ltd., near Lander, Wyoming.[11] A year later, on 7 April 1903, when the promoters discovered that it was legally hazardous for a foreign company to hold title to land in the United States, they incorporated another company under the laws of Wyoming, with the redundant name of Société Belgo Américaine des Pétroles du Wyoming of Wyoming,[12] afterwards called the Wyoming Belgo. The Wyoming Belgo's capital stock of $1.5 million was turned over to the parent Belgian Belgo.

With their corporate facade and treasury furnished, Lobell and his associates easily divined that their next promotional strategy would be guided in two directions. One, they would need the endorsement of a highly reputable geologist as to the value of their Wyoming lands. Two, a publicity campaign had to be launched in Europe to entice would-be investors and to inflate the Belgo stock. Their first plan was easily implemented. Sir Boverton Redwood, an internation-

---

companies, wrote a valuable history of the Salt Creek field, *Salt Creek: The Story of a Great Oil Field* (Denver, 1956). However, as the result of Roberts's heavy reliance on his personal recollections and files, the early history of Salt Creek is sketchily treated ("Notes for the Salt Creek History," Harold Roberts Collection, Petroleum History and Research Center).

11. C. W. Burdick, "Organization of the Belgian and American Belgo Companies, Acquisition of Land and Present Status," 3, manuscript, Midwest Oil Collection.

12. "Minute Book of the Société Belgo Américaine des Pétroles du Wyoming," Midwest Oil Collection.

ally renowned petroleum geologist and engineer, had visited Wyoming on his American tour of 1899. While his terse, laconic statements in his published account would give little hint as to his later enthusiasm,[13] evidently Wyoming greatly impressed the good scientist, for he furnished rhapsodic prose to the press in the form of letters to Rudi Landeur, about the tremendous petroleum potentialities of Wyoming.[14] Redwood even went so far as to offer to select the drilling sites from his London office!

To buttress Sir Boverton's zealousness, the Lobells selected a Wyoming geologist, Dr. Wilbur C. Knight, to sanction their plans. In contrast to Redwood, Knight was thoroughly conversant with Wyoming's minerals, having undertaken a survey of the mineral resources of Wyoming, the result of which he published in several state reports. In response to the Belgo company request on 6 July 1903, Knight issued a "Special Report on the Salt Creek Field."[15] Knight specifically focused his survey on the holdings of the Pennsylvania Oil and Gas Company, which Lobell had been urging his associates to purchase. While lacking the unrestrained enthusiasm of Redwood, Knight concluded his report optimistically, "Considered from every standpoint the Salt Creek field offers special inducements to capital . . . guaranteeing a safe investment that will yield good returns."[16]

Armed with the benedictions of experts, Lobell and company proceeded to their next step: a paper campaign in the European press, which became a war before it was terminated. Some time in the winter or spring of 1901–1902, Lobell employed a French journalist, Robert Charles Henri Le Roux, who wrote under the name of Hughes Le Roux, to

13. Boverton Redwood, *A Treatise on Petroleum*, I (London, 1913), pp. 94, 183.

14. "Letter Relating to an Interview with Dr. Boverton Redwood," F. E. Warren Letterbook, 2 February–11 July 1904, p. 433, F. E. Warren Collection.

15. Wilbur C. Knight, "Special Report on the Salt Creek Oil Field, Located in Natrona County, Wyoming, U.S.A., for Governor Noel Pardon of Paris, France" (Laramie, Wyoming, 6 July 1903), Wilbur C. Knight Collection, Western History Research Center.

16. Ibid., p. 6.

visit Wyoming and offer his observations on the petroleum conditions to the public. Le Roux published his "findings" in a small book entitled *Le Wyoming: Historie Anecdotique du Pétrole* in April 1904.[17] In view of his sponsorship, it is stretching the bounds of credibility to expect an objective account. We are not disappointed. In glowing, eloquent phrases, Le Roux relates the anecdotal, as he put it, history of the petroleum industry from the Drake Well forward. His accounts of the "golden wealth of the land" and the "social habits of the citizens" leave us a bit breathless. Evidently intoxicated by more than the high altitude, he recalls a high moment at the Interocean Hotel bar in Cheyenne with "your feet a little higher than knees, a cigar in the corner of your lips, and an important 'Bourbon Whiskey' within reach of your hand."[18] After gushing about the riches of the Salt Creek field and the marvelous efficiency of the Casper refinery, Le Roux concludes his narrative with yet another account at the London office of that great prophet, Sir Boverton Redwood. We hear again from the lips of Sir Boverton reassurances about the tremendous petroleum "deposits" in Wyoming.

Perhaps a bit dubious about the capability of the Le Roux manuscript alone to guarantee investor gullibility, the Belgian Belgo directors announced to the European press that an impartial Committee of Investigation would be appointed to examine the Wyoming property. Finally, it was decided that two members of this committee, Noel Pardon, former governor general of the French colonies and André E. Sayous, referred to as a "writer, doctor of law, and Professor at the École des Hautes Études," would tour Wyoming. In the spring of 1903, the Wyoming newspapers announced for the second time within a year the arrival of French visitors.[19] Pardon and Sayous traveled over Wyoming and the West; at

17. Hughes Le Roux, *Le Wyoming: Historie Anecdotique du Pétrole* (Paris, 1904). Wilson O. Clough has translated this volume and the André Sayous pamphlet (see note 21). See Wilson O. Clough, "Portrait in Oil: The Belgo-Américaine Company in Wyoming," *Annals of Wyoming* 61 (April 1969):5–31.

18. Le Roux, *Le Wyoming*, p. 44; Clough translation, Wilson O. Clough Collection, Western History Research Center.

19. Cheyenne *Leader*, 28 April 1903.

both Cheyenne and Casper they were guests of honor at "sumptuous" banquets.[20]

When the "Committee of Investigation" presented its verdict, in essence a complete endorsement of the Belgo company, they quite obviously ignored the writing of André Sayous, which appeared soon after his return to Paris. Under the title of "Le Wyoming and General Considerations on the 'Far West,' "[21] Sayous, in startling contrast to Le Roux, emphasized the hazards of investing in the Wyoming petroleum industry. "Every hole dug by prospectors is declared richer than a cave in the thousand and one nights."[22] Wyoming, he insisted, was an economic fief of the Union Pacific, "Its employees are numerous and in every electoral campaign they control not only the votes but also the capital."[23] As to the riches of Salt Creek, "There are numerous obstacles to putting this wealth into production." The chief of these, Sayous argued, was transportation and the Standard Oil Company. "It is difficult to put Lander in touch with civilization."[24]

Sayous's cautious and skeptical warnings seemed mild in relation to the next tract that appeared, this time not in Paris, but in Brussels. For the *Histoire de la Société Belgo-Américaine des Pétroles du Wyoming*, by Louis Magne, was laden with vicious attacks, vitrolic comments and sarcastic observations.[25] Little is known of Magne; he may have been a disgruntled stockholder or a competitor of the French-Belgian investment galaxy behind the Belgo company. Whatever his background, Magne's book systematically demolished Le Roux's work and the favorable press statement and prospectuses issued by the Belgo directors. Magne especially singled out Redwood's comments for castigation, insisting that the Belgo company had done little to improve their Wyoming properties. What was the evil genius behind the

20. Laramie *Daily Boomerang*, 3 May 1903.

21. André E. Sayous, "Le Wyoming and General Considerations on the 'Far West' " (Paris, 1904).

22. Ibid., p. 1, Clough translation, W. O. Clough Collection.

23. Ibid., p. 16.

24. Ibid., pp. 28–31.

25. Louis Magne, *Histoire de la Société Belgo-Américaine des Pétroles du Wyoming* (Brussels, 1904).

Belgian Belgo? "Publicity," retorts Magne. "Everything has served: articles of scientific appearance, the most colossal books, reports, interviews, the show of names and locations, the phantasmagoria of millions, the most audacious plans. . . ."[26] What immediate impact this war of words had on the Belgo stock is unknown, but by the spring of 1904, a Pyrrhonism regarding their stock issues pervaded the financial circles in European capitals.

Sen. Francis E. Warren of Wyoming discovered the disenchantment with the Belgo manipulations, when he received replies to his letters requesting a "confidential assessment" of the Belgo company from the United States consuls in Belgium, Switzerland, and France. From Paris came the news, "The Société Belgian Américiane . . . is strongly criticized; doubts are even expressed in careful and conservative circles as to the existence of the oil fields in question. Authorities consulted are of the opinion that the shares are not to be recommended as an investment."[27] From Brussels came word reminiscent of British understatement:

> I must say that the information obtainable locally respecting the concern in question is of a rather indefinite character, but the opinion predominates in financial circles that the ultimate outcome is exceedingly problematic, those principally interested in its promotion are widely known as shrewd financiers, but their time in the past seems to have been devoted to undertakings of a rather hazardous nature.[28]

From Geneva the confidential report held that in that city the Belgo operation had been merged into another speculative venture, the "Association Internationale." Floated at something over 100,000,000 francs the "Association Internationale" announced its raison d'être as dual in purpose: one, to build a railroad from the Mississippi River to the Wyoming oil fields; two, to construct a tunnel under the Alps

26. Ibid., p. 123.

27. J. K. Goudy to Francis E. Warren, 28 March 1904, F. E. Warren Letterbook, 2 February–11 July 1904, p. 427, F. E. Warren Collection.

28. George Roosevelt to Francis E. Warren, 25 March 1904, ibid., p. 429.

between France and Switzerland—both quite modest proposals from introverted promoters! Horace Lee, the Swiss
consul, concluded by observing the self-evident, "the 'Association Internationale' is a highly risky proposition even
by standards of Geneva."[29]

The Belgo directors replied to these rumors and attacks in
kind, dispatching a number of open letters and broadsides
throughout 1903 and 1904. One letter addressed to "our
friends and shareholders," emphasized that the press attacks
came from "jealous" financial interests engaged in a nefarious
plot to depress the price of the Belgo shares.[30] After this was
accomplished these "blackguards" would take over the company. In ringing sentences the Belgo officers explained that
it was their "duty to unmask this plan in order to warn our
friends against the trap thus planned." For the only alternative "would be to throw one's self in the wolf's mouth."[31]

While the claims and counterclaims flared on the Continent, back in Wyoming another type of publicity coverage
was well under way. Throughout 1903, monthly and more
frequent releases showed up in Wyoming newspapers on the
various plans of Lobell and crowd.[32] Most of them centered
on a proposed railroad, whose origin and destination mean-
dered over Wyoming, month by month. The one concrete
accomplishment of the Belgo company came in November
1903, with the announcement that Wyoming Belgo had purchased the refinery and land holdings of the Pennsylvania Oil
and Gas company.[33] The announced price was $350,000 cash
for one hundred sixty acres of patented land, innumerable
claims, and the refinery in Casper. As far as can be determined, this is the sole time that the Belgo officers paid cash

29. Horace Lee to Francis E. Warren, 28 March 1904, ibid., p. 428.

30. *Wyoming Industrial Journal* (October 1903), p. 106; Cheyenne
Leader, 19 March 1904, and London *Times*, 4 December 1903.

31. "To our Friends and Shareholders of the Société Belgo Américaine of Wyoming Petroleums," copy in F. E. Warren Letterbook, 2
February–11 July 1904, p. 432, F. E. Warren Collection.

32. Cheyenne *Leader*, 28 April, 2 May 1903; Laramie *Daily Boomerang*, 19 March, 17 March 1904.

33. *Wyoming Industrial Journal* 2 (December 1903):180–81.

for any property, a feat that was accomplished only after borrowing $331,000 from Count and Countess Roy de Puyfontaine of Paris. Lobell then issued a mortgage to the Puyfontaines for the lands, but withheld the refinery, asking for a personal payment of $50,000 from the Belgo directors for the inclusion of the refinery. Puyfontaine immediately instituted a suit, which was settled on 15 May 1905, with Lobell transferring the lands and the refinery to the Belgian Belgo.[34]

Far from being discouraged by the Puyfontaine debacle, on 1 May 1905, Wyoming Belgo vice-president, J. M. Laventhal, who was closely involved in Lobell's dealings, executed a mortgage to Lobell for $150,000, secured by the identical lands that had just been mortgaged to Puyfontaine; needless to say the count had no knowledge of this Lobell lien.[35] Lobell later argued that the $150,000 mortgage was in payment for services he had rendered on behalf of the Wyoming Belgo.

Five months later on 14 November 1905, the Wyoming Belgo, via Joseph Lobell, trustee, gave the Belgian Belgo a ninety-nine-year lease on all the lands heretofore owned by the Pennsylvania Oil and Gas Company.[36] For this magnanimous act, Joseph and Fred Lobell were given a substantial amount of Belgian Belgo stock and were designated as the American agents for the Belgian Belgo. As agents their duties encompassed the arduous tasks of making the annual assessment work in Salt Creek and managing the Casper refinery. Concurrently with the acquisition of the Pennsylvania company, Lobell put together the Belgo-American Drilling Trust, ostensibly for the purpose of drilling the Belgo holdings.[37]

34. C. W. Burdick, "Organization of Belgian and American Belgo Companies, Acquisition of Land and Present Status," pp. 2–3, Midwest Oil Collection.

35. "Transactions of Joseph H. Lobell in re. to the Salt Creek Oil Field," manuscript, ibid.

36. "Minute Book Société Belgo Américaine des Pétroles du Wyoming," p. 36, ibid.

37. S. A. Lane, whose company subcontracted the Dutch-Belgo Américaine Drilling Contract in Salt Creek, recalled that Lord Templeton told him that Joseph Lobell, "never will operate the Belgo-Américaine Drilling Trust—operation is not the purpose of Lobell's life"

As far as can be told, the Belgo-American Drilling Trust never put down one well in Salt Creek or elsewhere.

In the summer of 1905, the directors of the Belgian Belgo decided, in view of their restricted capital for development, to offer subleases to their stockholders and directors, provided that the lessees would pay the assessment and drilling costs, with a 15 per cent overriding royalty being given to the Belgian Belgo. A number of the leases on the Salt Creek lands were passed out from 1905 to 1909, but with two exceptions none of the lessees did any exploration.[38] The failure to find production, plus the drain on the Belgo treasury by the Lobells for costs involved with the annual assessment work, brought the downfall of the Belgian Belgo company in 1909.

However, by 1906, Lobell and his confederates in the Wyoming Syndicate realized that they had squeezed about all the profits they could from the various Belgo companies so they turned to new fields to conquer with the same tried-and-true techniques. Accordingly, Lobell sought out the forty-niner, Cyrus Iba, and for a $19,500 mortgage obtained from Iba a large number of unpatented claims in the heart of the Salt Creek field.[39] Looking for some place and someone to whom he could peddle these claims, Lobell now shifted his attention from Belgium to Dutch capitalists. At The Hague, he found what he considered a likely mark, Camille M. A. de Ryck van der Gracht,[40] who managed the funds of

(interview with S. A. Lane, 23 February 1958, Petroleum History and Research Center).

38. A French group under the company title of ASCO drilled several wells on Section 2, Salt Creek, on Belgo subleases; none were productive. A Swedish concern added to the cosmopolitan flavor of Salt Creek in 1907 by taking another sublease from the Belgo company. They also drilled on Section 2, finding water. Evidently this was enough to dampen Swedish spirits for this is the one and only time they are recorded in Salt Creek history (C. A. Fisher, "History of Well Drilling in the Salt Creek field in Chronological Order from 1889 to the Present Time," manuscript, Midwest Oil Collection).

39. "Testimony of C. W. Iba," transcript, Central Wyoming Oil and Development Company vs. William Henshaw, et al., 7:210–11, Midwest Oil Collection.

40. Very little is known of van der Gracht's life. A bachelor, he died

a Dutch investment group. Van der Gracht became so entranced with Lobell's description of Wyoming's petroleum wealth that he employed an outstanding Italian geologist, Dr. Cesare Porro,[41] to go to Wyoming to examine the Salt Creek geology.

Unlike Boverton Redwood, Porro was perfectly capable of holding his enthusiasm in check. The report he sent back to the Dutch is a model of geological examination. Porro had little doubt about the potential of the Salt Creek field; he even specified the site for the first well to be drilled. What bothered Porro were other intangibles such as the problem of transportation, markets, and the price of oil. Porro wrote, "If altogether considered, the price of oil, the cost of production, and unavoidable missresults [sic], [and] the production gives a profit, one could try to enlarge the field gradually."[42]

at The Hague on 26 July 1916, age forty-nine. H. L. Kruimel to Gene M. Gressley, 1 January 1958, Petroleum History and Research Center.

41. Everett De Golyer wrote of Porro, "His work covered almost the entire oil world of his time and was marked by notable successes. His location of the discovery well for Salt Creek is probably the first geological location for a big oil field in the United States and at the time of his death, he was probably the senior oil geologist for the world." Born in Milan on 17 March 1865, Porro was the son of Count Alexandro Porro, senator in Italy. He studied in the Lyceum in Turin, graduating from the University of Pavia in 1891. Later Porro did post-graduate work at the universities of Berlin and Strausberg. Royal Dutch Shell sent him to Sumatra in 1899, where his assessment and recommendations of geological structures proved so profitable for the Royal Dutch that his services were soon sought the world over. For the next two decades Porro worked for clients in Iraq, Iran, Rumania, Wyoming, Burma, California, Russia, South Africa, and Albania. He retired in 1924. Thomas Harrison, a geologist and life-long friend described Porro, the man, "A powerful figure of a man, somewhat taller than the average—pleasant, simple, friendly—he was an energetic, tireless worker. . . . In the field, he wore a dark green jean suit—coat and knee trousers, with nail clad shoes, the whole topped with a soft green crush hat. On occasion, he carried, strapped high on his back and shoulders, a green canvas knapsack of many convenient pockets. All were evident products of his Alpine background." Porro died in Milan on 1 December 1940 (Thomas Harrison, "Cesare Porro," *The Bulletin of the American Association of Petroleum Geologist* 36 [August 1952]:1681–86).

42. Cesare Porro, "Report on Salt Creek," p. 4. Thomas S. Harrison

Porro's measured remarks could hardly be interpreted as an impassioned endorsement of the Salt Creek field. Yet his very cautiousness, together with his assurances that the field was not "salted," soon converted the Dutch to Lobell's cause.

Subsequently, on 22 November 1906, the Petroleum Maatschappij Salt Creek of The Hague was incorporated with a capitalization of $1 million. The Dutch then negotiated a contract with the Wyoming Syndicate to buy 2,200 acres of land in the Salt Creek field as selected by Porro. Of the $1,250,000 purchase price, $250,000 was in cash, the remainder in stocks and bonds.[43] By April 1907, the Petroleum Maatschappij Salt Creek had delivered another cash payment of $100,000 plus $40,000 in bonds to Lobell and friends. The Dutch, as had the Belgians, decided to organize a Wyoming corporation with an identical name to hold their newly acquired oil lands. On 13 May 1907, the Petroleum Maatschappij Salt Creek of Wyoming, hereafter referred to as the Wyoming Maatschappij, was incorporated with $1 million capitalization.

Seventeen days later the Dutch Maatschappij entered into an agreement with Lobell's Belgo American Drilling Trust to drill one well to a depth of 3,500 feet, for $20,000, of which $15,000 was paid in advance.[44] A few days later Lobell subcontracted an expanded drilling contract with the Oil Wells Drilling Syndicate of London for fourteen wells.[45]

In May 1907, the Dutch Maatschappij sent out a young engineer, Coenraad Kerbert, to Casper to act as local manager.[46] In June, Kerbert hired a wagon and made the long

Collection, Petroleum History and Research Center, University of Wyoming.

43. "Corporation Record," Petroleum Maatschappij Salt Creek of The Hague, p. 8, Midwest Oil Collection.

44. "Memorandum, Transactions of Joseph H. Lobell in re. Salt Creek Oil Lands," Midwest Oil Collection.

45. Interview with S. A. Lane, 23 February 1958.

46. When Kerbert departed from Casper and the Petroleum Maatschappij in 1911, he went with Royal Dutch Shell first in Russia. In December 1919, he "escaped with so-to-speak nothing but my pants on and lucky at that." After Russia he spent the next twenty-some years

forty-mile trek to Salt Creek. What he saw then and over the next few weeks convinced him that all the titles in the Salt Creek field were suspect with the most questionable of all those originally held by Lobell and the Wyoming Syndicate. In association with Septimus A. Lane, the local representative for the Oil Wells Drilling Trust, Kerbert haunted the courthouse and held long conversations with his attorney. The more he uncovered the more upset he became, for the very titles conferred to the Dutch by Lobell contained double conveyances, undischarged mortgage liens, and a mosaic of other claims.[47] Kerbert's letters to The Hague were so discouraging that Van der Gracht went to Wyoming to personally survey the situation. His findings only amplified those of Kerbert. But what should they do? On the advice of their Casper attorney, G. R. Hagens, a new set of placer claims was filed by local citizens, covering the same land as conveyed to them by Lobell. These claims were then placed in a new corporation, the Central Wyoming Oil and Development Company, on 28 October 1907, with van der Gracht and Kerbert serving as officers. A year later, on 19 December 1908, the Central Wyoming company gave a ninety-nine-year lease to

---

with Shell in Sumatra, Venezuela, and the Middle East. When the Central Wyoming Oil and Gas Company sued William Fitzhugh and William Henshaw in 1916, they sent two attorneys and a stenographer to Russia to obtain Kerbert's testimony. They returned to New York with Kerbert's deposition on 20 July 1916. The accuracy and forthrightness of Kerbert's testimony proved valuable not only in the Central Wyoming case but in much of the subsequent litigation on Salt Creek. Fluent in eight languages, Kerbert married Constance Thomson-Stevenson of Bridlington, England, who died in Russia on 5 May 1917. He remarried on 7 July 1920, to Clara J. Stevenson of Windsor, England. Kerbert died in The Hague on 12 August 1958. His English friend and coworker, S. A. Lane, remembered Kerbert as a "first rate" engineer and manager, but personally as "kind of a busybody, very important, quite nice, rather fussy about his dress and things, rather a good entertainer and that kind of thing" (H. L. Kruimel to Gene M. Gressley, 1 January 1958; Coenraad Kerbert to Gene M. Gressley, 2 February 1958. Interview with S. A. Lane, 23 February 1958; Harry McCracken to Gene M. Gressley, 14 October 1958, all in Petroleum History and Research Center).

47. Interview with S. A. Lane, ibid.

the Dutch Maatschappij for a five-per-cent overriding royalty on the net production.[48]

Kerbert spent the winter of 1907–1908 "jumping" Wyoming Belgo claims, a description that would come back to torment him in a suit a decade later.[49] With the coming of spring, Kerbert began to push S. A. Lane to start drilling. Lane, a bit lethargic by nature, would not proceed until he heard from London. Unfortunately the Oil Wells Drilling Syndicate had encountered financial problems, so until it reorganized as the International Drilling Trust, there were no instructions being sent anyone.[50] Finally, after an exasperated Kerbert threatened suit, the drilling began on Section 23 in August 1908. By October 16, the well reached 1,050 feet, gushing in with a roar.[51] The "big Dutch" well, as it was ever after known in Salt Creek lore, did far more than substantiate the twenty-year-old dreams of Cyrus Iba and the fairyland prognostications of Joseph Lobell. For quickly the news of the Dutch well spread throughout the petroleum world, attracting capital and entrepreneurial talent that would inaugurate a new era for Salt Creek. No longer just a maze of fraudulent claims, Salt Creek now had proven wealth for the taking, and takers were plentiful.

Tout de suite, the Lobells, who correctly assessed the birth of the Central Wyoming company as an undermining of their rights, began attacking Kerbert in the board meetings of the Dutch Maatschappij. Actually the Lobells' pique with Ker-

48. "Minute Book of the Central Wyoming Oil and Development Company," p. 13, Midwest Oil Collection.

49. Kerbert in Guriev, Russia, on 16 June 1916, was asked the embarrassing question of whether he had written his Casper attorney on 26 November 1908, as follows, "About the jumping of more Belgo-American lands after January first, I shall write you in a few days." Kerbert conceded that the quotation was probably accurate (Kerbert Deposition, Central Wyoming Oil and Development Company vs. William G. Henshaw, et al., p. 152, Midwest Oil Collection).

50. Interview with S. A. Lane, ibid.

51. The "discovery" date has been open to considerable controversy; however, the diary of Frank Middaugh, an employee of the Dutch Maatschappij, establishes the above date ("Frank Middaugh Diary," C. L. Hendershot affidavits, William M. Fitzhugh Collection), Petroleum History and Research Center.

bert began three years earlier, ever since Kerbert convinced de Ryck to withhold some of the stock of the Dutch Maatschappij from the Lobells, thereby preventing the speculation that had been synonymous with the Belgo operations.[52] To protect himself, Kerbert returned to The Hague in the winter of 1909, determined to oust the Lobells from the board of the directors. After a two-month contest the Lobells surrendered —for a high price. They received, in addition to a cash payment of $108,000, the release of the previously promised $1 million in debentures and shares in the Dutch Maatschappij. In return the Lobells and the Wyoming Syndicate relinquished all future claims and mortgages on Dutch land in Salt Creek.[53] While this marks the official severance of the Lobells with foreign investment in Wyoming, by their continual legal sniping they were a factor to contend with for another decade.[54]

52. Kerbert Testimony, Central Wyoming Oil and Development Company vs. William Henshaw, et al., 1:175–77, Midwest Oil Collection.

53. "Corporation Record," Petroleum Maatschappij Salt Creek, 64–66, Midwest Oil Collection.

54. Lobell, for a decade after 1913, continued to harass the Salt Creek contestants, pyramiding one company on top of another. In 1913, he incorporated the Parkman Oil Company, then the National Petroleum Company, the United Oil Company, the Federal Oil and Development Company, Western Union Oil Company, and the Salt Creek Oil and Gas Company. Into each of these companies Lobell transferred personal claims, either mortgages, land or stock. Then with these companies as vehicles he proceeded to sue in succession Reed, Fitzhugh, the Stock family, and the Central Wyoming Oil and Development Company. In one of these suits, which involved the Executive Withdrawal Order of 1909, Henry McAllister, William Fitzhugh's attorney in Denver, wrote Fitzhugh upon returning to Washington, "It seems that one John H. Hobbs, formerly of Colorado Springs and Denver, and who is a promoter by vocation, has been trying to break into the Lobell proposition, and through Hobbs, Senator Thomas of Colorado began to show his fine Italian hand in the Department of Interior. The result of all this was that about the time Schuyler left Washington, Commissioner Tallman related to him a long tale of woe for which undoubtedly the Lobell people were responsible. More important was Schuyler's [Midwest Oil's attorney] recital of an interview with Townsend [Lobell's attorney], who again attacked you bit-

With the Lobell problem resolved, Kerbert returned to the United States strongly determined to push the drilling program as fast as funds would allow. Unfortunately, after the Lobell struggle the exchequer of the Dutch was almost exhausted. So low were the Dutch on funds that Kerbert had to take part of his salary in Maatschappij stock. In fact, Dutch directors had considerable doubts about going ahead with any drilling, for by the fall of 1909 they had exactly one well to show for a total expenditure of more than $315,000 cash and more than $1 million in debentures and stock. Kerbert, convinced that Lane and the International Drilling Trust would never complete their contract, stopped at Pittsburgh on the way west, purchasing two drilling rigs.

Upon reaching Casper, Kerbert announced the largest exploration and drilling program ever undertaken in the twenty-year history of the Salt Creek field. By December 1909, through Kerbert's persistent prodding, the Dutch had ap-

---

terly for the high-handed method which you had pursued in defeating Lobell, 'just as he was arranging for financing his enterprise' and then Townsend proceeded to make the remarkable proposition that this fight should be really between Lobell and you and that if the Midwest Company would keep its hands off, then Lobell would be willing to make an arrangement with the Midwest to take the same royalties or profits which you received under your contracts, which Townsend stated he had examined from the records at Casper. Briefly, Townsend, who first charged you with bad faith, then proceeded to out-Herod Herod by suggesting that the Midwest Company throw you out, remain neutral in your fight with Lobell, and then enter into contractual relations with Lobell substantially the same as you now have." The Wyoming Oil Fields Company negotiated a "final" settlement with the Lobells in 1919, which for all practical purposes removed the Lobells from Salt Creek, though their suits ran on for another four years. The total amount paid the Lobells under the Wyoming Oil Fields contract is not known; we do know that when the monthly payments finally ceased in May 1925, the Wyoming Oil Fields had disbursed over $800,000 to the Lobells (Henry McAllister to William M. Fitzhugh, 7 April 1915; G. R. Hagens to William M. Fitzhugh, 13 October 1911; Henry McAllister to William Fitzhugh, 7 April, 6 May 1915, William M. Fitzhugh Collection. Statement by Frederick J. Lobell, 6 July 1917, Midwest Oil Collection. Frederick J. Lobell to Charles W. Carlisle, 17 December 1915, 26 January 1916, Charles W. Carlisle Collection, Petroleum History and Research Center).

propriated another $60,000,[55] with the result that, as Kerbert proudly wrote them, they now had four productive wells. Ironically, the technological and financial vexations that Kerbert conquered in 1909 were overshadowed by a much greater threat to his company, specifically the activities of William M. Fitzhugh.

Tenacious, able, exasperating, with far more integrity than his transactions or his reputation allowed, by the time William Fitzhugh arrived in Wyoming in 1907, he had behind him a long illustrious career as a mining engineer. In common with many turn-of-the-century mining engineers, Fitzhugh at one point had offices the world over. Shortly after Spindletop came in, Fitzhugh was there obtaining leases that would still be in his family a half century later. Hearing rumors of oil wealth in northwestern Wyoming, Fitzhugh organized a group of California friends to provide his financial backing for exploration work in the Bryon field.[56] Then came the news of the "big Dutch" well at Salt Creek. Fitzhugh lost all interest in northern Wyoming, moving his entire operation to Casper. He first wandered over Salt Creek in the company of his surveyor, O. J. Midthun, in May 1909.[57] Four months later he returned to survey and develop the field in earnest.

Initially Fitzhugh discussed the possibility with Kerbert of buying the entire Dutch production, then transporting it by pipeline to the Pacific Coast.[58] This pipe dream was dropped when Fitzhugh became increasingly convinced that all of the Salt Creek titles were fraudulent, an opinion that became firmly fixed after conversations with G. R. Hagens,

55. Kerbert Deposition, Central Wyoming Oil and Development Company vs. William G. Henshaw, et al., p. 127, Midwest Oil Collection.

56. William M. Fitzhugh, "Chronological Statement of Facts Respecting the Relations between William G. Henshaw and William M. Fitzhugh as to Wyoming Lands, and also contractual relations between Fitzhugh and the Midwest Oil Company, the Reed Investment Company and Others," William M. Fitzhugh Collection.

57. Ibid., p. 3.

58. William M. Fitzhugh Testimony, Central Wyoming Oil and Development Company vs. William G. Henshaw, et al., 1:274.

the Casper attorney for the Dutch! Fitzhugh valued Hagens's advice so highly that he hired him away from the Dutch to assist him in jumping eighteen thousand acres in the Salt Creek field. What made this feat even more an accomplishment was that Hagens, as Fitzhugh's attorney, was jumping the identical claims that Hagens, as the Dutch attorney, had established when he advised the Dutch to create the Central Wyoming Oil and Development Company. Allegiances to clients were as transitory as dreams of riches at Salt Creek.[59]

While Hagens poured over the by now familiar land plats at the courthouse, Fitzhugh, through the winter of 1909–1910, worked feverishly to legitimatize Hagens's legal maneuvering. Never before had Salt Creek been the scene of so much systematic exploration. Fitzhugh employed forty to fifty men to survey the field and build reservoirs, bridges, and roads. Quickly he drilled four exploratory wells, not so much to find oil, but to establish the limits of the first-wall creek sand.[60]

Kerbert, perturbed more by the aggressiveness of Fitzhugh's organization than by the fact that he had jumped the Dutch claims (after all, Kerbert was an old hand at jumping claims), retreated to Holland for a round of meetings with his directors. When Kerbert returned to Casper in April 1910, he found yet another well-financed and coordinated adversary in the Reed Investment Company of Colorado Springs, Colorado.

One brief encounter with Verner Zevola Reed was enough to recall him forever. With a physical profile resembling F. Scott Fitzgerald and the dashing demeanor of one of Fitzgerald's characters, at one time or another Reed donned the masques of novelist, financier, labor negotiator, and bon

59. A half century later the bitterness engendered by Hagens's action lingered on in S. A. Lane's memory; he spoke in 1958: "In the meantime he had gone to our attorney and I don't know what he paid him, which he evidently did, and he turned around and said our titles were no good and he would work for Fitzhugh against us. Can you imagine that!" (interview with S. A. Lane, 23 February 1958).

60. William M. Fitzhugh Testimony, Central Wyoming Oil and Development Company vs. William G. Henshaw, et al., 1:276.

vivant.[61] In 1899, Reed acted as broker for the sale of the Independence mine at Cripple Creek to the British. Taking his nearly million dollar commission, he placed the majority of his new wealth in conservative securities and fled to Paris to live the good life on the banks of the Seine.

On 5 September 1910, Oliver Shoup, later governor of Colorado but on that day manager of the Reed Investment Company, stopped to visit with William Fitzhugh at his Salt Creek camp. Entranced with what he saw, Shoup wired Reed to come at once.[62] Having his fortune already in hand, Reed was far less inclined than his ebullient manager to gamble on Salt Creek oil, but he finally yielded to Shoup's entreaties. Back in Paris, Reed again brought the French to Salt Creek by organizing the Midwest Oil Company with the support of some of his French friends. Six million par value stock was issued in Midwest Oil, with Reed and his American colleagues in control of the majority of shares.[63]

With plenty of capital, Reed matched Fitzhugh's speed in getting underway at Salt Creek. By the spring of 1911, Reed had purchased two excellent claims from Fitzhugh, started construction on a refinery at Casper and, most important of all, began building a pipeline from Salt Creek to Casper.

61. For the life and times of Verner Zevola Reed, see two volumes by Marshall Sprague, *Money Mountain* (Boston, 1953) and *Newport in the Rockies* (Denver, 1961).

62. Long after he had left Salt Creek, Oliver Shoup put down a delightful memoir of his Wyoming years. Reed, imbued with a skepticism born from living through the boom days of Cripple Creek, was incredulous over the hourly reports of "gushers" coming in during his sojourn in a tent on the banks of Salt Creek. Shoup told the story: "Mr. Reed and party spent the night at the Fitzhugh Camp in Salt Creek. Reed became skeptical and suspicious. He knew very little about Hopkins, who had joined his organization since he had been living in France; he did not know much about Fisher, and all the rest of the party were entire strangers to him. During the evening, he was worried by the fact that the cook or the yardman, or someone, would come running to the house every few minutes and say, 'The Stock well is flowing,' or 'The Dutch well is flowing,' or 'No. 23 is spouting.' This caused Reed to become more and more suspicious" (Oliver Shoup, "When Salt Creek Roared," Oliver Shoup Collection, Petroleum History and Research Center).

63. "Minute Book," Midwest Oil, Midwest Oil Collection.

About a year from Reed's entrance at Salt Creek, a group of businessmen and bankers in Paris met with the directors of the bankrupt Belgian Belgo, offering to purchase all their assets. The bankers' proposition included delivering to the stockholders of the Belgian Belgo 75,000 shares in a new company, plus $100,000 in cash and settlement of all outstanding debts of the Belgo firm. This unexpected generosity was accepted with alacrity.[64] Subsequently, on 11 September 1909, the Franco-Wyoming Oil Company was incorporated under the laws of Delaware with a capital stock of $6,500,000.

Plunging into a broad promotional program, the officers of the Franco-Wyoming were as reluctant as Fitzhugh and Reed to be left out of the race for fortune. First they decided to accept their claims on faith until some of the litigation cleared up (seemingly a distant happening).[65] Second, they sought to rival Midwest Oil by building another refinery in Casper and a parallel pipeline from Salt Creek to Casper. Consequently by the end of 1911, the oil capital of Wyoming could claim two refineries and two pipelines! Within the short space of two years, the Salt Creek field had entered the ranks of the major producing fields of the United States. Still the Salt Creek title situation remained as confused as ever with the filing of suits and cross suits in the local, state, and federal courts.

Throughout the course of all this two-year frenzied enterprise, two events occurred that were external to Salt Creek, which depressed the spirits and the stocks of foreign investors. All prospecting for minerals, including petroleum, came under the federal placer mining law of 1897. In the era of Progressivism and conservation, scientists, politicians, and conservationists all in a chorus decried the waste, inefficien-

64. C. W. Burdick, "Organization of Belgian and American Belgo Companies, Acquisition of Land and Present Status," Midwest Oil Collection.

65. The method of handling title litigation in Salt Creek caused a wide split in the Franco-Wyoming board of directors. Some wanted to vigorously prosecute their claims; others desired to "assume" possession, letting their opponents contest their possession. The latter viewpoint prevailed, but the wounds from the dispute were still open at the time of the Paris Agreement.

cy, and fraud that they insisted were the natural accompaniment of the placer law. Responding to these pressures, plus the specific suggestions of his immediate advisors, President Taft on 27 September 1909 promulgated an executive order withdrawing from private entry over a million acres of mineral land in Wyoming and California.[66] Oil operators in Wyoming did not realize the profound import of this decision for several months after the order. When the news finally filtered through to Casper, Fitzhugh, Reed, and Kerbert, all received assurances from their attorneys that the order was undoubtedly illegal. In spite of these legal opinions, phrases revealing nervousness crept into their communications.[67]

Before they had a chance to fully recover their balance from the president's edict, another blow came, this time from closer home. On 30 August 1910 Edwin Hall, Wyoming state geologist, sent an open letter to the London *Times*, stating that he had received "a great number of letters, purporting to come from investors in oil companies who claim to own vast acreages of oil lands in this State, more especially in the Salt Creek field." Hall then went on, "It is my official duty to warn you, and protect innocent purchasers, from swindlers and from fraudulent stock dealers, so far as I can." With this declaration echoing in their ears, Hall explained that there was "a vast amount of illegal transactions in the petroleum lands in Wyoming." Pointing out the numerous abuses, specifically the practice of using "dummy" locators, Hall concluded by advising, "I am therefore of the opinion that the titles to these lands are not safe to say the least. . . . Kindly give this as much publicity as you can."[68]

66. Excellent accounts of the background of the withdrawal order can be found in: J. Leonard Bates, "The Midwest Decision, 1915, A Landmark in Conservation History," *Pacific Northwest Quarterly* 61 (January 1960):29–34; J. Leonard Bates, *The Origins of Teapot Dome* (Urbana, 1963); and Gerald Nash, *United States Oil Policy, 1890–1964* (Pittsburgh, 1968).

67. William M. Fitzhugh to J. D. Negus, 29 June 1910; Henry McAllister to William M. Fitzhugh, 29 January 1912, William M. Fitzhugh Collection.

68. Edwin Hall to Editor, London *Times*, 31 August 1910, State Geologists' Files, Western History Research Center.

Hall's last admonition was gratuitous. After his letter was spread across the financial pages of the *Times*, the stocks of the Franco-Wyoming and Dutch Maatschappij plummeted. The reaction to Hall's letter was as violent as it was instantaneous. Strong protests from the directors of the French and Dutch companies landed on his desk.[69] Kerbert and Lane wrote to their companies suggesting that their old and reliable friend Boverton Redwood be enlisted in rebuttal.[70] On 1 February 1911, Hall resigned; whether his resignation was forced or not is unknown; considering the furor, it seems likely. The foreign investors received a modicum of retribution when the next state geologist, C. E. Jamesion, sent a letter to the *Times* refuting Hall point by point.[71]

As the new year of 1911 broke over Salt Creek, a more chaotic situation would have been hard to imagine. First, there were four well-financed and managed groups contesting for control of the field: Fitzhugh and his California backers, the Franco-Wyoming crowd, the Midwest-Reed alliance, and the Petroleum Maatschappij. Add to this the several strong minor claimants and the ticker-tape-number title suits and cross suits, all of which threatened to tie up the profits of the Salt Creek field for an eternity. In addition to this jousting, the withdrawal order and Hall's letter promised to make

69. Ernest Ayrault to Edwin Hall, 6 December 1910; Camille M. S. de Ryck van der Gracht to Edwin Hall, 27 November 1910; ibid.

70. Interview with S. A. Lane, 23 February 1958.

71. C. E. Jamesion to Editor, London *Times*, 10 February 1911. Not all European reaction to Hall's letter was negative. Charles Walter, brother of Henry Walter, a prominent board member of the Belgo companies, could not refrain from expressing his delight over the discomfort of the Franco-Wyoming board. Charles Walter sent off a letter to Hall congratulating him on his stand against fraudulent activities in Wyoming oil! Further, Walter advised Hall that with his new-found reputation of high honesty, he would be in demand by all the companies in England desiring an expert's opinion. However, Walter's cynicism showed through: "In this connection pardon me if I call your attention to the fact that the dear British Public invariably appreciates and values an Expert's opinion and advice in accordance with the honorarium thereof. In England such run and must run into good solid figures. Verbum sap" (Charles Walter to Edwin Hall, 13 September 1910, State Geologists' Files).

future financing an extremely difficult, if not impossible, task.

The combination of these pressures in the summer of 1911 made an opportune time for some entrepreneur to bring some synergistic arrangement out of farrago. The answer came in the personage of Henry Myron Blackmer, president of the International Trust Company of Denver. "This man of the hour," as one of his close associates would later remember him, "could be a suave, congenial gentleman, a cold, hard-boiled banker, a friendly, story-telling host, as the occasion required."[72] Over the next two years Blackmer brilliantly displayed and exploited all these talents as he traded, cajoled, and needled the competing parties into a unified design.

The first sign of order glimmered through when the Franco-Wyoming and the Dutch Maatschappij in September 1911 transferred all their rights, titles, and interests in the Salt Creek field into a new company, the Wyoming Oil Fields Company.[73] This amalgamation pertained solely to their claims in Salt Creek; the other interests of both companies were totally excluded. Blackmer astutely pointed out to all Salt Creek contestants that it would be wise to resolve their title differences so that a united front might be presented to the government. An economic motive reenforced this political stratagem; because of the excessive intercompany boundary lines in the field, each firm, in an attempt to preserve its reserve, had drilled a prodigal number of off-set wells, which jeopardized the gas pressure for all of Salt Creek. To reform this situation, the Dutch and French exchanged acreage for the purpose of consolidating the holdings of each company into a smaller number of larger units. While they did not realize it, their action represented one of the first moves toward unitization in the United States.[74]

The next major breakthrough came when Blackmer convinced Fitzhugh and his main California associate, William

72. Harold Roberts Collection, Petroleum History and Research Center.

73. Wyoming Oil Fields *Record*, Midwest Oil Collection.

74. P. E. de Caplane to Ernest Ayrault, 11 October 1911. Wyoming Oil Fields file, Midwest Oil Collection. Interview with H. C. Bretschneider, 12 June 1958.

Henshaw, that it would be to their best interests to join Midwest Oil. Wherefore, on 14 July 1911, a tentative contract was drawn up for the sale of the Fitzhugh-Henshaw interests, subject to previous Fitzhugh contracts.[75] The agreement became finalized in September 1912, by a $325,000 payment by Midwest Oil.[76]

Blackmer's greatest victory came when Verner Z. Reed consented to go along with the reorganization plans shortly after the Fitzhugh-Henshaw concession. With some justification, Reed became suspicious of the interplay between Blackmer and his associates in the Reed Investment Company.[77] Only when Reed was firmly convinced that his investment would be protected did he yield to Blackmer's pleas.[78]

Now Blackmer could again turn to the French and Dutch with his backing consolidated, this time to urge them to join all the parties in Salt Creek by merging not only their land but also the refinery and pipeline into a new corporation.

75. Vaile, McAllister & Vaile, "Memorandum Relative to Fitzhugh-Midwest Contract and Right to Enforce Specific Performance thereof in certain Respects," William M. Fitzhugh Collection.

76. "Midwest Oil Company—W. M. Fitzhugh Agreement, September 14, 1912," Midwest Oil Collection.

77. Allusions and rumors were prevalent in the friction among the Midwest crowd in the immediate months preceding the Paris Agreement. Fitzhugh and his attorneys did their best to exploit this dissent in the Reed managerial structure (William M. Fitzhugh to Oliver Shoup, 17 December 1911, Fitzhugh Collection).

78. Reed's surrender may have been due in part to Fitzhugh's intimidations. In a breezy, blunt, blustering letter, Fitzhugh told Reed in unequivocal terms, "I am going to give you my candid opinion of the situation, first prefacing my statements by saying that the Midwest and Reed Investment Companies are so closely identified with my interest that their success is my success. Don't let us kill the goose that lays the golden egg, but let us get together and we can all make more money. . . . I can send to Europe certain official letters that would in my opinion completely block and stop any stock selling—but I think it would be inadvisable *provided* we can in any way combine—if we can't then I certainly will stop the stock sales." Coming as closely as it did on the heels of Hall's letter, this Fitzhugh missive must have sent shudders through Reed's spine. For one thing Reed knew about Fitzhugh—he did not bluff (William M. Fitzhugh to Verner Z. Reed, 18 December 1911, William M. Fitzhugh Collection).

After an extremely acrimonious holiday interlude of accusation and counteraccusation, a contract known as the "Paris Agreement" was concluded on 29 December 1913. Under its terms a new company, the Midwest Refining Company, was organized with a total capitalization of $20 million. Into this new firm would be placed both pipelines and refineries of the French and Midwest Oil. In essence the Midwest Refining Company would be the operating company for the Salt Creek field from production through marketing. Midwest Refining then agreed to purchase, for a twenty-year period, all the production from the major land units—Midwest Oil, the Reed Companies, and the Wyoming Oil Fields—purchasing one third from each firm.[79] The Paris Agreement brought the first peace that Salt Creek had ever had. The enormous petroleum market created by World War I, combined with the amazingly talented entrepreneurial group that Blackmer attracted, assured the phenomenal future of the Midwest Refining Company. All through the twenties, the Midwest Refining annual reports told one success story after another until the final merger into the Standard Oil Company [Indiana] in 1931.

As the French, Belgian, and Dutch financiers returned to their homes after the Paris Agreement, they could look back over their history in Wyoming with mixed emotions. Indeed, they may have asked themselves the question of whatever possessed them to risk their capital in Salt Creek. Simplistically, part of the answer resided in the promotional acumen of Joseph H. Lobell. Had Lobell been honest, less cleverly disguising the risks, obviously foreign investors would not have played the role that they did in Salt Creek. Ignorance and subterfuge were intimate allies in the birth of the Wyoming petroleum industry. Had the French and Dutch realized what the Standard Oil officials already knew, it is highly unlikely that they would have ever cast their eyes toward Salt Creek.

A more significant rationale behind foreign investment interest in Wyoming derived from the general financial milieu existing in their countries in the early years of the twentieth century. The savings of the French, Dutch, and Belgians

79. Paris Agreement, 29 December 1913, Midwest Oil Collection.

poured into world-wide investment in this era. In 1870, France had an overseas investment of fifteen billion francs; by 1914, this total had climbed to forty-five billion.[80] Prosperity was the dominant economic indicator, with France and the low countries experiencing a rise in prices of 40 per cent and a trade increase of 70 per cent. Moreover, a quarter of all French investment was channeled into Russia, where much of it was utilized in the lucrative Caucasian oil fields. Their Russian experience provided some of the French motivation in Wyoming.

However, their operational pattern differed in the two countries. When the French sent their francs to Baku, they also exported entrepreneurial managers and technicians. Until the last few months before the Paris Agreement, the French and Dutch for some reason did not find it necessary to send to Wyoming a cadre of managerial and technical talent. This failure, more than any other single factor, explains why the French, Belgians, and Dutch lost out in the scramble for dominance in the Salt Creek field.

How speculative had the French, Dutch, and Belgians been in Wyoming? From one premise, it has been argued elsewhere, any investment in the nineteenth- and early twentieth-century West was a highly risky proposition. Few ventures represented more of a gamble than the one the French and

80. For background on European economic growth and investment strategy in the 1870–1914 era see: Rondo F. Cameron, *France and the Economic Development of Europe, 1800–1914* (Princeton, 1961); David S. Landes, "French Business and the Businessman, a Social and Cultural Analysis," in Edward M. Earle, ed., *Modern France: Problems of the Third and Fourth Republics* (Princeton, 1951), pp. 334–51; Charles P. Kindleberger, *Economic Growth in France and Britain, 1851–1950* (Cambridge, 1964); David S. Landes, *The Unbound Prometheus* (Cambridge, 1969); John F. Laffey, "Roots of French Imperialism in the Nineteenth Century: The Case of Lyon," *French Historical Studies* 6 (Spring 1969):78–92; Warren C. Baum, *The French Economy and the State* (Princeton, 1958); Alexander Gerschenkron, "Social Attitudes, Entrepreneurship and Economic Development," *Explorations in Entrepreneurial and Economic Development* 6 (October 1953):1–15; and Bert F. Hoselitz, "Entrepreneurship and Capital Formation in France and Britain since 1700," in *Capital Formation and Economic Growth* (Princeton, 1956).

Belgians underwrote in the Belgian Belgo in 1904 or the Dutch in the Petroleum Maatschappij of 1907. What could be more speculative than investing in an oil field, with no market in sight for a thousand miles, with no way of transporting their oil from field to refinery, once they found it?

One of the numerous ghosts that hovered over the shoulders of the French and Dutch during the early days in Wyoming was the fear that one morning the behemoth Standard Oil Company would suddenly decide to swoop down on the Salt Creek scene. If they took any interest in these foreign phobias, how the executives of the Standard Oil must have smiled. For long before the French came to Salt Creek, in 1899, John D. Archbold, the president of Standard Oil, had directed three geologist-executives—Oliphant, Lufkin, and Eckbert—to examine the Pennsylvania Oil and Gas Company operation. In their report to Archbold, written from the Interocean Hotel in Cheyenne, Wyoming, on 14 June 1899, in one sentence they succinctly summed up the Salt Creek situation, "The Salt Creek valley is in our opinion a large area of probable producing territory, but until there is a pipeline and market for the oil, there will be no profit for the Pennsylvania interests or others."[81] It was hardly an assessment that would impress John D. Archbold to push Standard Oil into the Rockies.

Yet what Standard Oil justly scorned, due as much to World War I and H. M. Blackmer as anything else, turned out to be an astonishingly fertile investment for the French, Belgians, and Dutch; the extent of the remunerations we can not fully ascertain. We do know that by 1936, the Wyoming Oil Fields Company had paid their foreign stockholders over $12 million in dividends.[82] What percentage they reaped from

81. An account of French technology in the Caucasus is in the *Record Book* of A. Beeby-Thompson, 1898, A. Beeby-Thompson Collection, Petroleum History and Research Center. See also, A. Beeby-Thompson, *The Oil Fields of Russia* (London, 1904).

82. C. L. Lufkin, F. H. Oliphant and J. E. Eckbert, "Report on Wyoming, June 14, 1899," Carter Oil Collection, Petroleum History and Research Center. For more on Lufkin, Oliphant, and Eckbert's activities with Standard Oil, the reader is referred to the perceptive

their stock in the Reed companies, Midwest Refining, and the remnants of the Franco-Wyoming is not known. However, in relation to the general profitability of these companies, they undoubtedly far exceeded the returns on the Wyoming Oil Fields shares. Because the French, Belgian, and Dutch input into Salt Creek before 1911 had not exceeded a million and a half of actual cash flow, they undoubtedly considered their decision to go into Salt Creek one of their more prescient moments.

After the Paris Agreement, the French, Dutch, and Belgian influence and interest in Salt Creek waned. For a half dozen years, the artifactitious vestiges, a pipeline and refinery, remained as mute testimony to their *Chateau en Espagne*. If they reflected on things besides their rich dividends and memories, they could take satisfaction in having been a significant force in opening up one of the major oil fields in the United States. Some did recall: writing to his old friend, S. A. Lane, in 1926, Coenraad Kerbert sat in a hotel in Vevey, Switzerland, where he was on a holiday: "You say you are looking for another Salt Creek; are not we all? I have thought to leave Casper would be a moment always remembered with happiness. Now I only remember the nice times; the ill days are gone. If I locate another Salt Creek, I will send for you; will not you do the same?"[83]

history of Standard Oil by Ralph and Muriel Hidy, *Pioneering in Big Business, 1882–1911* (New York, 1955).

83. Coenraad Kerbert to S. A. Lane, 8 August 1926, S. A. Lane Collection, Petroleum History and Research Center. The above article is a reedited essay that appeared in *The Business History Review* 44 (Winter 1970), 498–519. Appreciation is extended to the editors for their graciousness in permitting the publication of this version.

Reclamation
and the
West via
Arthur Powell Davis

The traditional interpretation of the first two decades of the history of reclamation in the twentieth century is as precisely defined as it is frequently fallacious.[1] According to this historiography, a naive bib-overalled eastern farmer was lured to a caked, alkali desert, shown forty acres, and dared to make a living! Once he was ensconced in his tar-papered shack, the government, which had appeared so friendly and paternalistic in the East, suddenly forgot that he existed, leaving him to struggle as best he could with an unproductive soil, a locally nefarious banker, and an unsympathetic bureaucracy personified by uncompromising technocrats in the Reclamation Service. The government in Washington, as one shrewd Uncompahgre Project pioneer remarked, "had removed all the aces from the deck, for the unfortunate farmers."[2]

This impressionistic tale of woes of the homesteader is not entirely erroneous, but it demands so much qualification that to accept it without major revision would be to create another version of the agrarian myth. In retrospect, the astounding fact is that there was any reclamation program at all. The Newlands legislation, as we now know,[3] was an anomaly,

1. For reflections of this historiographical position see Benjamin H. Hibbard, *A History of the Public Land Policies* (Madison, 1965), p. 448; Roy M. Robbins, *Our Landed Heritage: The Public Domain, 1776–1936* (Princeton, 1942), p. 332; Donald C. Swain, *Federal Conservation Policy* (Berkeley, 1963), p. 78; Paul W. Gates, *History of Public Land Law Development* (Washington, D.C., 1968); Burl Noggle, "The Twenties: A New Historiographical Frontier," *Journal of American History* 53 (September 1966):299–314.

2. Interview, Dan Hughes, Montrose, Colorado, 28 June 1965.

3. An incisive dissection of the origins of the Newland Act is William

cleverly conceived by a conservation-minded, politically astute president and a crusading Nevada congressman. Suddenly, his fellow western senators, who had long trumpeted the virtues of private enterprise, found themselves in the bastion of public subsidy.[4]

In addition to the contest between public power and private interest, the reclamation program was rooted in a department that had suffered several scandals and innumerable political crises.[5] Secretaries, of varying ability and influence, came and went. Inevitably, they arrived with the announced purpose, as Secretary Lane put it, "of doing something about Reclamation,"[6] only eventually to leave the Service (and to be left themselves) in a state of frustration.

The Reclamation Service was so racked with political at-

Lilley III and Lewis Gould, "Western Irrigation Movement, 1878–1902: A Reappraisal," in *The American West: A Reorientation* (Laramie, 1966), pp. 57–76; see also Lilley, "Theodore Roosevelt and the Newlands Act" (manuscript, William Lilley Collection, Yale University, New Haven).

4. F. H. Newell recalled the formulation of the Newlands Act in his memoirs: "Mr. Newlands got into the habit of dropping into my office later in the afternoon and put into shape many suggestions for bills which he later introduced. . . . Roosevelt asked us to prepare a draft of the things which he might properly put in his first message to Congress. This we did during the next few days meeting frequently with George H. Maxwell and Senator Newlands and also discussing details with Charles D. Walcott then Director of the U.S. Geological Survey. The material as finally prepared was adopted by Roosevelt with little change and incorporated in his message of December, 1901." Newell, "A Man's Life," manuscript, pp. 63–64, Newell Papers, Western History Research Center, University of Wyoming, Laramie.

5. The literature on the scandals of the 1920s is as diffuse as it is erratic. Some of the more reliable tomes are those by John Ise, *The United States Oil Policy* (New Haven, 1926); Burl Noggle, *Teapot Dome: Oil and Politics in the 1920's* (Baton Rouge, 1962); Andrew Sinclair, *The Available Man* (New York, 1965); R. C. Downes, *The Rise of Warren Gamaliel Harding, 1865–1920* (Columbus, 1970); Robert K. Murray, *The Harding Era* (Minneapolis, 1969); J. Leonard Bates, *The Origins of Teapot Dome* (Urbana, 1964); T. Blake Kennedy, "Memoirs," manuscript, Kennedy Papers, Western History Research Center.

6. Arthur Powell Davis, "Memoir of the Reclamation Service," manuscript, A. P. Davis Papers, Western History Research Center.

tacks and internal dissension at the higher echelons that its efficiency was consistently impaired. The service seldom had the opportunity to concentrate all its efforts on its announced goal of making the desert bloom. The ordeal of the Reclamation Service was increased by congressional investigations and constant political harassment. Congress, spurred by the grumblings of its constituents on reclamation projects, found the service fair game, and would launch an investigation, a favorite congressional remedy to alleviate the pressure of protest and to provide the illusion that solutions would soon be forthcoming. By 1925, Congress had indulged itself in more than thirty probings into reclamation.

Plagued by dissension from within and attack from without, faced with enormous technological problems demanding imaginative engineering, the task of the Reclamation Service was hardly an enviable one. When the ex-Postmaster General, physician and protégé of Senator Phipps, Hubert Work,[7] assumed the mantle of the secretary of the interior from a New Mexican appointee who recently had fallen from grace, he had a ready answer to the eternal question of what was wrong with reclamation. Work discerned a simple syllogism: what the Reclamation Service required was a businessman. The current director, Arthur Powell Davis, though one of the country's most celebrated civil engineers, was obviously ill prepared in the world of high finance. Therefore, the solution was self-evident—fire Davis. After all, in the milieu of the 1920s, business and politics, always compatible, were intimately integrated.

On 16 June 1923, Secretary Work called Director Davis into his office and informed him that his position was being abolished.[8] Furthermore, the Reclamation Service would be

7. Biographical information on Hubert Work is available in *Who's Who in America, 1918–1919* (Chicago, 1918), p. 3032.

8. Davis, Memorandum, A. P. Davis Papers; Davis wrote to his associate, F. E. Weymouth on 16 June 1923: "This morning, about 20 minutes of nine, as I sat at my desk, I received a call to go to the Secretary's office and found him in his private room. As I entered he desired me to be seated and closed the door. He then told me that he had sent for me to inform me that he had decided to replace me with

christened with a new name, the Bureau of Reclamation, and as the commissioner of this bureau, the secretary was appointing a businessman and former governor of Idaho, D. W. Davis.

What Secretary Work did not anticipate was the violent reaction to Arthur Powell Davis's summary dismissal. Sensing a scandal, the press flashed sinister headlines, "New Ballinger Case in Offing,"[9] and "Power Interests Back of Davis Removal."[10] Several engineering societies adopted unanimous resolutions deploring Secretary Work's action.[11] Predictably, evangelistic conservationists and old Progressives rushed to Davis's defense. Gifford Pinchot termed the Davis firing "deplorable." The La Follette mouthpiece, *Progressive*, attacked Secretary Work in a scathing article: "Work knew nothing of Reclamation in its technical aspects and knows nothing now. . . . Work is an M.D. and looked after an insane asylum in Colorado, when he had time to spare from handling certain aspects of the Rockefeller interests in that State."[12]

Even former congressional critics of reclamation in the West, always attuned to a popular cause, took up the hue and

---

someone else. I expressed my appreciation of having been informed of this at first hand without having announcement come through others. He then assured me that he had mentioned it to no one yet and had not selected my successor, nor spoken to anyone for the place but said that he would probably appoint Governor D. W. Davis as Director. . . . He said this change had been in contemplation for over two years and that if his predecessor had been in office it would probably have been accomplished sooner. He also said that it was in response to a general public demand that a business man rather than an engineer be placed at the head of the Service."

9. *New Mexico State Tribune*, 11 July 1923.

10. New York *World*, 26 June 1923. Other editorial reactions, pro and con, can be found in the Rochester *Times-Union*, 30 June 1923; Cincinnati *Enquirer*, 28 July 1923; New York *Times*, 27 June 1923; Los Angeles *Examiner*, 25 July 1923; Philadelphia *Evening Public Ledger*, 21 June 1923; Boise *Idaho Statesmen*, 30 June 1923.

11. E. Howson to Davis, 12 July 1923; E. J. Mehren to Davis, 5 July 1923; John H. Dunlap to H. Work, 17 October 1923, Davis Papers.

12. "Reclamation Service in Scandal," *Progressive* 16 (March 1924): 14–27.

cry. Burton L. French, of D. W. Davis's home state of Idaho, wrote a sympathetic though thoroughly discreet letter, marking it "personal and not for publication."[13] Addison Smith, chairman of the House Committee on Irrigation and a friend of D. W. Davis, wrote a note of appreciation for A. P. Davis's past accomplishments, ending with the comment, "We are hoping something can be worked out."[14] During the uproar, Arthur Powell Davis was far from silent. Both publicly and privately, he added inflammatory statements to the controversy.[15] He darkly implied that private power companies were behind his removal—specifically, Senator Phipps, an ex-Carnegie associate and a large stockholder in several power companies.[16] Nor did President Harding ease the tension. On his fatal trip West, he addressed an audience at Spokane on the necessity for "unlocking" the natural resources of the West.[17] A year passed before the dispute cooled, by which time D. W. Davis was being shoved aside, not so gently, to make way for Elwood Mead, a renowned irrigation engineer.[18] By this time the entire affair had come to resemble an opéra bouffe.

Was Secretary Work justified in his announced belief that a business ethic was the sure catharsis to cure reclamation ills? Most historians have thought so; one authority of conservation in the 1920s has suggested that a "readjustment of bureau objectives was long over due."[19] Actually, Arthur Powell Davis had a far more sophisticated approach to recla-

13. Burton L. French to Davis, 2 July 1923, Davis Papers.

14. Addison T. Smith to Davis, 14 June 1923, Davis Papers.

15. As an answer to Work and his critics, Davis issued a small privately printed pamphlet entitled, "Statement of Arthur Powell Davis, July 11, 1923." Logically, if not so convincingly, Davis argued point by point the charges leveled at him by Work. He also furnished some of the "propaganda" for the Democratic National Committee's diatribe, "How Reclamation is Being Wrecked and Why."

16. Davis to Barry Dibble, 28 June 1923, Davis Papers.

17. *New Mexico State Tribune*, 11 July 1923.

18. A massive unpublished biography of Elwood Mead is in the J. T. Peterson Collection, Western History Research Center.

19. Donald C. Swain, *Federal Conservative Policy* (Berkeley, 1963), p. 78.

mation than either historians or his contemporary critics have conceded. Born in Decatur, Illinois, on 9 February 1861, Davis spent his youth at Junction City, Kansas, among, as he later recalled, "dry farmers and dry land."[20] In 1882, Uncle John Wesley Powell wired an offer of a position with the United States Geological Survey. Six years later, with a Bachelor of Science in hand from George Washington University,[21] he continued his rapid professional rise. By 1896, Davis was in charge of the Division of Hydrography, concentrating on obtaining comprehensive charts of stream measurements in the United States. He was given a leave of absence from this post to participate in the Isthmian Canal Commission. When the Reclamation Service was organized in 1902, Davis was appointed assistant chief engineer. Five years later, he received the designation of chief engineer, holding the office of director from 1914 to 1923.

In a skeletal profile of Davis's career, the complex and systematic public philosophy that he evolved during his lifetime in government service is obscured. True, his orientation was that of an engineer-technocrat, but his speculative rationality ranged far wider than the boundaries set by the graph paper on his drawing board. The crux of his social thought pivoted on "Georgian" economics.[22]

Fascinated by *Progress and Poverty*, which he first read during his adolescence, Davis missed few opportunities to

20. The biographical data on Davis is extracted from a "Biographical Memorandum" in the Davis Papers and *Memoir 438*, published by American Society of Civil Engineers.

21. Then known as Columbian University.

22. How far Davis followed the path of Henry George is illustrated by his address, "The Engineer's Future Solved by Single Tax." "The chief complaint among engineers is, that they neither receive the financial reward justly due to their importance in the community, nor the social recognition accorded other professions whose course of training is in no respect more difficult than the one of the engineer. . . . A slight change in our taxation method is all that is required. Exempt from Taxation every article of wealth owing its existence to human effort: retain nature's store for the benefit of all by taxing society created values and land to its full rental value," *Pacific Builder and Engineer* 12 (July 1914):32–36.

lobby among his associates for the single tax. His diary is sprinkled with notations of the single-tax meetings he attended, whether in Helena, Montana, or Orland, California.[23] In 1897, he gave public testimony to his fervent belief in the single tax by writing small throw-away pamphlets, of the type so popular in the age of reform, whether the cause was bimetallism or temperance. The title, *The Single Tax from the Farmer's Standpoint*, expressed ideas that were straight Henry George.[24] Especially intriguing, when viewing his later career, was Davis's strong espousal of the humanity of man, and his adoption of George's Jeffersonian idealization of the small homestead. In 1912, Davis wrote the godfather of the conservation movement, Gifford Pinchot, regarding the derivation of his personal conservation persuasion, "I consider the subject [conservation] in direct line with the gospel of Henry George as expounded in Progress and Poverty and other works, which shows that the rights of the individual and the rights of property are not in conflict, but that one can not be violated without violating the other."[25]

The import of this quotation for Davis's public philosophy was apparent: one could be in the yeast of political reform, yet stand foursquare for individualism. One could be for decentralized control locally of reclamation projects, and yet believe strongly in the value of centralized planning and over-all federal supervision. Friend and foe both missed this side of Davis's speculative thinking.

For all his championship of the single tax, Davis was as firmly committed as Nelson Aldrich to the inherent value of private property. Upon reading an essay by the eminent Dr. Lyman Abbott on the fallacies of the rights of property, Davis became infuriated. In an irate letter to the editor of *The Outlook*, Davis decried Abbott's position, "If the law can with impunity take away the products of our labor, it can in effect

23. Davis, Diary, 20 February 1911, 20 December 1916, 11 April 1917, 24 July 1918, Davis Papers.

24. Davis, *The Single Tax from the Farmer's Standpoint* (Minneapolis, 6 October 1897).

25. Davis to Gifford Pinchot, 14 May 1912, Davis Papers.

enslave us, and this is in fact the most important result of any system of slavery."[26]

Davis was far from an isolated instance of an engineer adopting the cause of Henry George.[27] The distinguished professor of civil engineering at Harvard, Lewis J. Johnson, went on the Chautauqua circuit for the single-tax program.[28] George Goethals, famous for his engineering feats on the Panama Canal, proclaimed his interest in Henry George. Even Frederick H. Newell, the first director of the Reclamation Service, told Davis that he saw "much of value in the single tax movement."[29] Frank Weymouth, longtime assistant chief engineer under Davis, discovered much that was "stimulating in the work of Henry George."[30] This is not to imply that professional engineers in America adopted *sine qua non* the single-tax theme, but is to suggest that a fruitful area of historical inquiry would be in the interrelationships between the single-tax movement and the engineer.[31]

In his political belief, Davis subscribed heart and soul to the Progressive creed. The humanistic, individualistic, anti-monopoly and middle-class tone of progressivism held strong appeal. He saw nothing incongruous or uncomfortable about bringing his single-tax gospel into the Progressive tent, nor did many of his fellow single taxers.[32] He endorsed the urban emphasis and municipal reform activities, even though he clung to the agrarian myth. The Progressive emphasis on human dignity and opposition to overt class consciousness were especially favorite faiths of Davis's personal convic-

26. Davis to Editor, *The Outlook*, 8 July 1919.

27. The impact of George is detailed in Steven B. Cord, *Henry George: Dreamer or Realist?* (Philadelphia, 1965).

28. Lewis J. Johnson, "The Single Tax in Relation to Public Health" (Cincinnati, 1915).

29. F. H. Newell to Davis, 7 January 1915, Davis Papers.

30. Frank Weymouth to Davis, 9 December 1923, Davis Papers.

31. While George's able biographer mentions little about the impact of single tax on engineers, he does provide insight into George's thoughts on irrigation. Charles A. Barker, *Henry George* (New York, 1955), p. 199.

32. Barker, *Henry George*, pp. 621–22.

tions. He was a thorough-going small "d" democrat. Horrified by the inefficiency and stratification of any organization, he wrote an open letter to a fellow engineering society official attacking the military rank consciousness.[33]

Although his ideas on military education may have been unorthodox, he followed wholeheartedly in the mainstream of the Roosevelt-Pinchot conservation movement. In missives to Gifford Pinchot and James R. Garfield, Davis outlined his position on conservation in doctrinaire terms. In a letter to Pinchot from Helena, Montana, he wrote the same shibboleths that the entire country was hearing from the conservationists.

> I have, in fact, little interest in conserving anything for the temporary benefit of a few "dollar chasers." The broader principle of conserving all natural resources for the benefit of all persons is a cause for which, in common with many others, I should be glad to sacrifice anything which would materially contribute to its progress.[34]

Over the years Davis steadfastly held to the beliefs inherent in the conservation evangelism. The practicalist spirit, the strong executive, the divorce of politics from administration, and the Taylorite emphasis on efficiency were all principles he would reiterate time and time again to his associates. When Sen. Oscar Underwood had the temerity to propose a political candidate for a position in the Reclamation Service, Davis administered a moralistic dressing down to the good senator.[35] To load one's staff with political appointees was not only disastrous to the Service from the standpoint of esprit de corps, which he romanticized, but was definitely inefficient.

Davis bristled most at the inefficiency of political manipulation. Any small reservoir of patience was quickly exhausted when he found himself confronted by the pork barrel,

33. Davis to B. J. Arnold, n.d., Davis Papers.
34. Davis to Gifford Pinchot, 14 May 1914, Davis Papers.
35. Davis to Secretary of the Interior, 25 October 1913, Davis Papers.

political pressure from the water users, and congressional meddling.[36] Davis never appeared to realize that lecturing senators and water users was perfectly permissible if one was not concerned about the next appropriation or about grass-roots intrigues to have one fired. In addition, he evidently saw nothing paradoxical about utilizing the support of conservationists as a political fulcrum.[37]

This, then, is the portrait of an engineer who personified the Reclamation Service for more than two decades. More than any single individual, Arthur Powell Davis was responsible for the formulation and execution of administrative policy from 1913 to 1923. Damnation for the Service's failures, as well as praise for its success, would be focused on Davis's inflexible leadership.

Anyone tracing the early history of the Reclamation Service cannot help but be impressed with (or depressed by) the constant turmoil marked by bureaucratic in-fighting and political attacks. Reminiscing in his later years, A. P. Davis could remember only one secretary in the long line of secretaries passing through the Interior Department who im-

36. Davis lamented to Elwood Mead, "About half of my testimony yesterday was combatting in one form and another the idea of en-grafting the infiltration plan on the pending legislation. Two or three members of the Committee desire this for their States and will oppose the bill unless it contains it, while the majority favor the bill in any event; but a few of them would like to put this in either on their own account or to gain votes, and Mr. Smythe was of the opinion that it would be wise to do so. I told him I thought not, because if anything contemplating this were in the bill there would be immense pressure for extensive operations of this kind in more than half the States and we would make a colossal failure if that plan received the sanction of Congress" (Davis to Elwood Mead, 12 June 1919, Davis Papers).

37. Davis consistently implored Pinchot and Garfield to vigilantly watch "special interest" legislation. Even when he was no longer in government service, he kept a steady barrage of communications going. In 1924, he harangued Garfield, "When I was dismissed from the Service I informed all inquiring friends that I was personally bene-fitted and had no grievance to be redressed, but urged efforts to prevent further disorganization of the Service. The hammering the Secretary got from the press in general and engineering societies prevented any drastic action for some time" (12 June 1919, Davis Papers).

pressed him favorably, James P. Garfield.[38] This was an understandable preference as Garfield was a confidante of the Roosevelt-Pinchot "conservation club." On the basis of administrative ability alone, any impartial observer would have to concede that the procession of secretaries was hardly a distinguished lot.[39]

Ineffectual leadership only compounded the personality clashes and internal power struggles among the upper strata of the Service.[40] From 1913, when Secretary Lane took office, until the summer of 1916, when Davis emerged as uncontested director of the Service, perpetual reorganization was the order of the day.[41] Secretary Lane inaugurated the bu-

38. A scathing assessment of Secretary Lane's administrative ability was made by John Ise. "A fair argument might be built up to show that he was one of the most dangerous men that have ever held the office of Secretary of Interior" (Ise, *The United States Oil Policy*, p. 336).

39. Of course, the most devasting internal "explosion" in the Department of Interior was the Ballinger-Pinchot feud. The Reclamation Service was affected, but the controversy is far too involved for the present discussion.

40. In memorandum after memorandum, Davis compiled an almost daily diary of the interservice struggle. The most pertinent are: "Memorandum—June 1914"; "Memorandum with Secretary Land and Mr. Ryan, July 23, 1915"; "Memorandum, May 6, 1915"; "Memorandum of an Interview with Secretary Lane, November 22, 1915"; "Memorandum to Secretary of Interior, December 1, 1915"; A. P. Davis to F. K. Lane, 30 January 1916; and "Memoirs of the Reclamation Service," all are in the Davis Papers.

41. Even the usually charitable Newell lamented in his autobiography, "Secretary Lane however to the great disappointment of all, surrounded himself with men of at least questionable character and the feeling that they must find something wrong filled his mind with distrust. He was induced to encourage complaints from the landowners of the Reclamation projects and was soon flooded with vague statements distorted and abusive. These quite swept him off his feet and finally he concluded to have a series of public hearings. These were held at the Capitol and everyone with a grievance was invited to be present. . . . The Service itself was in constant turmoil. Secretary Lane had a curious obsession regarding executive duties, having served for many years as a member of a commission he was greatly impressed with the desirability of dividing authority and of debating every kind of question which came up" (Newell, "A Man's Life," pp. 86, 87, 88, F. H. Newell Papers).

reaucratic civil war by undermining Director F. N. Newell.[42]
A longtime government servant, Newell was one of the most
respected civil engineers in the United States.[43] A pioneer
advocate of reclaiming arid lands, Newell had worked closely
with Senator Newlands in the drafting of the 1902 legislation.[44] Secretary Lane insisted that because of the political
pressure from the water users, he was left with no alternative
but to demote Newell. Suspicious of Lane's motives, and interpreting the attack against Newell as an attack against the
Service, Davis violently disagreed.[45] Later Davis goaded the
secretary into admitting that Newell's demotion resulted
from Lane's jealousy and personal insecurity. W. A. Ryan,
a longtime business associate of Lane's, had been brought
into the Service as comptroller. When Davis, during one of
his innumerable clashes with the secretary, chided him about
Ryan's defensiveness, the secretary said that "this attitude
was due to Mr. Ryan's hatred of the Reclamation 'machine.' I
asked him what he meant by this expression and he stated,
Newell had built up a strong personal machine loyal to him
and to nobody else, and that machine was disloyal to Ryan
and the Secretary. I vehemently denied this."[46] Lane then
moved to gain control of the Reclamation "machine" by clipping the power of administrative centralization of the Service.
In June 1913, the secretary appointed a five man commission,
of which Newell was a member, to run the Service, with the

42. On the Newell dismissal, Davis reminisced, "Shortly after my
return to Washington, the Secretary sent for me and I met him for
the first time in his office. He broached the subject of the Reclamation
Service and stated that a great deal of complaint had come to his
notice from water users and others concerning the administration of
the Reclamation Service; that it seemed to have no friends either on
the projects or in Congress, and there was special complaint against
Mr. Newell, the Director" (Davis, "Memoirs of the Reclamation Service," Davis Papers).

43. Profuse biographical data on Newell are available in his auto-
biography "A Man's Life," F. H. Newell Papers; interviews with
Newell's associates by A. D. Rodgers III are in the Rodgers Collection,
Western History Research Center.

44. Newell, "A Man's Life," pp. 63–66.

45. Davis, "Memoirs of the Reclamation Service."

46. Ibid.

peremptory comment, "This is not to be a one-man organization."[47]

The swiftly changing political and administrative realign-
ments of the next three years are beyond the scope of this
study, but the main configurations are easily traced. By the
summer of 1914, even the docile Newell had accepted his
fate and departed.[48] Davis then added the office of director
to his position as chief engineer. During 1915 the bitterness
that had built up over the past two years erupted. The problem that had to be resolved was deciding who was going to
run the Service. Secretary Lane, perceptive enough to realize
Davis's immense loyal support within the Service plus his
endorsement by conservationists and Progressives, surrendered in the spring of 1916 to all of Davis's demands.[49] The
Davis victory was signaled by the resignation of the chief
of construction, Williamson, and the chief account, McCoy,
two of Davis's most bitter antagonists.

Now with power coupled to his titles, Davis decided that
the Service required another revamping. When his longtime
friend and assistant chief engineer, F. E. Weymouth, heard
of the rumored reorganization, he fired a letter off to Davis
with the anguished plea:

> I believe that any reorganization of the Service at this time
> is to be deplored. There have been so many changes in the
> Service during the past few years that I fear any reorganiza-
> tion . . . will leave the Service so demoralized that it will not
> be possible to conduct it to the credit of the government,
> the water users, or those responsible for the success of the
> Act.[50]

47. "Memorandum with Secretary Lane and Mr. Ryan, July 23,
1915," Davis Papers.
48. Commenting on Newell's resignation, the Orland *Register* editorialized, "It was unfortunate for Newell that he was evasive in discussing the work of his office; there is nothing evasive about Davis."
49. "Memorandum of changes suggested to bring the Reclamation
Service into harmonious relations, making it possible for the present
Director to remain," Davis Papers.
50. F. E. Weymouth to Davis, 23 September 1917, Davis Papers.

Whether Weymouth's plea altered Davis's musings is not known. One fact is certain—the Service continued its historic pattern of administrative shuffling for the next twenty years.

A major political issue facing the Service from its inception and one tightly interlocked with the administrative shuffling was the unceasing pressure from the water users' associations. Every secretary who had dreams of revising the goals of the Service utilized the political discontent of the water users as a *locus standi* to implement his personal plans.

In turn, the water users' political scene was inseparably bound up with the Service's embryonic vision of transforming the desolate desert into a flourishing garden. On few occasions has there been a more extravagant example of the agrarian myth in full blossom.[51] What is surprising is that the "scientific" engineer succumbed to the myth as fervently as the most opportunistic politician. Neither Davis's personal diaries nor his private correspondence indicate the slightest dissent with the agrarian myth. Bracketed with the fantasy of white clapboard homes surrounded by verdant vegetation was the Benthamite philosophy of the "greatest good for the greatest number." In 1905, the eminent director of the U.S. Geological Survey, Dr. Charles Walcott, speaking to the appreciative audience of the Thirteenth National Irrigation Congress, said of the reclamation funds, "The general allotment of funds has been made with a view to the greatest benefit to the greatest number, and from the broad standpoint of the welfare of the country as a whole."[52]

Five years after Walcott's enthusiastically applauded address, Gifford Pinchot echoed the Benthamite formula in his definition of the principles of conservation, "The preservation of our resources are for the benefit of the many and not

51. The literature focusing on the agrarian myth is vast; the classic treatise, which inevitably appears in footnotes, is Henry Nash Smith, *Virgin Land: The American West as Symbol and Myth* (Cambridge, 1950).

52. Cited in Leahme Brown, "The Development of National Policy with Respect to Water Resources" (Ph.D. dissertation, University of Illinois, 1937), p. 95.

merely for the profit of a few."[53] One of the most melodramatic expressions of twentieth-century agrarian fantasy appeared in *Hampton's Magazine* in 1912.[54] The ubiquitous author, Frederick Palmer, wrote the biography of a downtrodden eastern clerk caught up in the silver-lined dream of a small homestead in the West. Palmer rhapsodized:

> You know the type. He was one of the hundreds of thousands of nerve-raw weary city clerks, who with a growing family, had given up trying to save a cent from his salary. Every fiber of his body, of his wife's body, of the bodies of his three children called for the land and fresh air. He lay awake torturing his brain for some way in which to improve his condition.[55]

From the government agent the downtrodden eastern clerk discovered that "his fairest dream of opulence" could be realized.

The end of Palmer's agrarian drama is as predictable as the finale of a contemporary Zane Grey novel. After three years, our hero has a "house nearly paid for and his forty acres including water rights are worth a hundred dollars an acre. Muscles have padded his once skinny bones, his hands are calloused. He rejoices in the independent citizenship of a property holder."[56] Palmer's article goes on to point out that Newell and the Reclamation Service have fulfilled the American destiny; "they have given a rare vehicle with which to work out the New England town meeting idea in a broad and progressive modern spirit."

Palmer's soliloquy of paradise pointed up one of the most serious defects in the reclamation law; namely, who could be denied an opportunity of fulfilling his own personal dream? There was a complete lack of administrative apparatus by which to screen prospective homesteaders. At first blush, this omission might have appeared surprising, for seldom has

53. Quoted in M. Nelson McGeary, *Gifford Pinchot* (Princeton, 1960), p. 87.
54. Frederick Palmer, "The Service that Makes the Desert Bloom," *Hampton's Magazine* 26 (June 1911):699–712.
55. Ibid., p. 699.
56. Ibid., p. 701.

any administrative official been allocated as broad a discretionary power as the secretary of the interior under the Newlands Act.[57] He had the authority to determine the size of the farm unit, the water charges, the amount of private land to be included in a project, the selection of the project size, and the budgeting of reclamation funds.

The answer was deeply ingrained in the American democratic tradition. Statesmen and administrative bureaucracy alike had insisted that reclamation would create homes for thousands of landless citizens.[58] How, then, in the face of this agrarian myth in full cry would they deny applicants, even when these aspiring homesteaders had no previous farming experience and had inadequate capital?[59] They could not and did not; to have done so would have been as patently undemocratic as it was impolitic. Any congressman sponsoring a "selection" provision in the Newlands Act would have been thought to be suffering from political schizophrenia, or worse.

F. H. Newell, after noting that more than 75 per cent of the "first comers" had departed from the projects within three years, cryptically summed up the problem from the Service's viewpoint. "In proportion, however, as the land owners under the reclamation projects have been lacking in ability, strength, experience and good health and other essential qualifications, to that degree, the result has fallen below the standard set."[60]

Another innate defect in the reclamation legislation sur-

57. An enlightening discussion of the investure of powers in the Secretary of Interior under the Newlands Act is traced in Leahme Brown, "The Development of National Policy with Respect to Water Resources," pp. 90–92.

58. Daniel Boorstin, in his eclectic work, *The Americans*, has a suggestive passage: "America, then offered a novel opportunity to 'create property' owners, and no governmental power was more important than the power to give title to pieces of the New World" (*The Americans* [New York, 1965], p. 249).

59. A strong antidote to the fable of the agrarian myth in reclamation, with a heavy economic-technical slant, is Roy E. Huffman, *Irrigation Development and Public Water Policy* (New York, 1953). An extremely able discussion of water resource development in the West can be found in Norris Hundley, *Water and the West* (Berkeley, 1975).

60. F. H. Newell, "Twenty Years of Reclamation," in *A Survey of Reclamation* (New York, 1923), p. 19.

faced soon after the projects were initiated. The projects, financed from the public land sales of the seventeen western states, were idealistically to be apportioned to each state in ratio to their proceeds from land sales. The injudiciousness of this arrangement was obvious. A state with the largest land sales would receive the largest number of projects, regardless of suitability of their sites. There were modifications to this theoretical position, but the provision still resulted in considerable embarrassment to local politicians and to the Service.[61]

No aspect of the reclamation program caused more acrimonious debate than the repayment clause of the Newlands Law.[62] Water users on the projects accused the government of "paternalistic tyranny," often a *non sequitur* in itself. Reclamation officials charged the project settlers with fraud and political harassment.[63] Under the 1902 law, the project costs were to be repaid in ten annual interest-free installments. After five years, it became obvious that the repayment schedule was unworkable, unrealistic, and openly flouted. By 1912, when a national association of water users was organized, political pressure by disgruntled settlers became so strong that Capitol Hill could no longer ignore the protest.[64]

Water users systematically catalogued their grievances in an inundation of letters to the Reclamation Service and to

61. One of the more intelligent and nonemotional discussions of the "ratio" provisions of the Newlands Act can be found in Peterson, "Ellwood Mead," J. T. Peterson Collection.

62. A most exhaustive study of the repayment problem is Peggy Heim, "Financing the Reclamation Program, 1902–1919" (Ph.D. dissertation, Columbia University, 1954).

63. The Reclamation Service insisted that each project manager maintain a month by month (often day by day) history of his project. Though frequently selective as far as data incorporated, these histories are revealing as to the difficulties between the Service and the water users. "Klamath Project, Oregon-California, 1905–1925," Project Histories and Reports of Reclamation Bureau, National Archives; "Grand Valley, 1902–1923," Sinclair Harper Papers, Western History Research Center.

64. In 1914, the Reclamation Extension Act was passed, which extended the repayment period from ten to twenty years. Numerous "extensions" have been authorized since the 1914 act.

their congressmen. In short, they demanded an extension of repayment schedules, the firing of specific "highly irritating" reclamation officials, full control of projects by water users' associations, and "reevaluation" of construction costs in the future.[65]

The users' most vociferous complaint centered on estimates of construction.[66] They argued that the Service, on the basis of estimates, duped the settlers into believing that their repayment schedules would be considerably lower than they proved to be. They claimed that project expenditures were unreasonably high because of the Service's inefficiency in construction and operation. In addition, the forty-acre per person limitation thwarted any possibility of economic success.

Year after year the Reclamation Service rebutted these charges. In 1913, Director Newell decided that a blueprint of "responsible" answers could be highly useful in replying to the users' accusations. Accordingly, he drafted a forty-point rejoinder to be circulated among the project managers. The first laconic item observed, "The accompanying memorandum is sent for information or advice concerning the recurring criticism of the Reclamation Service. This reaches its peak at times when there is a change in the office of the Secretary of Interior."[67]

Actually, as Arthur Powell Davis noted to his friend Morris Bien, the Service had little use for this blueprint, no matter how glowingly drafted.[68] Imaginative answers were of little

65. Davis, "Diary," 5 January 1921; 20 October 1916; and 23 April 1917; the Davis diary is crammed with cryptic statements about the difficulty of repayment and the obstreperous actions of water users. There are numerous sources reflecting the dissatisfaction with the repayment policy: Davis, "Memorandum on the Rio Grande Project," Davis Papers; F. E. Schmitt, "Letters from a Reclamation Reconnaissance," in *A Survey of Reclamation*; F. E. Warren to Frank Mondell, 16 September 1914, F. E. Warren Papers, Western History Research Center.

66. Heim, "Financing the Federal Reclamation Program, 1902–1919," pp. 123–25.

67. Newell, "Memorandum on Periodic Criticism of the Reclamation Service," 14 March 1913, Davis Papers.

68. Davis to Morris Bien, 9 June 1913, Davis Papers.

help in responding to the yearly petitions of water users. Regarding the low estimates, Davis conceded that cost often exceeded original estimates, but the original estimates referred to did not include many of the construction features that water users later demanded that the Service take over—drainage systems, for instance. As an example, Davis cited the Rio Grande Project, where it came "as a great surprise, when finally, the officers . . . after much jockeying, announced they could make no payments" until they were assured credit for the cost of several canals the users had built and which the Service took over.[69] Second, the users refused to consider the inflationary rise between the 1902–1905 base period, when most of the estimates were calculated, and the final completion date.[70] Third, in some cases construction difficulties had increased costs beyond original expectations.[71] Frank Weymouth, assistant chief engineer, summed up the problem in a communication to Davis:

> I think it must be admitted that the early estimates were as a rule too low, but most of the increase in cost was due to the taking on of more additional work than was at first outlined and to the rise in prices of labor and material, and in many cases the cost of operation and maintenance for a long period of years was added to construction costs.[72]

The water users' unceasing political maneuvering to avoid or delay the repayment schedule angered Davis. In a vitriolic letter to Secretary Lane, in 1916, he noted that for six years the users on the Salt River Project had been enjoying the "bounty" of irrigation, without making any repayment, which Davis argued, "is productive of great criticism and embarrasses the Service in collections on all of the projects."[73] Two years later, when the Yuma Project users were lobbying for repayment relief, Davis confided to Pinchot, "I wish you could see your way clear to call on him [Lane] and inform

69. Davis, "Memorandum on the Rio Grande Project," Davis Papers.
70. Davis, "Memorandum on the Cost of Reclamation Projects," Davis Papers.
71. Ibid.
72. F. E. Weymouth to Davis, 8 December 1923, Davis Papers.
73. Davis to Secretary of Interior, 1 September 1916, Davis Papers.

him that such action will be followed by wide publicity and I believe you can save the cause of Reclamation from disaster."[74]

As to the charge that the government left the settler stranded once he was on the project, Davis staunchly insisted that this was just not true. He was especially piqued by the accusation that the Service slighted the agricultural developments on the projects.[75] Davis pointed out that in 1910 Secretary Ballinger had requested that the agricultural responsibilities (which were nebulous enough in the Newlands Act) of the Reclamation Service be transferred to the Department of Agriculture.[76] If agricultural programs were languishing, blame the Department of Agriculture or Congress for insufficient appropriations, not the Service. Critics and historians have largely ignored Davis's contention.

No single censure irritated Davis personally as much as the indictment of inefficiency. This criticism challenged the professional engineer's creed, especially when efficiency was being deified by the age of Taylorism, scientific management, and technocracy.[77] Colonel House, in his highly overrated novel, *Philip Dru*, has his chocolate soldier hero mouth the platitude, "There was no doubt that there was enormous waste going on, and this he undertook to stop, for he felt sure that as much efficiency could be obtained at two thirds the cost."[78] Regardless of the success of unctuous Philip Dru, House was parodying the contemporary vogue on efficiency.

As director of the Service, Davis, in press and before Congress, continually testified to the efficiency of his engineers. One of his proudest boasts was that the Service had escaped all charges of graft.[79] Just before leaving his position in June

74. Davis to Gifford Pinchot, 5 May 1918, Davis Papers.

75. Agricultural assistance offered by the Reclamation Service is outlined in "Klamath Project, Oregon-California, 1905–1925," Project Histories and Reports of the Reclamation Bureau, National Archives.

76. Davis to Calvert Townley, 27 August 1923, Davis Papers.

77. For the age of efficiency in the age of normalcy, see Samuel Haber, *Efficiency and Uplift* (Chicago, 1964).

78. E. M. House, *Philip Dru, Administrator: A Story of Tomorrow* (New York, 1920), p. 168.

79. Even his severest antagonists testified to the incorruptibility of

1923, he wrote the project manager at American Falls, Idaho, "Probably the one thing most regretted by big business is the successful and economic operation of public utilities by the nation, the States or municipalities, and this is always combatted by the statement that public works can not be done efficiently or economically."[80] Davis invested his manager with the responsibility of continuing the fight against "horrendous forces."

This then is the schematic framework of reclamation policy as molded by Arthur Powell Davis within the political tensions and compromises of his age. What import did this rationale have for the West? First of all, reclamation became inseparably entangled with evolving twentieth-century federalism. The private versus public power issue, which troubled Davis, was but a microcosmic contest of state decentralization versus federal centralization.[81] Historically the West has been bitterly opposed to federal suzerainty over the public domain, jealously regarding all public land as a part of the state's fief. Yet, as numerous commentators have observed, western spokesmen have adopted a dichotomous attitude toward federal bounty.[82] On the one hand they ve-

the Service. "The Reclamation Service has unquestionably been one of the best administered bureaus of the government with no taint of politics, graft or intentional wrong" (H. H. Brook, "Difficulties and Complaints of the Farmer," in A Survey of Reclamation, p. 31).

80. Davis to Barry Dibble, 11 May 1923, Davis Papers.

81. Provocative discussions of private vs. public interest are in Grant McConnell, Private Power & American Democracy (New York, 1966); Gerald Nash, State Government and Economic Development (Berkeley, 1964); E. Louise Peffer, The Closing of the Public Domain (Stanford, 1951); Richard G. Baumhoff, The Dammed Missouri Valley (New York, 1951); Gerald Nash, The American West in the Twentieth Century (Englewood Cliffs, N.J., 1973); Neal R. Peirce, The Great Plains States (New York, 1973); Dean E. Mann, The Politics of Water in Arizona (Tucson, 1963); and Samuel P. Hays, Conservation and the Gospel of Efficiency (Cambridge, 1959).

82. The commentary on colonial schizophrenia is available in the following: Thurman Arnold, Folklore of Capitalism (New Haven, 1937); Joseph Kinsey Howard, Montana: High, Wide and Handsome (New Haven, 1943); Wendell Berge, Economic Freedom for the West (Lincoln, 1946); Avrahm G. Mezerik, The Revolt of the South and West (New York, 1946); Walter P. Webb, Divided We Stand (New

hemently denounce grants from Washington, while on the other hand they accept federal largesse with alacrity.[83] The West has denounced federal withdrawals from the domain, yet lobbied incessantly for liberal legislation in utilizing public lands.[84] Sen. Francis E. Warren from Wyoming, in an astonishingly revealing letter to one of the constituents, unraveled the subtleties of western states' rights:

> The disposition of the public domain has been marked by two conflicting theories. One, and I believe the correct theory, contemplates getting the public lands into the ownership of the individual as rapidly as may be done in accordance with public land laws. . . . The opposing theory contemplates the retention by the federal Government of as great an area of public land as can possibly be retained. . . . This theory threatens to undermine all property rights in the West.[85]

What was the prospect for the future?—not an optimistic one from the good Wyoming statesman's viewpoint. Senator Warren did not believe in a "surrender policy." He withstood the pressure for further federal retention and control of western resources, believing that the individual should obtain ownership of the land and all that it contained.[86] The Wyoming senator was first and foremost a political realist.

What Senator Warren desired was federal subsidy to remove the risk for private profits. Newlands lobbied for public dividends from public investment. While the Newlands political theory prevailed, the settlers defeated the public profit philosophy by refusing to reimburse the public purse. Why should the settler ignore the long-established tradition of

York, 1937); Bernard De Voto, "The West Against Itself," *Harper's* 169 (August 1934):355–64; and Gene M. Gressley, "Colonialism: A Western Complaint," *Pacific Northwest Quarterly* 64 (January 1963): 1–8.

83. A brilliant discussion on the economic implications of federalism is in Harry N. Scheiber, "The Condition of American Federalism: An Historian's View," Committee Print, Subcommittee on Intergovernmental Relations, Committee on Government Operations, U.S. Senate, 89th Cong., 2d sess., 15 October 1966.

84. Philip O. Foss, *Politics and Grass* (Seattle, 1960).

85. Warren to Cola W. Shepard, 5 May 1914, F. E. Warren Papers.

86. Ibid.

raiding the federal treasury? Where was the precedent in history to reverse capital flow from western citizens to the federal exchequer? In the final analysis, the western settler pragmatically adopted the best of both worlds of Senators Newlands and Warren. He grasped the federal subsidy and put it into his personal pocketbook. In doing so, he was hardly unique, for he was merely following a traditional pattern. Nor could western states offer any alternative; the plain fact of the matter was that the states were neither economically nor administratively capable of amassing the resources to launch a comprehensive reclamation program.[87]

As Arthur Powell Davis sorted the papers in his files prior to leaving the Reclamation Service in June 1923, Secretary Work began selecting the task force of experts for his famous "fact-finding" committee.[88] These "fact finders" were invested with formulating an answer to the now hackneyed question, "What is wrong with reclamation?"[89] The irony of this query was that everyone concerned—settler, engineer, and politician —realized the deficiencies and prescribed remedies.

For the politician and the settler the most convenient scapegoat was the Reclamation Service. So successfully did they advertise the "failures" of the Service that their viewpoint has triumphed historically. Undeniably, the engineer never became adept at playing the role of politician. Even his assignment contained a professional paradox. The reclamation engineer, a creature of a technological-industrial civilization, had been designated as an instrument to perpetuate the myth of an agrarian society. As technocrat he had performed his mission with professional competence. If anyone would have

87. See Gerald Nash's brilliant analysis, *State Government and Economic Development* (Berkeley, 1964).

88. The "fact finders" carried the formal appellation of "Committee of Special Advisors on Reclamation." The membership consisted of Thomas E. Campbell, James R. Garfield, Oscar E. Bradfute, Clyde C. Dawson, Elwood Mead, and John A. Widstoe.

89. Newell sarcastically noted in his autobiography, "In October Secretary Work appointed a small committee designated as 'fact finders' but which was popularly known because of the pessimistic way in which their report began as the 'fault finders'" (Newell, "A Man's Life," p. 108, F. H. Newell Papers).

thought to ask, "What is right with Reclamation?" the obvious and almost only response would have been that the reclamation projects were technological successes. One engineering problem after another had been met and conquered.

Federal reclamation had been, in the words of the "fact finders," an "experiment conceived in a spirit of wise and lofty statesmanship."[90] Regardless of conception, they were precisely correct in suggesting that reclamation had been an experiment, but one born in political opportunism and nutured in political controversy.

The reclamation legislation and administration represented one of many attempts to merge the conflicting ideologies of private and public interest, of local decentralization and federal centralization. By the mid-1920s, the compromise constructed between the centrifugal pull of the states and the centripetal magnet of the federal government threatened to collapse. Only in the coming decades when a stabilized bureaucracy emerged, buoyed up by a body of vested congressmen resting on an articulate provincial power basis, did the reclamation program become assured. In sum, reclamation developed into one of those innumerable compromises of vested interests in a federal power structure. If reclamation appeared doomed in the 1920s, the participants soon discovered—if they were not already convinced—that the solution resided in politics, not in technology.

As a democratic experiment in federal-state adjustment, the first two decades of reclamation held enormous significance as a harbinger of the multipurpose water-resource schemes burgeoning in the era of the New Deal.

90. "Federal Reclamation by Irrigation," Sen. Document 92, 68th Cong., 1st sess., p. xi. This essay, subject to some editing, originally appeared in *Agricultural History* 42 (July 1968):241–58. My appreciation to Professor Shideler and the Agricultural History Association for permission to incorporate this version.

GOS,
Petroleum,
Politics,
and the West

On a hot, muggy, oppressive Sunday afternoon in June of
1933, George Otis Smith, current chairman of the Federal
Power Commission and sometime director of the United
States Geological Survey, sat at his desk in his home near
Rock Creek Park in Washington, D.C.

Writing one of his round-robin letters to his children, he
felt in a philosophical mood. In the past week Smith had completed two-and-one-half years as chairman of the Federal
Power Commission and thirty-seven years in public service
"as a fact-finding scientist and a fact-using executive."[1] Mus-
ing about the success of his life, he attributed a lot of his
personal achievement to the simple fact that he had always
been independent. "I am thankful that I was not brought up
to trade as the politicians do," he wrote, "I guess I was born
free, and, so far as these years in Washington go, I have not
sold myself for the sake of position, power, or any material
gain—and I may add there are grafters for power, as well
as for cash."[2]

George Otis Smith's introspective meditation on that June
afternoon was precisely correct. Few men in Washington
have wielded the weapon of independence with such finesse
or have received as great a reputation for integrity. Smith was
first and foremost a scientist, cherishing the scientific method
as strongly as any physician ever treasured the Hippocratic
oath. During the days of the Teapot Dome scandal, a reporter,
with a degree of incredulousness, asked Smith how he had

1. George Otis Smith, Diary, 25 June 1933, George Otis Smith Collection, Western History Research Center, University of Wyoming,
Laramie (hereafter cited as GOS, Diary).
2. Ibid.

managed to keep the Geological Survey above suspicion for so many years. Smith found nothing mysterious in his tactics; he quickly replied, "The method was simple enough—it was doing things the straight forward way and not playing for position either with Congress or the Secretary's office or the general public, but simply trying to deliver the goods."[3]

Undeniably and unequivocally, George Otis Smith had announced his creed. Up to a point, that is: what he did not say, nor could be expected to state, was that if he was not a politician, he was a first-rate diplomat. Time and again in his delicate maneuvering between Washington bureaucracy and Wall Street financiers, he displayed a Lord Cecil-like skill.

A scientist, a diplomat, what were the other tenets of the Smith faith? Paramount to his theological view of natural resources was his fervent belief in conservation. The Smith conservation ideology was in the classic Progressive sense. He was not a preservationist and he had no objection whatsoever to the proper utilization of the country's resources. Although never politically in the Progressive camp, he did insist, as did Pinchot and his followers, that this utilization must be efficient and scientifically planned. Waste horrified him as much as it did the most doctrinaire conservationist.

Indeed, Smith attempted with above average success to maintain what he considered was a politically balanced position in conservation's spectrum, a posture that frequently confused friends and foes alike. One March day in 1924, Secretary of the Interior Hubert Work suddenly blurted out that he regarded Smith "somewhat of a radical conservationist." With his usual composure and aplomb Smith calmly replied to the secretary that the question was altogether a matter of "geography." He noted that "in the West such a charge might be true, while in the East I had been regarded as not radical enough." Smith conceded, "I suppose my views would be quite popular in the vicinity of the Mississippi River, but either West of there or East of there I was subject to criticism."[4]

Smith quickly exploited the opportunity of reviewing his

3. GOS, Diary, 23 February 1924.
4. Ibid., 15 March 1924.

personal history on the definition of conservation. Smith hurriedly returned to his office to pick up his copy of the Ballinger-Pinchot hearings. Rushing back to Work's office, he read his testimony to the bemused secretary:

> Mr. Smith: When I speak of well-meaning conservationists I now speak respectively—that is the kind of conservationist I would like to be considered myself. I believe in conservation.
>
> The Chairman (Senator Knute Nelson): Let me then ask a preliminary question. Is it not a term that is hard to define?
>
> Mr. Smith: Well, I do not want to be called a conservationist, unless they allow me to define the term.
>
> The Chairman: Proceed.
>
> Mr. Smith: The first use I made in an official report of the word "conservation" was about ten years ago, when I was speaking against the waste of an expendable natural resource —that is, artesian water in a certain basin in the State of Washington—and reporting on that I used the term of "conservation of the water resources." I think that the term "conservation" is opposed not only to the waste of an expendable resource, but also to the nonuse of a nonexpendable resource, like water power or agricultural land. To me conservation means utilization and development. It means utilization with maximum efficiency and a minimum waste.
>
> Mr. Graham: Mr. Smith, just there. The word "conservation", of course, implies preserving for somebody or other. . . .
>
> Mr. Smith: It is to be conserved for some one to use.[5]

Putting his Ballinger-Pinchot hearings down, Smith rested his case with the secretary of the interior by emphasizing that in the fifteen-year period since he had sat in the St. Paul courtroom his definition of conservation had remained constant. He conceded that "either I was right then, as now or I have simply failed to make any progress during these years."[6] Smith then urged Work to decentralize the entire administrative structure of the function of the Department of Interior in conservation. Emphasizing that conservation

5. U.S., Congress, Senate, 61st Cong., 3d sess., 1910–1911, Senate Document 39, Volume 6, pp. 3338–39.

6. GOS, Diary, 15 March 1924.

"like charity" begins at home, he added that the localization of conservation would result in a proper balance given to the engineering and economic phases of conservation, phases that were often lost in the muck of controversy surrounding the social and political questions in conservation. Smith wisely refrained from pointing out to Work that he had given testimony on the decentralization concept at the Ballinger trial. After all, discretion, if not valor, dictated that one did not overemphasize to one's superior that Work's perception was fifteen years in arrears.

In his devotion to the scientific and efficient use of natural resources Smith would have been applauded by the most dedicated enthusiastic conservationist. Where he decamped from the followers of Pinchot was over the matter of accent. In conservation, as in his life-style in general, Smith was a middle-of-the-roader. He argued that it was not only unpolitic, but unscientific, to take a radically nonnegotiable stance on the philosophy of conservation.

Coupled to his ideology of conservation, Smith consistently opted for a Benthamite approach to the consumption of natural resources. In doing so he was echoing his neighboring bureau chief Arthur Powell Davis as well as many other conservationists. In a speech to the western oil men at Colorado Springs in 1929, Smith reminded his listeners that "there need be no antagonism in the interest between the large body of consumers and those interested in the production of this essential fuel. The greatest good to the greatest number over the longest period is the economic goal sought."[7] It is difficult to imagine a flatter endorsement of Bentham.

Two years later in a letter to his son, Smith again reiterated the Benthamite rationale in describing a controversy that whirled around the construction of a power plant on the Columbia River. Smith discovered that because of abnormal haste in engineering, a $300,000 budget overrun had occurred. Smith seized the occasion to lecture his engineering department on the responsibility to the general public, identifying them as 150 million investors. He terminated his sermon with the note, "it is sometimes hard for us to realize

7. Ibid., (n.d.) March 1929.

the millions of investors in power are the clients of our [Federal Power] Commission just as truly as the 25 million customers."[8]

During the decade of the twenties few bureaucrats had as influential a role in putting forth a personal definition of conservation's empiricism as did George Otis Smith. As director of the United States Geological Survey from 1907, as chairman of the Coal Commission, and later chairman of the Federal Oil Commission, advisor to the Federal Oil Conservation Board, and finally chairman of the Federal Power Commission, Smith, from the Olympian seat of a distinguished scientist, had an unrivaled opportunity to lobby for conservation. When this short-of-stature, slight-of-build, partially graying, gentle-demeanored scientist sat down before a congressional committee to offer testimony, congressmen listened. In an age of magnified political and economic scandal, Smith's independent, scholarly insistence that his only vested interest was the public welfare may have sounded naive, even unbelievable, but above all it was refreshing. So consistent was his pronouncement, so untarnished was his image that few congressmen or even presidents cared to dispute his statements.

Of all the natural resource areas, it was in petroleum that Smith had the optimum opportunity to evolve and refine his doctrine of conservation. From the moment Smith became director of the Geological Survey, he pushed vigorously and successfully for the withdrawal of government land containing petroleum reserves, insisting that the day would soon arrive when the navy would be converting to liquid fuel.[9] Throughout the twenties there were few months that passed that a periodical or the press did not carry one of Smith's pronouncements on oil conservation. Always contending that public opinion was one of the most potent weapons the Washington bureaucracy commanded, he unceasingly did everything in his power to mold and sway public will.[10]

8. GOS to Joseph Smith, 1 September 1931, GOS Collection.
9. GOS to Henry L. Doherty, 12 June 1924, GOS Collection.
10. Not that Smith ever underestimated the difficulties involved in public education; he once jotted in his diary, "Educating these American people is a terrible task. It is hard enough for those of us who

It is a decided understatement to note that petroleum conservation in the United States has had a highly volatile and uneven history.[11] From the very birth of the industry when oil shot in streams down Pithole Creek in western Pennsylvania, oil men have been decrying the waste, the sin of undisciplined exploitation of oil. By 1890, the rise in production and consumption scared a number of state legislatures into adopting conservation measures of varying intention, scope, and enforcement.

These state statutes on conservation in the main converged on five types of policies of conservation. First, there were what might conceivably be called the universal statutes of conservation, such as those in California where the total producing formation in the Midway Field was protected against water infiltration. Second, there were statutes aimed at prohibiting specific instances of waste. Indiana legislation, for instance, required the confinement of gas after two days of open flow on a discovery well. Third, there were the so-called common purchaser laws, which were adopted in Oklahoma, Texas, Arkansas, and Louisiana. These laws would suddenly appear when producing companies affiliated with pipeline organizations would run all of their oil in periods of overproduction, while their neighbors in the same field sat idly by, unable to market their production. Fourth, the common purchaser laws were quickly followed in Texas annd Louisiana by well-spaced legislation. Commonly under these codes a state agency would be designated the power to indicate where wells should be located in a pool, which, of course, resulted in greater conservation of production. Fifth, states such as Wyoming and Oklahoma passed legislation governing the amount of wasteful production of natural gas.

In spite of this plethora of state conservation measures, by

feel the responsibility of educating cabinet officers" (GOS, Diary, 18 October 1924).

11. Literature abounds on the history of petroleum policy and debacles of the early twentieth century. Two of the most competent, pertinent, and useful monographs are J. Leonard Bates, *The Origins of Teapot Dome* (Urbana, 1963); and Burl Noggle, *Teapot Dome, Oil and Politics in the 1920's* (Baton Rouge, 1962).

1920, scientists, government leaders, and a select few of industry leaders were becoming increasingly convinced that uniform federal regulation of the petroleum industry was essential. First came the Delphic warnings of George Otis Smith, who claimed that within a decade the petroleum reserves of America would be exhausted. Smith was joined in his chorus of conservation by other industrial leaders, particularly Henry L. Doherty, Earl Oliver, Warwick Downing, and E. W. Marland, who all denounced the waste and foolhardiness of the current practices of oil production. Finally, military leaders, especially the navy admirals, predicted national disaster unless adequate reserves were on hand for the fleet.

With this wellhead of pressure accumulating for national action, one would have thought that the political path through Congress would have been smooth, if not clear. Just the opposite was true: industry opponents of conservation were far more numerous than were proponents of conservation. In fact, overwhelming antipathy to conservation pervaded the board rooms of the American Petroleum Institute until 1926–1927.

Why did the executives of the petroleum companies have such an aversion to conservation? Their motives were intertwined with the exceedingly complex montage that was the petroleum scene in the 1920s. Some oil men would have argued that they were not against conservation per se, but only the Smith-Doherty brand.[12] Others would have brought forth the age-old cry of laissez-faire that the industry through voluntary cooperation was perfectly capable of self-policing.[13] Still others would have maintained that the sad state of the industry derived from the erratic political madness that kept their industry boomeranging between the dogma of New Nationalism and that of the New Freedom. These executives would have stressed that economics and politics, like oil and water, do not mix. How could anyone reconcile the regulation

12. An excellent discussion of the forces propelling petroleum conservation can be found in Gerald Nash's ably written volume, *United States Oil Policy, 1890–1964* (Pittsburgh, 1968), pp. 72–111.

13. M. L. Requa to GOS, 27 January 1926, GOS Collection.

of the New Nationalism with the reliance on competition and individual entrepreneurship inherent in the New Freedom?

If they had any insidious thoughts about the irrationality of their position when they contributed to favorite party coffers at election time, they quickly banished these insidious inferences. Yet these executives did have a point. Few in or out of government could divine with any precision what the Coolidge administration did favor in petroleum policy in 1923. Slowly there were ample portents that if Coolidge did not want to court big business, he at least had no objection to flirting with it. So these leaders reasoned, why hurry to embrace the straight-jacket of conservation when the president might fix his Vermont stare on other issues.

Three years later the entire petroleum scene was swiftly changing into what amounted to a rapprochement between government and the eastern petroleum industry. The surface sources for this sudden switch were easily discerned. Uppermost was the simple fact that President Coolidge decided to act. Rebounding from the successive exposés in the Teapot Dome case and other scandals that seemed to the president to go on forever, Coolidge finally realized that he had to expunge the Republican party, simultaneously besmirching the Democrats. In essence, he had to seize the morality issue and assume the uncomfortable mantle of Don Quixote, while his party sloshed in oil.

Furthermore Coolidge was as horrified as George Otis Smith at tales of enormous dissipation of petroleum.[14] Always one for bread and circuses, as long as the bread was in communion-sized bites, Coolidge could not intellectually or morally justify waste in any industry, while at the same time he so emphatically advocated economy in government operation. Moreover, standing on the twin issues of prosperity and normalcy (or at least a becalmed, some would have said anesthetized, society), Coolidge could not risk the double jeopardy involved in the economic collapse of the petroleum industry.

On the issue of profit, Coolidge and the industry were of

14. J. Edgar Pew to Hubert Work, 21 September 1925, GOS Collection.

one mind. When all the smoke wafted from the corporate board rooms, the one dramatic issue that remained was declining profits. Reduced dividends were more responsible for the tandem arrangement between government and industry than all the lamentations of the conservationists or the two-sentence monologues of silent Cal. Even ultraconservative petroleum dynasties could be transformed into wild-eyed conservationists if that would result in higher dividends, because it was obvious to industry leaders in the mid-1920s that their business was in a decided slump. Overproduction increasingly threatened to glut the market, forcing prices steadily downward. In addition it was apparent to all that voluntary agreements and state statutes had failed to plug the flow of oil. Technological advances had enabled production and exploration to find oil faster than conservationists could propose solutions or a national market be developed.

With prices in some locales in the Southwest listed at fifteen cents per barrel, the industry became ready, even eager, to listen at last to federal proposals for conservation. Whether the officialdom of the American Petroleum Institute was receptive to federal action or not, President Coolidge succumbed to the entreaties of George Otis Smith and Henry L. Doherty on 18 December 1924, establishing the Federal Oil Conservation Board. Dictating from a memorandum furnished by Smith,[15] Coolidge in his literal, staccato style, reviewed the waste, the economic instability, and the needs of military security, ending with the hardly startling conclusion that all of these needs depended on a sensible petroleum conservation policy. Again at Smith's suggestion, Coolidge mollified the API by underlining that the primary duties of the board initially would be investigative.[16] The board was charged with holding hearings, gathering evidence and sponsoring studies. Composed of the secretaries of interior, com-

15. After meeting with the president in July 1924, Smith came away from the conference remembering the Coolidge command, "You must help get these government people and these industry spokesmen together on this waste problem" (GOS, Diary, 3 July 1924).

16. Memorandums to Secretary Work, 23 August 1924, GOS Collection.

merce, navy, and war, the board was called upon to issue a report that would offer guidelines for federal and state conservation legislation.

Smith had been aware for several months that Coolidge was seriously considering the establishment, via executive fiat, of a federal investigative oil board.[17] Upon receiving the official news, he dashed off a letter to his good friend, Henry L. Doherty. While exuding optimism, Smith cautioned Doherty not to expect too much from the board's "meditation."[18] Nevertheless he and Doherty both could and did bask in the limelight of Coolidge's action. They had, with very little outside assistance, convincingly educated the president of the United States on the sins of overproduction and the corresponding virtues of conservation. Now, as Doherty commented to Smith, "we must gird our loins for the battle."[19]

A most remarkable association, this buccaneering Wall Street financier and the erudite government scientist! In many ways it was as unlikely an entente as one could imagine between the worlds of government and business. Nervous, volatile, brilliant, impetuous, this Henry L. Doherty, who by his own admission "had not seen the inside of a school room since I was twelve,"[20] forged a gigantic oil-utility empire. Scholarly, patient, diplomatic, with little interest in this world's goods, George Otis Smith threw his energy into pushing his scientific schemes through the bureaucratic jungle.

And yet their mutual attraction is easily appreciated. Both men of high integrity, they had been crusading for many of the same goals of conservation for most of their professional lives. George Otis Smith had formulated the policy (for which President Taft assumed credit) of the petroleum land withdrawals in 1909.[21] A decade after Smith's advocation of the public lands withdrawal, Doherty began to campaign

17. GOS to Henry L. Doherty, 19 April 1924, GOS Collection.
18. GOS, Diary, 22 March 1924.
19. GOS to Henry L. Doherty, 20 December 1924.
20. Henry L. Doherty to GOS, 17 January 1925, GOS Collection.
21. Henry L. Doherty to James A. Veasey, 6 August 1927, James A. Veasey Collection, Petroleum History and Research Center, University of Wyoming, Laramie.

with revivalistic fervor to put, in his favorite phrase, "the petroleum industry on a sound and proper basis." With conservation as their first commandment, each saw in the other an entrée to unfamiliar territory. Smith definitely desired a friend in the counsels of the petroleum industry; Doherty valued a guide in the palace court on the Potomac. In the beginning, it was a marriage of common concerns, which grew over the years into a solid friendship.

After exchanging a lengthy series of correspondences from the fall of 1923, the two decided to get together in early 1924. Smith jotted down a lengthy description in his diary of his first, impressionable visit to Doherty's New York penthouse.[22] Walking into 24 State Street, facing the Battery, Smith took an elevator to the thirteenth floor, walking up two short flights of steps. He found himself "facing a door, colonial in design with side lights and all the trimmings that you would expect to see on Bancroft Place."[23] Smith was ushered into the music room, where his host, adorned with a grizzled gray beard and suffering from a slight arthritic stoop, soon entered. From this first encounter, Smith never ceased to be amazed at the enormous energy of the founder of Cities Service. Doherty, so Smith quickly observed that first evening atop a skyscraper, was "a driven man." After a quiet dinner, the two men talked late into the night, sitting in front of two enormous bay windows overlooking Lower New York Bay. Smith came away from that evening more strongly convinced than ever that "he is an outspoken man and more alive to the [conservation] situation it seems to me than any other oil man."[24]

Over the next four years, while their correspondence never became more familiar than "Dear Dr. Smith" and "Dear Mr. Doherty," the philosophical scientist and the business tycoon formed a close rapport. By the time of their first introduction, Doherty, as Smith, had fashioned a systematic scenario encompassing the entire range of petroleum production.[25]

22. GOS to Rossiter W. Raymond, 23 May 1912, GOS Collection.
23. GOS, Diary, 7 June 1924.
24. Ibid.
25. Ibid.

Doherty was even more convinced than Smith that at the nation's current rate of use, the domestic reserves would be exhausted by 1932. On occasion at API meetings Doherty fairly shouted at his colleagues that they were consistently overestimating the country's undeveloped pools. Furthermore, as if this were not bad enough, the oil industry uniformly underestimated domestic consumption. In 1925, Doherty wrote Smith that three recent developments—heating of homes with oil, the switching of railroads to liquid fuel, and the growth of the trucking industry—assured an oil crisis by 1930.[26]

Doherty perceived the wrangle of conservation in very elemental terms; "The whole controversy is based on whether we have an adequate supply of petroleum and whether there are avoidable wastes. The Brigadier Generals of the Industry say we have a super-abundant supply and there are no appreciable or avoidable wastes."[27] When he heard such pronouncements "out of the mouths of the babes of industry spokesmen," Doherty was incredulous. Such statements, he insisted, were irresponsible. In letter after letter of Doherty's, one phrase or its variation kept outcropping: "This country bids fair to become a pauper nation so far as oil is concerned."[28]

What did Doherty propose to do about this sad situation? Over the years, he had evolved a fairly schematic offensive on overproduction and petroleum conservation practices. First, he discerned the problem, as did Smith, in terms of one

26. Doherty wrote James A. Veasey in the summer of 1927, "Since 1919, I have spent a great deal of time and brain effort to try and get the petroleum industry on a sound and proper basis. If my time is worth anything and if my brain is worthy of anything, the same amount of time and brain effort should have produced a good sized fortune if it had been applied to my own business. I finally worked out a program for the oil industry which covered practically every feature of it from production to the final marketing of the product. Unfortunately such a controversy has raged over the feature regarding production that almost everybody lost sight of the fact that my work covered a much wider scope" (Henry L. Doherty to Veasey, 25 July 1927, James A. Veasey Collection).

27. Henry L. Doherty to GOS, 1 December 1925, GOS Collection.

28. Ibid., 15 September 1925.

of education of the public, of the petroleum industry, and of the government. Through the director of the Geological Survey, Doherty now had a place on the government carousel. On almost any pretext Smith invited Doherty to Washington, and on several occasions, both during the hearings of the Federal Oil Conservation Board and after, they personally presented Doherty's proposals to government figures.[29] Via Smith's intercession, Doherty had private conferences with Coolidge, Secretaries Hoover and Work, and an assorted array of admirals. Intriguingly enough, this oil man who was scorned by his own fraternity as a senile radical received a very favorable reception almost everywhere he went in Washington. After a meeting with Doherty, President Coolidge told Smith, "That man makes sense."[30]

Long regarded in the industry as something of an eccentric at best, Doherty enjoyed his trips to Washington. It restored one's perspective to find people who did not automatically assume you were demented. In fact his negative role became so blatant in industry circles that Doherty began turning it into humor. After an especially vitriolic meeting of the API board of directors, Doherty walked up to A. C. Bedford, chairman of the board of Standard Oil of New Jersey and an especially favorite bête noir of Doherty's, and proceeded to

29. Ibid., 28 June 1924. In the spring of 1971, William Bellano, President of Occidental Petroleum Corporation, told the writer, "Whether this country knows it or not, we are a have-not nation" (Interview with William Bellano, Los Angeles, 9 March 1971).

30. Smith commented in his diary, "I think I have pulled every wire so far toward giving Mr. Doherty a chance to put his plans across, and my speech at Tulsa ought to help." A few months later, Smith noted, "I am not having an easy time, however, in getting as much action on the part of Cabinet officers as I could desire, but I am still trying to arrange a conference between Mr. Doherty and the Secretaries of War, Navy, Interior and Commerce." Smith finally maneuvered not one but two meetings with these Secretaries in February of 1925. He then arranged a lunch for Doherty with Admirals Hilary P. Jones and H. H. Rousseau in April 1925. "These naval officers were so impressed with Mr. Doherty's personality, and I think some good seeds were sown" (GOS, Diaries, 20 September, 6 December 1924; 25 April 1925).

inform Bedford that he, Doherty, had more influence than any other single API director. As Doherty gleefully chortled to Smith, "I explained that I had only to vote yes on any proposition and the other members of the board would immediately vote NO."[31]

If Doherty's impact on the petroleum industry appeared negligible, his personally sponsored research on the scientific problems of petroleum conservation were enormously successful. He set up a Cities Service research laboratory at Bartlesville, Oklahoma, under the able direction of C. E. Beecher, one time Bureau of Mines engineer. At Bartlesville, Beecher recruited a competent group of petroleum engineers to launch a comprehensive inquiry into the methods of secondary recovery. Conceiving the experiments going on in Beecher's laboratory as a foundation for his pet conservation proposals, Doherty followed closely the calculations coming out of Bartlesville. In fact, so intense was his interest that his eight-to-ten page letters strained Beecher's patience.[32]

Nevertheless a mutual respect developed between the two men over the years; and as the studies poured forth from the Bartlesville laboratory Doherty's faith in Beecher was more than justified. By 1927 Doherty had ample evidence to prove what he had been saying for a number of years, that under the current wasteful production techniques as much oil remained in the ground as was being brought to the surface.[33] Specifically, his scientists demonstrated that the movement of oil in a virgin field is possible only by reducing the surface tension and viscosity and by maintaining the gas pressure.

Having convinced himself and his friends in government, the challenge became how could he win over the petroleum industry to acknowledge the revolutionary impact of his secondary recovery findings. Why not copy the advertising methods, those miracle workers of mass marketing in the twenties, and obtain the endorsement of "a star." Following

31. GOS, Diary, 11 July 1925.
32. Ibid., 28 March 1925.
33. Interview with C. E. Beecher, 26 February 1958, Bartlesville, Oklahoma.

up this idea Doherty commented to Smith, "If some petroleum engineer of outstanding reputation could make a statement that he believed five times as much oil could be produced from the Bradford sands as ever has been produced, it would be a very effective argument for conservation."[34]

Whether Doherty ever found his distinguished petroleum engineer to play celebrity or not, he soon advocated another path "to my dream of an orderly petroleum production." With his usual emotional fervor, Doherty propounded that while he held no brief for the myopic petroleum executives, they were not entirely to blame for the chaotic state of the petroleum world. Rather the national and state legislatures should be censured for drafting legislation that was "amazingly unrealistic and foolhardy." Doherty recalled that the banking system had been handicapped for years by laws that forced them to sell government bonds. He saw an analogous situation in the petroleum industry, where there was a bramblebush of conflicting statutes. Doherty believed that the strange bashfulness of oil executives to enter the political arena to remedy these abuses was due to the fear that "the subject might become a political football or made worse by impractical reformers."[35] Reading his political barometer, Doherty may have accurately forecasted the rationale behind the petroleum industry's reluctance to advocate wide sweeping reforms. However, it did not explain why the petroleum lobby exhibited little shyness in pushing for other types of helpful legislation such as less taxation, longer leasing periods, ad infinitum.

While Doherty was making his weekly journeys to Washington both to court the bureaucracy and to be present at the Oil Conservation Board hearings, Smith was active in directing the board probe. Besides holding the public hearings, the board sent a multitude of questionnaires to leading petroleum executives. Smith especially tried to make certain that both independents and major corporations were repre-

34. Henry L. Doherty to Hubert Work, 3 July 1925; Henry L. Doherty to GOS, 16 December 1925, GOS Collection.
35. Ibid., 15 September 1925, GOS Collection.

sented. Although the questionnaires requested specific information, frequent rambling replies reflected the confused state
of the thinking of the industry.[36] The board's queries focalized
on various conservation practices. One, what direction should
be given to curbing waste? Two, what is your estimate of
overproduction in 1924? Three, how could the "brakes" be
put on the discovery of new pools, particularly in view of the
rapidly developing technology of exploration? Four, what
would be the demand for petroleum in the future? Five, could
coal replace oil as a domestic fuel? Six, under the present
production methods, would you care to give your personal
assessment of the amount of waste? Seven, do you see overproduction being slowed by technical innovations or alter-
nations in legislation governing oil production?[37]

Although they could not even feign astonishment, Smith,
Doherty, and the members of the Federal Oil Conservation
Board were dismayed by the answers to the questionnaires.
The majority of the respondents refused to admit that there
was any "unnecessary" waste, further that a degree of waste
was inevitable, and finally, companies should be commended
for the great amount of money and effort they had allotted
to reducing waste.[38] Smith refrained from commenting on
the answers, but he must have smiled at the internal incon-
sistencies in these responses. If waste was minimal, why
should corporations be bestowed kudos for their efforts? How
much energy, money, and time could they expend on a non-
existent problem? Replying to the rest of the questionnaire,
most petroleum executives found little overproduction at the

36. The secretary of the Federal Oil Conservation Board and a
longtime Smith friend, E. S. Rochester, drafted and provided overall
supervision of the board's questionnaire. In condensing the replies to
the questionnaire for Smith, Rochester sarcastically appended a post-
script on his report, "If these men run their companies in the same
muddled way they answered their questionnaire, there can be no doubt
that the oil industry is in serious trouble" (E. S. Rochester to GOS, 9
October 1925. GOS Collection).
37. Ibid., 8 June 1924.
38. Federal Oil Conservation Board Questionnaire, draft and text,
GOS Collection.

present moment; they argued for less not more legislation; and there was a decided division of opinion on how much of the energy market coal would absorb.

In only one area, and that represented a by-product of the questionnaire, did industrial leaders express any uneasiness over their economic plight. Many leaders conceded that they were afflicted with too many retail outlets,[39] resulting in maldistribution, but even here the industry "brigadiers" suggested that in time the uneconomical distribution of petroleum through outlets on every street corner would correct itself. In aperçu, the industry spokesmen advocated laissez-faire, their house was in order.

From the preliminary and subsequent final reports of the Federal Oil Conservation Board,[40] it is obvious that the board refused to surrender to the petroleum industry. They not only reiterated but intensified their warning about the depletion of petroleum reserves: they prophesied that petroleum resources would be exhausted within six years.[41] Then after reviewing the future sources of petroleum supply—including improved secondary recovery methods, conservation of new fields, oil shale, and foreign imports—the report ended with a ringing invitation for more cooperation between industry and government.

This clarion call for a gentlemen's agreement echoes not only the personal philosophy of the board's members, Hoover, Wilbur, and Work, but also, of course, of President Calvin Coolidge. George Otis Smith dashed off a note to his son

39. Résumé of the Federal Oil Conservation Board Questionnaire replies, 9 October 1925, GOS Collection.

40. Anxiety especially over the surplus of marketing facilities shone through the replies of Alexander Deussen of Marland Oil Company; Earl Oliver, Independent, Ponca City, Oklahoma; M. N. Poe of the Ohio Oil Company; William R. Wallace of the Utah Oil Company; and H. C. Bretschneider of the Midwest Refining Company. Smith thought the less integrated the company the less worry over marketing. This may have been partially true, but many of the majors such as Standard Oil of California and Texaco also had decided apprehension over the abundance of retail outlets.

41. *Report of the Federal Oil Conservation Board to the President of the United States, September, 1926* (Washington, 1926).

to the effect that he was very well satisfied with the report, as he should have been since he composed the first three drafts.

How optimistic Smith could be in 1924 about a possible shoulder-to-shoulder stand of industry and government is a moot question. Typically Smith perceived the business tycoon of the twenties as neither devil nor saint. Throughout his service on the Coal Commission in 1922, he jotted down in his diary a steady stream of opinions pertaining to the "antics" of both labor and capital. After one unusually exasperating conference with one of the "coal barons" of Pennsylvania, Smith wrote his son a snippy comment, "while I refrained from criticizing administrative methods. . . . I see little difference between the theoretical long distance bureaucratic control from Washington and the actual long distance autocratic control from New York City."[42] Continuing, he wrote, "yet no one is more vehement in support of private initiative than the presiding genius of the Delaware and Hudson group." A great deal of the difficulty of both labor and capital could be ascribed to neurotic behavior, "The trouble with operators as I size it up, and it is also partly true of the miners, is that they are hard-boiled and thin shelled as well."[43]

Three months later another terse commentary came from Smith's pen on the businessman's moral attributes; he graphically depicted one executive he ran into in New York "as the heavy pyramidial type somewhat like Nast's cartoon of Bill Tweed. His build is that of the successful man of big business, and I have long thought that he typifies what is most dangerous in big business, marked ability actuated by a decidedly reactionary spirit."[44] However, Smith refused to blanket the eastern financier with righteous condemnation. Once on a trip to see Doherty in New York, he arrived a little early for his appointment. Taking the time to walk up and down Wall Street, Smith reflected, "I suppose some people regard me as reactionary, but Wall Street does not affect me as it does Senator La Follette. I am really not only impressed

42. GOS to Joseph Smith, 5 June 1926, GOS Collection.
43. GOS, Diary, [n.d.] 1922.
44. Ibid., 24.

but inspired by walking the few steps from Trinity Church to the United States Sub-Treasury."[45]

By 1931, with the deepening pall of the depression hanging over the land, Smith's meditation on capital versus labor turned to humanistic considerations. Coming back to his home from a long congressional hearing, Smith noted to his son, Joseph, "The fact is, I don't need wild Senators to convince me of the selfishness of businessmen; the tame captains of industry and especially their corporals tell me all about it."[46] Smith tended to interpret the difference between capital and labor as a matter of resources, not of human spirit. "Of course, you know I believe that capital deserves its wage and I put it right on par with labor's right to a wage. But, why not realize and admit the difference between the capitalists, big or small, and the workmen, skilled or unskilled, is a matter of tightening up the belt and withstanding the depression." In this crisis Smith descanted "for one thing, the eggs of the capitalist are commonly well distributed, those of the laborer almost without exception are in one basket."[47]

George Otis Smith's judicious appraisal of the business community was sorely tried in the immediate months following the publication of the Federal Oil Conservation Board's report. First he became enmeshed in the settlement of the nullified Teapot Dome and Elk Hills leases. The second disturbing event was a scathing broadside and broadscale attack of the API on the board's report. Nine months before the president conceived the Federal Oil Conservation Board, he appointed an oil commission of experts—R. D. Bush of the Bureau of Mineralogy of California; Rear Adm. Hilary P. Jones, president of the Navy General Board; and the ubiquitous George Otis Smith. The Oil Conservation Board's specific investiture charged them with the task of studying ways and means of conserving and providing storage for naval oil reserves.

The president had resorted to an ancient political maneuver—when embroiled in a political cauldron quickly install

45. Ibid., 26 January 1924.
46. Ibid., 30 September 1924.
47. Ibid., 23 August 1924.

an investigative committee. Coolidge shrewdly calculated that he could use this opportunity to overcome the discontent over oil policies being expressed by Congress and quell fears arising from the Teapot Dome hearings. Since the middle of January 1923, when he had had a long discussion with the president, Smith had been waiting for the announcement of the oil commission. In the January tête à tête, Coolidge had sketched what he had in mind; then he asked Smith to draft a memorandum and to nominate two other men to serve on the commission with him. At the first meeting of the commission with Coolidge, Smith "counselled moderation" about extending the inquiry beyond the requirements of military needs, specifically the navy.[48] While he refrained from commenting directly, the president would obviously consider the commission a tremendous success if Smith came up with a workable reserve policy, especially a scheme that Coolidge could use to seize the political initiative from Congress.

In many ways the oil commission became the most frustrating assignment that George Otis Smith ever received in his government tenure. Undertaking what he originally discerned as a six-month probe, the weary assignment drug out until the eclipse of the twenties. Within the first year he had to undergo three physically wearisome transcontinental trips to California for "a first hand examination of this mess." Once in California he found the situation so ensnared with local and national politics, neolithic executives, and plain stupidity that Smith for a brief moment uncharacteristically wondered if he should not return home.[49] When he opened the first meetings of the commission with the California operators at Kettleman Hills, he announced that the commission had come to listen, not to recommend.[50] "I am trying to avoid even the

48. GOS to Joseph Smith, 19 June 1931, GOS Collection.

49. Ibid. Smith concluded his letter sadly, "Well writing this letter clears my head a bit, tho, it doesn't lift the load off my heart, for I am bitterly disappointed in my mining friends; these days of overproduction and unemployment test a man's soul, and some men do not pass the exam, with high marks."

50. At a conference with the president in the spring of 1924, some of the admirals pressed Coolidge to widen the power of the commission to encompass the future requirements of industry and transportation,

word investigate," he wrote to Doherty, "for it is a constructive study that we wish to make preparatory to submitting recommendations to the President and his executive advisors. Let others investigate—we will try to inform ourselves."[51]

Although Smith was undoubtedly sincere in his desire to listen sans comment, the California oil men refused to accept this approach. Insisting that they wanted answers plus help from the commission, they turned the meetings into shouting contests. The oil company executives had specific questions for which they demanded precise replies. The Beldridge Oil Corporation, for instance, wanted to know whether they could offset drill the Pacific Oil Company's lease on Section 34. When they were told that they would have to wait for a decision until the matter could be studied, they responded with huffy comments from the Beldridge vice-president, who loudly announced that the committee was transparently biased in favor of the Pacific Oil Company.[52]

As if harassment by corporate executives were not enough vexation, much to his intense annoyance Smith discovered that the Department of Interior had in the past and was at that very moment issuing mineral prospecting permits on government land directly adjacent to the naval reserves. Again in a marvelous low-keyed tone, Smith noted, "I find that it is a matter of wide comment that the government is endeavoring to maintain reserves, and at the same time is leasing its lands to operators who are going to develop and drain additional oil."[53] Smith found it decidedly uncom-

---

as well as the navy. Coolidge and Smith objected; Smith chortled in his diary, "I felt that our little group of three has full enough to do to look after the United States Navy and its future, and I almost smiled when the President put this same idea by saying that there was a danger of spreading out over a subject too thin, and he therefore cautioned moderation in our extending our investigation beyond naval requirements" (GOS, Diary, 19 April 1924).

51. GOS to Henry L. Doherty, 22 April 1924, GOS Collection.

52. Smith wrote to Doherty, "Although we do not intend to have formal hearings on this subject, we are anxious to have free discussion and personal conferences with leaders in the petroleum industry" (GOS to Henry L. Doherty, 19 April 1924, GOS Collection).

53. The Beldridge corporation's obstinacy frustrated all who be-

fortable to have to concede to the California oil men that the Washington bureaucracy's right hand did not know what its left hand was up to. Smith should have taken some satisfaction that within six days of his official protest in both a telegram and letter to Secretary Work, the Department of Interior's leasing ceased.

Slowly, ever so slowly, Smith began hammering out a workable arrangement with the operators. Selecting the divide-and-conquer stratagem, Smith and Bush drafted agreements with a few of the more amenable Kettleman Hill's companies, then used these documents as a basis for discussions with the more intransigent executives. Although complex and acrimonious negotiations clouded over the fact, actually Smith's petroleum conservation diagram in California represented the essence of simplicity. He first convinced Secretary Work that the economic interests of both landlord and producer were identical in regulating flush production. With this official benediction in hand, he evangelically lobbied with the operators for the attainment of explicit objectives. In order to reduce drainage and compact the naval reserve, he advocated, first, the exchange of acreage, principally between the Standard Oil Company and the Pacific Oil Company; second, the creation of a no-man's land bordering the naval reserves that would be exempt from drilling; third, until this area could be cleared, a royalty be paid the government from the wells currently producing there; fourth, in a few random cases, the government purchase or trade enumerated private tracts adjacent to the reserve.[54]

All in all, it comprised a conservation design that was neither hidden nor intricate; yet it took over five years and a disasterous depression to force the oil industry to implement

---

came ensnared. W. C. Mendenhall, chief geologist of the United States Geological Survey, told Smith, "The hoped-for acceptance by the Beldridge Company of the proposal to limit drilling activities has not materialized. Messrs. Pomerene and Roberts have advised the Admiral that they do not regard the bringing of a suit as within their jurisdiction" (W. C. Mendenhall to GOS, 3 July 1924, GOS Collection).

54. GOS and Hilary P. Jones to Hubert Work, 1 May 1924, GOS Collection.

it. Visiting Kettleman Hills in 1930, Smith could not help noticing how cordial his reception was in comparison to former years.

> They [the oil men] are on our side now. . . . and have forgiven me for the stand I took a year ago opposing their ideas of plunging ahead regardless of the market. . . . That reckless spirit has always characterized the oil game, and any rules that ran counter to the old pace of haste and waste naturally were resented as un-American, which is the last word in opposition.[55]

Concurrently with facing down that "reckless spirit" in California, Smith found that back in Washington the Federal Oil Conservation Board's hearings were receiving slashing vilification from the American Petroleum Institute. The directors of the API appointed a Committee of Eleven for the express purpose of discrediting the board's hearings and preliminary findings. Trotting out their own experts, the Committee of Eleven began a point-by-point rebuttal to the board's conclusions. Their entire case had previously been made by oil men, indeed many times. The Committee of Eleven announced that petroleum reserves were almost limitless, that overproduction was a fabricated charge of bureaucratic mythologizers and of those insidious individuals who would sell America short.[56] The Committee of Eleven argued that any surplus petroleum that occurred in the future could easily be cured by economic adjustments. All would be right with the world if the government would only quit tampering with industry. The Committee of Eleven preached these beatitudes to whoever would listen.[57]

Smith viewed the frantic efforts of the API with his usual detachment, although on occasion he did become incensed. At the end of August 1925, Smith scribbled in his diary that the Committee of Eleven would have a difficult time "explain-

55. Ibid.
56. Arguments pro and con on this California program appear in: GOS to R. D. Bush, 14 June 1924; GOS to R. C. Patterson, 25 October 1925; GOS to R. D. Bush, 24 April 1924; and GOS to Hilary P. Jones, 29 April 1924, GOS Collection.
57. GOS, Diary, July [n.d.], 1930, p. 2.

ing the recent slump in gasoline prices if there is not too much oil and gas being produced this year, as well as for the year past."[58] Henry Doherty, characteristically, could not be that introspective. Writing from Battle Creek, Michigan, where he had gone to be treated for a combination of arthritis, neuritis, and nervous collapse, he lambasted the Committee of Eleven, "I would like to use a softer word but it is impossible to describe this report except as a fraud upon the public."[59]

In all the clamor of accusations and counteraccusations, there was a note of levity introduced by the renowned geologist, Everett L. DeGolyer. De Golyer could not resist poking fun at both the API and Washington. In a witty letter to George Otis Smith, with "abject apologies to Don Marquis," DeGolyer advanced his perspective through Marquis's redoubtable cockroach "archy":

> . . . carefulcalvin had just appointed one of those georgeotissmithions to investigate and all the big oilmen appointed a committeeofeleven to guide and help and smother if it could georgeotissmithion before it hit them and the committeeofeleven said hotdog the problem is to get the geologists before the georgeotissmithion gets them and so the committeeofeleven got the geologists together and bossed them—and well should have bossed them for didnt they pay them and the committeeofeleven said boys who is your boss and the guesstimators said you are curse you and the committeeofeleven said hotdog boys you used to do some amateur guessing when werent looking now do some real professional guessing. . . . henriell do [doherty] do not be foolish says mehitabel you ribald mechanical cousins will keep drinking the juice as long as it lasts which is likely to be a damnsight longer than henriell and georgeotissmithion thinks but not so long as the committeeofeleven says and the indominitable

58. GOS, Diary, 29 August 1925. Earl Oliver in Oklahoma heard the Committee of Eleven's arguments one evening in Oklahoma City; he quickly sent a letter off to Smith, "I know that I am prejudiced, but I believe that any unbiased observor of the Committee of Eleven's tactics would not be fooled by their speeches—they are just too one sided to have side appeal" (Earl Oliver to GOS, 6 August 1925, GOS Collection).

59. Henry L. Doherty to GOS, 4 March 1925, GOS Collection.

mind of man will find a substitute remember how the boot-
leggers saved us after mr. volstead?[60]

It is doubtful whether Henry L. Doherty fully appreciated
DeGolyer's burlesque, but George Otis Smith immensely enjoyed it, so much so that he sent copies around to friends for
weeks later. After firing off the report of the Committee of
Eleven, the directors of the API met and came to the same
conclusion that Henry L. Doherty had reached on another
affair a year previously. They needed an attorney of high
prestige and unassailable reputation to plead their case at
the oil board hearings. Charles Evans Hughes met these ster-
ling qualifications. Having just resigned as secretary of state
the Olympian Hughes was available for hire.

The announcement of Hughes's employment by the API
amused Smith for he thought the industry had fallen into a
sand trap. Smith gossiped in his diary, "It is understood in the
inner circles that Mr. Hughes took the job of counsel and
adviser under the pledge that he should be given full authority to determine questions of public policy." Smith concluded
the joker in the deck came when, "if a difference of opinion
should arise it would be the poorest time for the industry re-
actionaries to break with their advisor whose employment
constitutes their pledge to the public."[61]

Of course endemic in these comments was George Otis
Smith's own high regard for the integrity of the former secretary of state. Smith could not imagine that Hughes could
have anything but a broader panorama of conservation than
did the API directors. Smith, in his wildest imagination,
could not conceive that Hughes was the type of man to take
tribute as a vassal of any vested interest. Mark Requa, an
able geologist who flitted in and out of Washington on a
number of assignments, explored the Hughes appointment
in another light. Requa commented to Smith: "Hughes now,
of course, is the 'big boss' of the Petroleum Industry. They
gave him a blank check and it is for him to make the program

60. E. DeGolyer to GOS, 13 January 1926, GOS Collection.
61. GOS, Diary, 30 January 1926.

which the Industry must follow." Requa continued, "I am firmly of the opinion that the industry has set a milestone that marks an inevitable increase in the intimacy with Washington. I do not believe they will go back, or can go back, to the old order of disassociation."[62]

As it turned out both were wrong. Smith overestimated Hughes's character. Requa misassessed the impact of Hughes's appointment on government-industry relations. On Thursday, 26 May 1926, Charles Evans Hughes made his long heralded address at the public hearings of the Federal Oil Conservation Board. Hughes's rambling remarks closely parrotted the API line. Indeed his speech could have come off the mimeograph machines of the public relations stall in the API offices, or perhaps from the Philadelphia headquarters of J. Edgar Pew. After reviewing the report of the Committee of Eleven, the history of conservation and overproduction á la Hughes, he came to the venerable conclusion that petroleum resources would be best utilized if industry were just ignored.[63] Voluntary representation meant the way and the light. Hughes embedded his arguments in constitutional terms dwelling on why one type of legislation after another would be unconstitutional. He concluded by emphasizing the value of scientific research for the progress of conservation.

A cambric tea performance: not only had nothing new been added in the way of constructive suggestions, but Hughes left little doubt as to who paid his retainer. Anyone familiar with Smith and Doherty could easily have predicted their reactions to the Hughes address. Smith laconically noted in his diary that the Hughes presentation had little in the way of "constructive contributions to satisfy most of us."[64] Three days after the Hughes statement, Doherty told Smith that he remained in a state of shock, "I am at a loss to know

62. M. L. Requa to GOS, 27 January 1926, GOS Collection.
63. For those intrigued enough to want to read this philippic, see *Public Hearing, Federal Oil Conservation Board, May 27, 1926* (Washington, D.C., 1926), pp. 2–23.
64. GOS, Diary, 29 May 1926.

how these men could ever bring sufficient influence to bear upon him to induce him to allow himself to be put in the position of endorsing that report."[65]

What Smith, Doherty, and many other observors failed to perceive was simply that the Hughes speech had little long-term impact. Another age, another generation might have been impressed with Hughes's championship of laissez-faire. In 1925, involving these hallowed incantations of leftovers from Adam Smith sounded more than a little anachronistic.

For a string of facts would not yield to rhetoric. Regardless of what the API leadership said in public, overproduction plagued the entire industry, but especially the midcontinent and California producers. The industry, whether admitted or not, was unable to cope with that surplus. With the exception of spasmodic relief, a soft market had been the petroleum industry's way of life for several years. Economic factors were forcing the oil executives into a consanguineous relationship with government. In retrospect, from the standpoint of industry, the dark, sad side of Hughes's testimony came from a miscarried opportunity. Instead of capturing this golden moment to polish their public relations image by championing conservation and donning the clothes of enlightened public statesmen, they opted the untenable, unpopular position of being despoilers of the country's natural resources.

What made the API position even more ironic was that within months after Hughes stood up at the oil board hearings they were covertly, if not overtly, moving toward the sponsorship of legislation to leash both overproduction and waste. Actually there had been rumors of change in the API stand on conservation as early as 1924. The ever-hopeful Doherty related to Smith that from a few oil company officials he had received "hints" that "conservation is not the ugly word it once was."[66] While Doherty's seismic soundings of executive attitudes may have been premature,[67] by 1925–

65. Henry L. Doherty to GOS, 30 May 1926, GOS Collection.

66. GOS, Diary, 23 August 1924.

67. Ever sensitive to any soundings they received importing a change in the API sentiment, Smith's diaries and Doherty's correspondence are full of rumors on petroleum leadership and conservation.

1926 Smith was receiving similar intelligence from friends inside and outside the industry. With high hopes that he could convert the favorable industry sentiment that he was receiving into a ground swell, he asked for and received an interview with John D. Rockefeller, Jr. Regarding his reception as more of an audience than an informal visit, Smith hurriedly summed up the petroleum scene as he saw it. Rockefeller sympathized with Smith's dissertation on conservation but remained noncommittal. After leaving Rockefeller's office suite, Smith recorded in his diary, "I did not come away with a feeling that I had necessarily changed the attitude of the whole petroleum industry."[68]

If Smith failed to enlist Rockefeller in the conservation crusade, by late 1926 it little mattered, for other compulsive forces were massing that the industry could not ignore. A combination of declining profits, public castigation of waste and fraud, and the needling of federal officials and industry "gadflys" convinced the officials of large corporations that it was necessary to take some action, and soon. In addition to receiving these pressures, the industry was bombarded with

Reporting in his diary on a visit in January 1925 to the Atlantic City meeting of the API directors, Smith disclosed, "Both Mr. [J. Edgar] Pew and Mr. [Otto] Donnell [President of the Ohio Oil Company] talked at length with me to the effect that there is no over production of oil and gas involved in present methods. I cannot believe that in taking this attitude that the industry is in perfect health will help either the patient or those who seek to suggest remedies." Three months later, Smith thought he detected signs of a change, "Mr. Doherty agrees with me that there is somewhat of a general shift in the attitude of the principal oil men toward the President's Conservation Board. They are coming to realize what I have contended right along that the President has given the industry a fine opportunity to improve its conditions before the public." The Hughes performance dashed Smith's judgments on the enlightenment of the API. By 1928, Smith discerned, as others did, a new mood with the API forsaking their previous anti-conservation position. After a Tulsa dinner of the Mid-Continent Oil Operators Association, Smith returned to his hotel room and opined in his diary, "The oil industry has availed itself of the privilege usually accorded to womankind—that of changing its mind. Had you heard what I hear you might well remark, the 'sinners have repented'" (GOS, Diaries, 17 January, 28 March 1925; 26 October 1928).

68. GOS, Diary, 20 January 1925.

the age-old demands for efficiency and naval requirements that could no longer be waved away as the babbling of alarmists. The question that increasingly became debated centered on precisely what legislation should be enacted. A very vigorous struggle ensued between those who favored state regulation and those who insisted on federal control.

One of the more amazing scenarios of the petroleum drama in the twenties was how swiftly diminished the histrionics over conservation, only to rise over regulation. Except in the West, by 1927 petroleum potentates were reluctantly surmising that some type of conservation program was inevitable. The more serious question was, who would formulate and enforce such a comprehensive conservation plan? Throughout the rest of the twenties a very vitriolic barrage was kept up between the champions and the adversaries of federal legislation and regulation.

The unitization of petroleum fields was one point on which all agreed. The combining of all producing interests in a field under one company's management with the attendant benefits of controlled gas and oil production was not only more efficient but in fact the only solution from a legal and economic standpoint. Yet this did not remove the issue of who should enforce unitization, the federal or state governments.

One man who could be expected to have both a firm opinion and a well-formulated plan of action was Henry L. Doherty. Firing off one letter after another to friends and foes, Doherty seemingly missed few opportunities to press for his current enthusiasm. One of his favorite targets, James Veasey, resided in Tulsa, Oklahoma, where he served as general counsel for the Carter Oil Company. The Veasey-Doherty correspondence revealingly exposed the subtleties of the federal-state argument. Doherty started out with the premise that the "highest type" of conservation consisted of the retention and preservation of gas pressure in an oil formation, based on the now-proven assumption that more oil would eventually be recovered. Next Doherty emphasized that petroleum represented a "wasting" asset, therefore an irreplaceable natural resource, upon which our military force had absolute dependence. Then as the coup de grâce to his argument Doherty pointed out that since oil was indispensable to national security, Congress, under delegated war powers, could enact laws for the preservation of gas pressure. Finally, if Congress had this power in wartime, it should be empowered in peace under the identical rationale that it maintains the nation's military establishment.[69]

A corollary to his sponsorship of federal regulation was Doherty's innate fear of state action. He found it inexplicable that so many within the petroleum fraternity desired state statutes. In one of his many lengthy epistles he informed Veasey:

> State legislation is dangerous and the greatest danger is when bills are passed under the so-called police power of the state. . . . I still hold that the Federal Government has ample power to legislate under its war powers and take away all powers from the states that in any way interfere or attempt to dictate as to oil production.[70]

To other petroleum executives, such as W. C. Teagle, president of the Standard Oil Company of New Jersey, who feared regulation of any kind, state or federal, Doherty took another tack. Insisting that the present "wild overproduction" would eventually lead to the adoption of conservation measures, Doherty suggested, why not try to direct this regulation? If the oil industry abdicated its leadership, Doherty strongly persisted that "dictation by the state and federal governments will come with control over all features of the oil business."[71]

69. Doherty's ideas are scattered with buckshot frequency throughout his correspondence. Among those germane to the specific topic are Henry L. Doherty to Hubert Work, 3 July 1925; Henry L. Doherty to James A. Veasey, 25 July 1927; Henry L. Doherty to GOS, 8 June 1924; Henry L. Doherty to GOS, 15 May 1924; Henry L. Doherty to GOS, 1 December, 16 December 1925, GOS and James A. Veasey collections.

70. Henry L. Doherty to James A. Veasey, 25 July 1927, James A. Veasey Collection.

71. Henry L. Doherty to Walter C. Teagle, 15 December 1925, GOS Collection.

Doherty frequently found the silence deafening; the petroleum establishment was not about to concede the argument, at least openly. Too wise a politician to attack the state defenders,[72] Smith quietly dwelled on the point that on the basis of past performance, what evidence could be offered that the states had either the desire or competence to prosecute conservation laws? Actually for Smith the essential issue revolved around the efficient and wise use of national resources. He would willingly go along with either federal or state regulation as long as it proved effective. His good friend Mark Requa could not be this optimistic about state enforcement: "As to your statement that if we must have regulation it should come from the federal government and not from the state government there can be no argument about this, and therefore I have been very critical of the efforts of some of our legal minds to prove the inability of the federal government to regulate."[73]

Requa, Doherty, and Smith found their answers to petroleum conservation in federal legislation. As much as any one person could, James Veasey typified the proponents of voluntary state legislation. In a spirited flurry of correspondence with Doherty, Veasey conceded that voluntary self-imposed policing of the oil industry had failed. As much as he tried to rationalize, Veasey had to agree with Doherty's verdict

72. George Otis Smith seldom left his diplomacy or his political sixth sense at home when he negotiated with the oil industry spokesmen. However, he never endorsed political opportunism, and occasionally he yearned for a triumph of economics over politics. Recalling in his diary in 1929, "This is, perhaps, a good place to stop and record what President Coolidge said to me on this subject about five years ago, the day after he was nominated for President. We were having a chat on coal, water-power, oil, etc. and he asked me how efficiency in the use of gasoline could be brought about. My answer was, 'only by making it worth while,' and I went on to say that I thought the country would be better off with 50-cent gasoline. 'Yes,' came back the President, 'You are probably right as an economics proposition—but I wouldn't want to be running for office.' I think however, he usually regarded good economics as good politics, but as I observe them, most politicians reason that whatever is not good politics must be, Q. E. D., bad economics" (GOS, Diary, 31 May 1929).

73. Mark L. Requa to GOS, 3 September 1927, GOS Collection.

that "all it takes is one wildcatter to wreck havoc with voluntary agreement." Still Veasey could not, would not, consent to a "federal bureaucracy in Washington running the oil industry in Oklahoma." [74]

Veasey based his brief on the twin arguments of constitutionalism and mechanism. Taking the by now venerable constitutional glossating on the division of powers, Veasey quoted the founding fathers at length. With school masterish style, he outlined the ramifications of the Tenth Amendment for Doherty. All matters of local concern were reserved to the states; the federal government had vested control of all issues of national import; and finally, all other subjects of national scope were vested in all the people. Veasey, leaving little room for dissent, wound up his treatise, "I am so convinced myself that the business of producing oil is local in character, and therefore within the sphere of state legislation and not national that I should be untrue to myself if I were not to urge this vigorously." Not that Veasey was enamored with the permanency of constitutional law. He emphasized to Doherty, "I say this upon the basis of our present understanding of constitutional law. The Lord alone knows what our conceptions may be in the future." [75]

Switching from constitutional theory to local conservation problems in the oil fields, Veasey again found Doherty puppeteering in fairyland. Veasey quickly agreed with Doherty on the importance of natural gas pressure to oil recovery; furthermore, it was undebatable that if one lessee released gas pressure, he was to that extent impairing the production from his neighbors' land. Veasey acknowledged that if one producer was actually wasting and recklessly dissipating gas, legislation to conserve the gas would be legitimate. However, suppose instead of squandering his gas the operator had justifiable use for the gas—could he be legally deprived from selling, for instance, his own gas? Veasey thought not. [76]

74. James A. Veasey to Henry L. Doherty, 10 August 1927, James A. Veasey Collection.

75. Ibid.

76. James A. Veasey to E. Ward Bannister, 14 October 1927, James A. Veasey Collection.

Veasey was highly skeptical as to whether a police statute could be enforced under the doctrine of neighborly conduct. Veasey was also concerned about another legal detail. In the unlikely event that such a police statute would be declared constitutional, could such legislation take the next step and require the reintroduction of gas into a well or a similar type of secondary recovery measure? In essence, what would be the distinction between a statute to enjoin a neighbor's production and one that would demand affirmative action to preserve oil flow?[77]

Veasey's sophisticated legal theory may have meant little to the oil fraternity in general. However, they had little trouble in understanding, at least in simplistic terms, federal overlordship versus state independence. One Rocky Mountain operator put it pungently to his Denver attorney, "If, as you say, regulation is coming regardless of what we do or say, by God, it must be by the states not by those ———— ———— ———— in Washington."[78]

Though not always relying on as expressive a language, western oil producers heavily endorsed such sentiment. The Casper, Wyoming, *Inland Oil Index* ran a series of editorials sporadically throughout the twenties, protesting "fallacious estimates of oil reserves," and "the inequities of conservation legislation." The editor of the *Index* went even further than most Westerners in decrying any regulation, whether by federal or state government. "Under the states' police powers . . . statutory regulations and conservation measures bordering upon and indicating the possibility of complete control of the oil industry in a few years aided by the evolution of public sentiment."[79] For editor A. L. Hazlett, 1984 was just around the corner in 1929.

Not all western editors feared "Big Brother" in Washington as much as did the editor of the *Inland Oil Index*, but many of them resented the epithets flung at them by, as

77. James A. Veasey to John Brennen, 2 August 1927, James A. Veasey Collection.
78. R. Taylor to Warwick Downing, 16 October 1930, Warwick Downing Collection, Petroleum History and Research Center.
79. *Inland Oil Index*, 26 April 1929.

Hazlett put it, "The Doherty-minded do-gooders." Three months after the *Index* editorial, the *Mining Congress Journal* editorialized that they were much in favor of the removal of waste, but that the George Otis Smith estimate that the country had lost $250 million in production was patently ridiculous. The *Journal* adamantly insisted, "If the business as a whole is profitable then that competition which brings to the consumer the lowest cost material is of great advantage to the country and not one in which governmental assistance is needed."[80]

Although the editor of the *Mining Congress Journal* did not seem to realize it or, perhaps more accurately, care to admit it, a sizable number of western oil men would have disputed his conclusion on profitability. The economic morass of the western oil industry darkened in 1929, regardless of editors' prophecies. Fumbling about for a solution to overproduction, President Hoover refused to consider any national legislation limiting overproduction, on the basis that such a move would only encourage price fixing and monopolistic trends. Repudiating the move to relax antitrust enforcement and declining to set forth a national petroleum plan, Hoover seemingly had only one workable alternative open to him. Reverting to his 1923–1924 scheme, the president suggested that the enlightened way to oil conservation would be through a voluntary cooperation via an agreement among the states (which was eventually called the Interstate Oil Compact).[81] In so doing, Hoover finally acquiesced to the entreaties of API leadership. Requa and Smith, who would have been far happier with a national regulatory effort, for the moment applauded the presidential action. At least Hoover had moved!

To sound out western sentiment for an interstate agreement, Hoover sent Smith on a two-week 9,600-mile tour in

80. *The Mining Congress Journal* 15 (July 1929):517.

81. George Otis Smith in a January 1924 entry in his diary had commented, "Secretary Hoover is pushing the idea of a co-operative action by the States in advancing the superpower idea of interconnection and a larger degree of unity of action as between States and between utility companies" (GOS, Diary, 7 June 1924).

April 1929 to call on the governors of Oklahoma, California, Texas, Utah, and Wyoming. Another presidential envoy, Mark Requa, followed up Smith's effort with calls on the governors of Texas and Oklahoma. Although the reports from these visitors were far from favorable,[82] the president asked Secretary of the Interior Lyman Wilbur to call a conference of western state governors and other concerned individuals at Colorado Springs on June 10.

Smith had deep reservations about the possibility of any constructive action coming out of the Colorado conference. His visits with governors in the West had been very discouraging. In a dispiriting letter to Mark Requa, the usually optimistic Smith analyzed the western mentality. Since the time of his youth as a member of the Geological Survey, Smith had discerned in the West a "Three Musketeer" psychology, all for one and one for all with nothing for anybody else. Writing in 1909 to his good friend, H. Foster Bain, later director of the Bureau of Mines, Smith commented, "I find that a good deal of the point of view with regard to public land is, as you suggest, that they ought to be freely given to whoever will take and occupy them."[83] Twenty years later in his report to Secretary Wilbur on his western governors' swing, he found to his disgust little change in western attitudes. "One trouble with these people out in the public land states is that everyone who voted for Hoover thinks he ought to have a piece of the public domain, and there simply isn't enough public land to acquire."[84]

82. Smith found the political machinations going on in the West very disillusioning: "The discussion of the curtailment of production, however, was colored by anxiety over the price of gasoline. The political side of the matter is always brought into view, and the economics turned to the wall, when I am talking to politicians just as too many of the oil men see present profits rather than future economics of the business." Then he added a remarkably revealing afterthought, "I, of course, have faith in my own views, because my eyesight is clouded by neither profits nor politics." Even more remarkably, few acquaintances of George Otis Smith would have quarreled with that introspective observation (GOS, Diary, 31 May 1929).

83. GOS to H. Foster Bain, 24 May 1909, GOS Collection.

84. GOS, Diary, 31 May 1929.

This self-centered, exploitative, "inalienable right to participate in Uncle Sam's land," he found acutely obnoxious when he tramped over a couple of oil boom areas in California and Wyoming. One evening he hurriedly scratched in his diary, "There is everywhere the desire to let Lawyer Tom, Storekeeper Dick, and Small-town Loafer Harry take a chance on an oil permit, not to develop, but to sell to someone who will develop."[85]

For Smith this malady represented the crux of the matter; he was not in 1929, nor had he ever been against the proper efficient utilization of the country's resources, but he did rile against "the hit and run land office hangers on" and all the connotations of this gambling neurosis. Smith also rebelled against the western petroleum executive who seemed to him to be perpetually panhandling the government. "These oil men are very human, I have found, and however outspoken may be their objectives to a paternal government, they are very fond of candy and usually ask for something to be handed out to make them good."[86] He did assign substantial blame to the oil industry's lack of statesmanship for the industry's malaise. To a man raised on the edge of the Maine woods, this selfishness did not make sense, economically or politically.

The Westerners continued to perform in their theater of the absurd, as far as Smith could divine, at the Colorado Springs conclave. Disgustedly he wrote Doherty that most of the delegates arrived in an angry mood, they stayed petulant and left huffy. Why Smith expressed surprise at the delegates' demeanor is an enigma. Highly annoyed over Hoover's recent withdrawal of the public domain from future oil leasing, the delegates came to Pikes Peak to vent their venom on the president's emissaries and program. The meeting turned into a well-mannered brawl, especially in the "hall" conferences. Typically the small operators spilled their spleens on the dominance of the majors. Clinging to the principle of flush production, the independents were not now nor in reality ever had been in a humor to listen to a sermon

85. Ibid.
86. GOS, Diary, 8–9 October 1930.

on conservation. The intransigent attitude of the western governors and their constituents was even more instrumental to rendering the conference impotent. The age-old animus against the Washington bureaucrat telling Westerners how to run their region surfaced numerous times throughout the Colorado Springs deliberations. In a couple of years, caught in the slough of the depression, some of these identical spokesmen would listen with eager receptiveness to the words of wisdom (and dollars) from Washington, but in the summer of 1929, they thought they could afford the luxury of independence.

After the debacle of the Colorado Springs meeting, the Federal Oil Conservation Board retreated from further attempts to curb oil production until 1931. Then, with the assistance of economic disaster and unleashed gushers of east Texas, the Interstate Oil Compact eventually became a reality.

The Colorado Springs gathering terminated George Otis Smith's last major policy foray in the petroleum industry. It had been an extraordinary journey. A scientist foremost and always, he had adroitly sidestepped the costly political infighting. A diplomat with a high appreciation of comon sense and tenacity, he impressed both his government associates and industry acquaintances with his unswerving dedication "to the common good." Now the isolation that he had suffered in former years had vanished; he could write in the autumn of 1930, "I used to be somewhat lonely in my conservation attitude, but now the conservation policy is common property, but I'm still the only one to take his conservation straight, undiluted with private interest."[87] George Otis Smith could take satisfaction, as few could, in having played a major role in the conservation of the nation's petroleum resources, more of a role than his contemporaries sensed, or than historians would later realize; he had indeed been born free—and even more he stayed in that Rosseaullian state.

87. GOS, Diary, 15–16 October 1930.

The Senator
from Wyoming,
FDR, and the
Supreme Court

A shiny new LaSalle, carrying the senior senator from Wyoming and his wife, sped west along the Lincoln highway across the cornfields of Iowa and the prairies of Nebraska in the early autumn of 1937.[1] Their destination, Cheyenne, was reached twenty-five hours and twenty-five minutes after they had left their Chicago hotel. Why was the senator in such a hurry to make a hegira home? A persistent reporter asked Senator O'Mahoney, during a brief stop in Omaha, if they were "hurrying home to lay the groundwork for the President's visit." The senator's good wife quickly answered, "Perhaps 'alay' is the better word."[2]

While O'Mahoney was shopping for his new auto in the Windy City, one of his office staff phoned him that President Roosevelt's ten-car special train was headed for the West with the first designated stop at Cheyenne. It required little imagination on the part of O'Mahoney to realize that the president's trip to the West was aimed at administering some old-fashioned political medicine to the unruly senators who had recently manhandled the president's prestige by over-

1. One of the advantages and hazards (as James Farley recently observed, "It has been over 36 years since that important period in our history and as memory plays tricks with us it is impossible to recall incidents") of contemporary history is the availability of the reminiscences of those who participated in the events. The writer is extremely indebted to those participants who read this essay and shared their recollections, as well as to fellow historians who offered their critiques. Inclusively they were: Benjamin V. Cohen, Alan Coombs, Hugh Cox, Barry Crouch, James Farley, Carl McFarland, and Robert O'Neil.

2. Press coverage of O'Mahoney's cross-country race was extensive. The above quotation is from an account in *Time*, 4 October 1937, p. 11.

whelmingly rejecting Senate Bill No. 1392 to reform the judiciary, the bill commonly referred to by its enemies as the Supreme Court packing bill.

The senator's endurance dash across a third of the continent was not in vain. Arriving a day ahead of Roosevelt's entourage, O'Mahoney joined the "citizens' welcoming committee" as the unexpected but much appreciated guest. When the local dignitaries boarded the president's car, no one seemed to enjoy the little "joke" more than Roosevelt, who boomed out, "Hello, Joe! Glad to see you!" Then graced by both Wyoming senators on either side of him, the president informally chatted to the assembled Wyomingites, ignoring both the personage of O'Mahoney and the issue of the Supreme Court!

O'Mahoney relished the hospitality of the president's train for seven hours, finally taking his leave at Casper, Wyoming. O'Mahoney was firmly convinced that Roosevelt had every intention of publicly spanking the senior senator from Wyoming in his hometown. Just as obviously, the trip to the woodshed had been foiled by an alert senator and his staff. Three days after the president's visit, he wrote to a friend in New York: "Later developments today indicate more clearly than ever that the response of the people of Cheyenne and Wyoming to the President's visit upset a well-laid plan. Democratic County chairmen are now receiving from Joe Guffey's office, under the date of September 23, copies of his [Guffey's] radio broadcast for distribution." O'Mahoney then continued, "The timing seems to make the inference clear that a blast from the high command was expected here. Governor Miller's telegram [to presidential aid McIntyre saying that he assumed Senator O'Mahoney was invited to accompany the president], copies of the *Wyoming Eagle* of Friday morning and my unexpected presence threw them off their stride."[3]

If the president believed in ominous omens, he should have taken the Cheyenne faux pas as a Delphic signal of worse to come. For his western swing amounted to a preview of his

3. Joseph C. O'Mahoney to Francis P. Garvan, 28 September 1937, Joseph C. O'Mahoney Papers, Western History Research Center, University of Wyoming, Laramie.

now-famous and disastrous purge of congressional opposition, a purge that served only to enhance a declining popularity. But President Roosevelt had little inclination to muse
about the occult on his western journey. He was plain angry!
The three states the president's train first rattled across—
Nebraska, Wyoming, and Montana—were the homes of
three senators—Burke, O'Mahoney, and Wheeler (not as
euphonious as the later chant, Martin, Barton, and Fish), all
of whom had vigorously opposed the reorganization of the
judiciary.

The main configurations, if the details are still only shadowy conjectures, of the now-infamous "Court-packing" plan
are well known.[4] Frustrated by the Supreme Court's declar-

4. The two most comprehensive accounts of the Court plan (although of uneven merit) are Joseph Alsop and Turner Catledge, *The
168 Days* (New York, 1938), and Leonard Baker, *Back to Back: The
Duel Between FDR and the Supreme Court* (New York, 1967). Many
New Dealers and their counterparts have reminisced about the events
of 1937; some of the more useful are: Harold Ickes, *The Secret Diary
of Harold L. Ickes* (New York, 1954), Vol. 2; Robert Jackson, *The
Struggle for Judicial Supremacy* (New York, 1941); Donald R. Richberg, *My Hero* (New York, 1954); Samuel I. Roseman, *Working with
Roosevelt* (New York, 1952); Raymond Moley, *After Seven Years*
(New York, 1939); *Roosevelt and Frankfurter: Their Correspondence*,
annotated by Max Freedman (New York, 1967); George Creel, *Rebel
at Large* (New York, 1947); Charles Michelson, *The Ghost Talks* (New
York, 1944).
Biographies and analyses of specific aspects of the judicial contest
abound: Professor William E. Leuchtenburg is currently engaged in
writing a comprehensive history of the Court plan; his brilliant investigation of the genesis of the disenchantment with the judicial review is in "The Origins of Franklin D. Roosevelt's Courtpacking Plan,"
in the *Supreme Court Review*, ed. Philip B. Kurland (Chicago, 1966),
347–95. For other discussions see: F. Alan Coombs's highly competent
dissertation on O'Mahoney is essential, "Joseph Christopher O'Mahoney: The New Deal Years" (Ph.D. dissertation, University of Illinois,
1968); Richard T. Ruetten, "Burton K. Wheeler of Montana: A Progressive Between Wars" (Ph.D. dissertation, University of Oregon,
1961); Merlo J. Pusey, "FDR vs. the Supreme Court," *American Heritage* 9 (April 1958):24–27; E. Kimbark McColl, "The Supreme Court
and Public Opinion: A Study of the Court Fight of 1937" (Ph.D. dissertation, University of California at Los Angeles, 1953); Barry A.
Crouch, "Dennis Chavez and Roosevelt's 'Court Packing' Plan," *New*

ing a series of major New Deal legislation unconstitutional, Roosevelt, after long wavering, determined to counterattack. But what weapons should he choose? Finally, Attorney General Homer Cummings cleverly seized on the issue of age, a device all the more appealing since one of the most conservative justices, McReynolds, had urged a similar court reform plan in 1914.[5] "This answer to a maiden's prayer,"[6] as the president referred to Cummings's suggestion, was conceived in ultra-secret sessions and camouflaged as a reform of the entire federal judicial system. Roosevelt selected the morning of 5 February 1937 as the time for the announcement of his bombshell, first to a group of congressional leaders and then at a press conference. Initially both the leadership and the rank-in-file of Congress were stunned. But they recovered quickly, with angry mutterings in the cloakrooms of "dictatorship," "subversion of the judiciary," and "destruction of the democratic process."

The salient features of the subsequent six months of controversy have been replayed by a number of the participants and historians: the tremendous pressure, pro and con; the violent public reaction; the host of radio "talks" by both sides; the shrewd antiadministration leadership of Burton K. Wheeler; the granite silence of the Republican minority gloating over the opposition scrapping; finally, the artful letter of Chief Justice Hughes to the Judiciary Committee, which destroyed step by step, with cold logic the entire raison d'être of the Court plan, laying it bare for what it was—a cleverly, all too cleverly, contrived rotation of the Supreme

---

Mexico Historical Review 42 (October 1967):261–80; Alpheus T. Mason, *Brandeis, A Free Man's Life* (New York, 1946); William E. Leuchtenburg, "Franklin D. Roosevelt's Supreme Court 'Packing' Plan" in *Essays on the New Deal*, ed. Harold M. Hollingsworth and William F. Holmes (Austin, 1969), pp. 69–115; Eugene C. Gerhart, *America's Advocate: Robert H. Jackson* (New York, 1958); A. T. Mason, *Harlan F. Stone* (New York, 1956); Merlo J. Pusey, *Charles Evans Hughes* (New York, 1952); and George Wolfskill, *The Revolt of the Conservatives* (Boston, 1962).

5. McReynolds had excluded the Supreme Court justices from his plan in the 1914 proposal.

6. Alsop and Catledge, *The 168 Days*, p. 36.

Court. In a sense, all that followed Hughes's letter was anti-climactic: the long drawn-out filibustering hearings; the refusal of "the chief" to compromise and the demise of Joe Robinson, the administration's field-general who literally worked himself to death. As with many battles, the final echo faded away quickly at the end of July with the Senate motion to recommit bill 1392.

The first major full-scale revolt against Roosevelt's leadership had ceased. The president had been handed the defeat by his own party, a bitter pill for the ego of any political leader, but especially so for one who less than a year previous had received an overwhelming victory at the polls—a mandate that Roosevelt was convinced gave his carte blanche "To move ahead," with the New Deal, only to discover to his mortification that the check bounced.

What of Sen. Joseph O'Mahoney's role in the Court fight? Roosevelt could have reasonably expected that he had a loyal lieutenant in the senator from Wyoming. As a strategist in the 1932 landslide, O'Mahoney had been of the "select" members of Jim Farley's cortege. As a reward for his efforts, O'Mahoney had been named the first assistant postmaster general.[7] He resigned a short time later, when Gov. Leslie Miller of Wyoming appointed him to fill the unexpired term of the late Sen. John B. Kendrick. Subsequently, O'Mahoney was elected to a full term in 1934. Again in the 1936 election, he had been numbered among the anointed high command guiding the campaign in the West from the Biltmore Hotel headquarters in New York.[8]

7. O'Mahoney, far from coveting the office of first assistant postmaster general, regarded the post as a political Siberia. Years later, he recalled his exchange with Jim Farley after the 1932 election: "He (Farley) was looking out the window on Madison Avenue. I said, 'Jim, who's the First Assistant Postmaster General now?' There was a great silence, and he turned around. He said, 'I get what you mean, but I still want you to be First Assistant Postmaster General'" (Joseph C. O'Mahoney Transcript 14 Oral History Research Office, Columbia University).

8. Writing three years after the 1936 election, Raymond Moley recounted a luncheon engagement with Roosevelt: "It was a completely pleasant occasion. I was asked for advice about the campaign trip—

The answer to O'Mahoney's position on the Supreme Court reveals not only considerable about the senator from Wyoming, but also about the ideals of western progressivism in general. One historian briefly comments, "Quite clearly, O'Mahoney took his position with respect to the Supreme Court matter on principle."[9] That Senator O'Mahoney stood on principle there is little dispute, but the statement belies the complexity of O'Mahoney's motives in opposing the Court plan.

O'Mahoney arrived at his decision of "principle" only after a long period of anguish and torturous self-examination, an ordeal marked by considerable doubt and hesitation. In the space of a year, he went from outright defiance of the Supreme Court to a complete break with Roosevelt. Second, the motivations behind his stand in the Court fight mesh closely with his economic philosophy so forcefully enunciated as chairman of the Temporary National Economic Commission. Third, on several occasions during the long, hot Washington spring and summer of 1937, O'Mahoney instituted overtures to compromise with the executive, only to be rebuffed or sidetracked.

From 1936 on, the evolution of O'Mahoney's thinking on the Supreme Court can be easily traced. In letter after letter to his personal friends he argued his case, at times almost as if he were trying to convince himself. Shocked by the AAA decision, he wrote one confidant, "It seems to me there is only one clear course to follow." What was that unequivocal path? "Congress should exercise the unquestionable power which it has under the second clause of Section 2, Article III of the Constitution, and by regulation provide that no law exacted by the Congress may be declared unconstitutional by the Supreme Court except by unanimous vote."[10] Further-

another friendly gesture—and I answered with the recommendation that Senator Joe O'Mahoney be taken on the Western campaign trip to help with speeches. Joe was taken" (Moley, *After Seven Years*, p. 349).

9. T. A. Larson, *History of Wyoming* (Lincoln, 1965), p. 350.

10. O'Mahoney to Charles M. Kearney, 16 January 1936, O'Mahoney Papers.

more, Congress should then defy the Court by turning right around and "re-enact the AAA." How different O'Mahoney's insurgency sounded just one year later.[11]

When one of his correspondents in Wyoming, the wife of the publisher of the Casper *Star-Tribune*, dissented with O'Mahoney's position, the senator refused to budge. In schoolmaster fashion, he reminded her that "the Constitution creates a government of three coordinate branches, ... the judicial, therefore, is only one-third of the whole." Then, O'Mahoney pounded on, was it not logical that "When two of the co-ordinate branches of government have deliberately come to the conclusion that a particular law is necessary in the public interest, that law should not be permitted to be overthrown by less than the full vote of the third branch."[12]

Senator O'Mahoney's constitutional theory could not have been more in tune with the most avid New Dealer. In justice to him, while a New Dealer without apparent reservation, he was undoubtedly reflecting a heritage of progressivism rather than total adoption of the liberal baggage of the thirties. Yet as 1936 wore on, O'Mahoney continued his attack on the judiciary. As a trial balloon, early in the year he delineated the unanimous decision of the Supreme Court scheme before a group of wildly cheering Democrats at a Detroit Jackson Day banquet. The uninhibited reception accorded his Detroit speech so encouraged O'Mahoney, that upon returning to Washington, he outlined his ideas in a formal memorandum to the president.

11. Who influenced him? When did he alter his position? And why did he make the change? All these are questions that must be asked regarding O'Mahoney's switch on the Court bill that took place over a thirteen-month period. I have endeavored to unravel O'Mahoney's motivation in the above essay. Alan Coombs proposes that Senator Borah, who had experienced a similar change of mind, may have been the decisive personage in O'Mahoney's rethinking. Hugh Cox believes that there is some indication that Senator Wheeler may have influenced O'Mahoney's reevaluation. Both views may be correct; my own opinion is that O'Mahoney, for reasons outlined above, decided he had no other course open to him (Hugh Cox to Gene M. Gressley, 3 February 1969, author's collection).

12. O'Mahoney to Mrs. Earl Hanway, 11 January 1936, O'Mahoney Papers.

A bold and dramatic stroke that would probably appeal to the nation would be to defy the Supreme Court by:

a.) Urging upon Congress a law to deprive the Supreme Court of the authority to declare any statute unconstitutional save by a unanimous vote.

b.) To immediately pass a new agricultural bill, . . .

c.) (This) avoids the delay and difficulty involved in a long campaign for *a Constitutional amendment*.[13]

O'Mahoney's enthusiasm must have been dampened by the president's reply, which merely acknowledged his epistle with thanks.[14] For the time being, Roosevelt was keeping his own counsel. But is it any wonder that the president made a mental note that here was a senator that he could count on in the future? Instead, less than nine months later, O'Mahoney was forcefully advocating to the president the merits of a constitutional amendment!

All through 1936, O'Mahoney continued to hammer away at the vexatious iniquities of judicial review, split decisions, and the nullification power of the Supreme Court.[15] To his former business associate and astute attorney in Denver, Warwick Downing, O'Mahoney commented that suggestions to deprive the Court of all jurisdiction except on an unanimous basis pervaded the Washington atmosphere. O'Mahoney said

13. The italics are mine. "For consideration of the President," O'Mahoney to Franklin D. Roosevelt, 10 January 1936, O'Mahoney Papers.

14. Franklin D. Roosevelt to O'Mahoney, 16 January 1936, O'Mahoney Papers.

15. Typical of O'Mahoney's thinking during this period is a letter he wrote to Rev. J. D. Salter, of St. Marks Episcopal Church, Casper, Wyoming. "I did say that, in my opinion, Congress has the constitutional power to require a unanimous opinion in order to invalidate a law enacted by the concurrence of Congress and the President. There is good reason to believe that had such a law been on the statute books in 1857 the Civil War could have been avoided, for the Dred Scot Decision holding the Missouri Compromise unconstitutional on grounds very similar to that on which the AAA decision was based, was rendered by a divided Court. The dissenting opinions of the minority in that case, supported wholeheartedly by Abraham Lincoln and the newly organized Republican party, were, as you may recall, not at all unlike the dissenting opinion of Justice Stone in the present case" (O'Mahoney to Rev. J. D. Salter, 20 January 1936, O'Mahoney Papers).

that most of the reasoning in support of such a move came from the conviction that the framers of the Constitution did not intend to give the Court the power of judicial review. He dissented, "Personally I cannot avoid the conclusion that the right is inherent under a written constitution." However, O'Mahoney contended, "It should not be overlooked . . . that this question never arises except when the Supreme Court has happened to enter the political field."[16]

As the autumn approached, O'Mahoney's efforts and interest riveted on the election. Touring the West as Jim Farley's representative, he campaigned "one hundred per cent" for the New Deal. Intriguingly enough, from August on he said little about the Supreme Court, either pro or con.[17]

After the November landslide, O'Mahoney again began writing to friends about the necessity of accomplishing the "President's program, particularly legislation to correct economic injustices."[18] On 19 January, he attended a victory preinaugural dinner at the White House, where he was seated on Mrs. Roosevelt's left. All in all it was a gala affair, with rounds of toasts, plentiful stories—an ether permeated with the warm glow of success.[19] Senator O'Mahoney, by his con-

16. O'Mahoney to Warwick M. Downing, 22 January 1936, O'Mahoney Papers.

17. Of course the president made little reference to the Supreme Court either. In light of later developments the omission is understandable.

18. O'Mahoney to George W. Tucker, 22 November 1936, O'Mahoney Papers.

19. The warmth of the preceding evening still lingered on when O'Mahoney reported in his diary: "In his (Roosevelt's) most felicitious [sic] manner he began by saying that the first of the three toasts could be drunk only by two persons present, whereupon saying that without the work of the guests there assembled, at 12:30 the next day he and Mrs. Roosevelt would not have been able longer to remain in the White House, he offered to toast the entire staff. The remark was, of course, greeted by deprecatory murmurs for all present well knew that their labors had served only to help, not to make the campaign, and that the President himself was his own greatest support. However, when he had finished, Mrs. Roosevelt and the President raised their glasses while all present enjoyed what the cartoonists call the thrill that comes once in a lifetime" (O'Mahoney, Diary, 20 January 1937, O'Mahoney Papers).

tributions to the recent campaign, as well as the recognition that he had received, had every reason that evening to feel embraced as part of the official family. Indeed, he had considered himself a member of the "Little Cabinet."

Just sixteen days later, O'Mahoney initiated the divorce between himself and unequivocable support of the New Deal. On the morning of 5 February, the president called in his congresssional leaders and cabinet members to read the Court message which he would send to the Hill at midday. Incredulous and stunned, the congressmen left the White House almost not believing what they had heard. Roosevelt then turned to his next pleasurable task of informing the press—"the most jubilant press conference he had ever had."[20]

Regardless of Senator O'Mahoney's immediate reaction, his response at hearing the news was one of studied discretion. He made no quotable remarks such as that of Congressman Hatton Sumners, whose comment to his colleagues upon leaving the White House, "Boys, here's where I cash in my chips," appears in almost every account of the Court fight and was bantered around Washington cocktail parties throughout the contest. Nor did O'Mahoney make any gestures akin to that of Vice-President Garner, who left the podium during the reading of the president's message, holding his nose with one hand and pointing thumbs down with the other one. The senator from Wyoming kept his own counsel; only slowly over the next few weeks to close friends and associates did he make his consternation known. First, his disenchantment with the president's handling of the mechanics of the Court plan meshed with that of disgusted senators on both sides of the aisle. The president's secrecy deeply irked him, "The unfortunate phase of it is that not one of his Congressional leaders were counselled [sic] until the very day the message was sent up."[21] The patent subterfuge of using age and overwork as the motives for judicial reform, "which has fooled no one, and now threatens to imperil his entire

20. Alsop and Catledge, *The 168 Days*, p. 66.
21. O'Mahoney to T. K. Cassidy, 23 February 1937, O'Mahoney Papers.

program,"[22] was unvarnished hypocrisy. As he wrote to his friend and fellow Wyomingite Thurman Arnold, "The whole mess smells of Machiavelli and Machiavelli stinks!"[23]

Later O'Mahoney summarized his more fundamental criticisms in a long letter to his close confidant, Tracy McCraken, Wyoming Democratic leader and publisher. "I am not writing for publication, because the time has not yet come I think for me to speak, but rather to let you know what the situation is in Washington." O'Mahoney pointed out that what support there was for the Court bill came from "loyalty to the President rather than enthusiasm for the proposal." The opposition O'Mahoney claimed was so deeply infused, "I am very much inclined to the opinion that this marks the beginning of the party realignment, . . . I predicted to you long before the election as a very likely development during this term."[24]

O'Mahoney succinctly enumerated his main objections to the Court proposal, objections that he had recently offered Roosevelt. First, "everyone" admitted there was really no provision to permanently "infuse" young blood into the judiciary. Second, the bill made no substantive alteration in the problem of judicial review. Third, and most disheartening to O'Mahoney, even if the bill passed, "it gives no assurance whatsoever that the legislative program to be adopted will be upheld in the case of an attack by the Courts."[25] O'Mahoney said that Roosevelt even acknowledged the correctness of these criticisms.

He lamented, "We, therefore, find ourselves asked to pass a bill which is at best only a temporary expedient." In addition, O'Mahoney reasoned, if there was no compromise and the bill failed, "then it is difficult to foresee the accomplishments of any aims of the administration." He then di-

22. Ibid.
23. O'Mahoney to Thurman Arnold, 8 March 1937, Thurman Arnold Papers, Western History Research Center.
24. O'Mahoney to Tracy McCraken, 6 March 1937, O'Mahoney Papers.
25. Ibid.

gressed into the problems of "practical" politics. "Take for example the sugar bill," a bill that had been introduced just five days before, "Its passage is essential for the sugar beet producers, yet if the President is defeated it would open the way for the bill to be invalidated by the Court." O'Mahoney ended by enunciating what was really the horns of his dilemma, "Obviously, those of us who would like to see a liberal program enacted into law, but who do not like the *appearance* of the attack upon the independence of the judiciary are confronted with the necessity of making a most serious decision. So I conclude this letter to you with an exclamation point and a question mark!?"[26]

Over the next few weeks, O'Mahoney balanced precariously on his own improvised political teeter-totter, moving little to the left or right, for his early reprehensions on the Court bill remained with him. Roosevelt's modus operandi, unmasked by the opportunism of the bill's provisions and the undermining of the independence of judiciary, continued to haunt Joe O'Mahoney's conscience. Speculatively O'Mahoney faced in the Court bill a paradox that ensnared others with Progressive convictions. He could be as fervent as George Norris in believing that the judiciary should be responsive to the people and the democratic process. He could even concur with Norris's judgment that the Supreme Court, by its recent decisions,[27] had "stacked" the deck against the common man. O'Mahoney could not, regardless of the provocation and justification, advocate the demolition of the

26. Joseph C. O'Mahoney to Tracy McCraken, 7 March 1937, O'Mahoney Papers (my italics).

27. Norris was uneasy about the Court plan; he definitely disliked the president's tactics as much as O'Mahoney. In his rationalization for supporting Roosevelt, he contended, "There is a great outcry against 'packing' the Court. But the Court in many recent decisions had been packed, in effect, against the common man, against the people, against the nation trying to save its life. Monopoly, special privilege, the interests of predatory selfishness have lost their old commanding influence at the White House and the Capitol. They are making their last stand in the federal courts" (*New York Times Magazine,* 30 May 1937, p. 3. Quoted in Norman L. Zucker, *George W. Norris* [Urbana, 1966]).

judiciary to achieve these "humanitarian" ends, thereby up-
setting the delicate power balance he felt must exist between
the three branches of government. Unlike his good friend,
Senator Wheeler, there is no evidence that he desired congressional dominance over the executive and the judiciary,
but undeniably O'Mahoney was troubled by presidential
initiative and judicial veto in relation to congressional legislation.

Roosevelt's muscular display of power and realpolitik maneuvering in Congress deeply disturbed him. Pragmatically,
O'Mahoney was painfully aware where he would be as to influence with the New Deal establishment and the economic
cornucopia pouring forth, if he openly participated in thrash-
ing the president. Far more than those sugar producers would
be jeopardized!

In the noble moments he could disdain the threat of banish-
ment from the federal largesse, but there were other personal
considerations that refused to vanish. Jim Farley had been
his friend and mentor, he had worked enthusiastically for
Roosevelt in two elections.[28] O'Mahoney was acutely aware
of the political adage, nothing is more rewarded than loyalty,
nor more punished than disloyalty. The question mark remained. Somehow to escape this moat of political obscurity,
with his principles intact, became O'Mahoney's prime pre-
occupation after 5 February. As the battle grew hotter between Roosevelt and Congress, the paradoxes that seemed
so evident in January melted away in July.

The one shining hope that he grasped almost immediately
and clung to with all absorbing tenacity, until the last vestige
of compromise faded, was the instrumentality of a constitutional amendment. Fourteen days after Roosevelt's "awful
shock," as the president labeled it to Frankfurter, O'Mahoney

28. Charles Michelson in his extremely useful autobiography assessed the O'Mahoney-Farley relationship. "O'Mahoney was under deep
obligation to Farley. He had been brought into the national field as
Farley's first assistant postmaster-general, which gave him a spring-
board from which he vaulted into the senatorship" (Michelson, *The
Ghost Talks*, p. 175).

received an invitation from the White House to discuss the Court plan. In this interview, O'Mahoney pressed diligently for an amendment that would limit the terms of all federal judges to fifteen years, make their salaries subject to the income tax,[29] and provide for compulsory retirement at the age of seventy-five—all of the substantive measures, O'Mahoney argued, that Roosevelt wanted. How the president must have been bemused, perhaps even amused, by the senator in front of him—was this indeed the same man who had written him just a few months before about the dangers of a long drawn-out amendment process?

Undaunted by the president's coolness, O'Mahoney returned from his conference with Roosevelt, sat down at his desk and dashed off a draft of the amendment he had just so eagerly propounded. In his covering letter to the president, O'Mahoney unfolded the rationale behind such an amendment. "All the critics of the proposed judiciary bill declare that no action should be taken without reference to the people."[30] Who could argue then that the better part of wisdom as well as valor dictated taking advantage of this sentiment? "This affords you the opportunity to challenge, and in my opinion successfully, all of them (the critics) to cooperate in securing the immediate submission to conventions in the several states."[31] O'Mahoney optimistically concluded by reassuring the president about the chances of passage, "It takes no prophet to predict that the liberal forces which rallied so strongly behind you last November would come to your aid now in procuring the ratification of such an amendment."[32] Characteristically Roosevelt replied, "Dear Joe, Many thanks for yours of February nineteenth. Am an optimist as you

29. The Court's "self-exemption" from the income tax had long annoyed O'Mahoney. Discussing the legal shuffling in the Supreme Court, he reminded Warwick Downing, "that the Court did not hesitate to declare that the salaries of its members could not be taxed by Congress under the income tax" (O'Mahoney to Warwick Downing, 18 January 1936, O'Mahoney Papers).

30. O'Mahoney to Franklin D. Roosevelt, 19 February 1937, O'Mahoney Papers.

31. Ibid.

32. Ibid.

know, but I think you are a worse optimist than I am!"[33] The president was counting on those liberal forces to rally around the White House, but with different placards than those envisioned by the senator from Wyoming.

Furthermore, regardless of his own recent conversion to the amendment process, O'Mahoney should hardly have been surprised that Roosevelt brushed aside his proposal.[34] In fact, O'Mahoney had had ample warning of the president's thinking. Writing in his diary the next day after the famous 1937 victory banquet at the White House, O'Mahoney recalled Roosevelt's objections to the constitutional amendment process. "In the course of the conversation," O'Mahoney wrote, "the President was explaining to Senator Guffey his attitude toward a constitutional amendment. . . . pointing across the table to me, he said, 'Joe and I think alike upon this subject.' "[35] Roosevelt, O'Mahoney remembered, went on to say that he believed that an amendment would have little chance of passing the necessary state legislatures.[36] The president argued that it would be especially foolhardy to leave an amendment to the winds of fate for the 1938 elections, "without the advantage of the factors which enter into a presidential campaign."[37] O'Mahoney was far from oblivious to the translation of these political smoke signals, for in the distillation of these comments he read the same signs so many did—"the manner in which the President discussed this subject seems to leave no doubt that he entertains no thought of a third term."[38] This prognosis of Roosevelt's thinking on a third term was a major faux pas committed by proponents, as well as opponents, of the Court plan.

33. Franklin D. Roosevelt to O'Mahoney, 20 February 1937, O'Mahoney Papers.

34. This may be another illustration of Roosevelt's ability to charm his guests into believing that they heard what they came to hear. O'Mahoney, aware of this Rooseveltian trait, should not have been misled by the president; on the other hand, he desperately desired an escape from the imbroglio.

35. O'Mahoney, Diary, 20 January 1937.

36. Ibid.

37. Ibid.

38. Ibid.

Probably because the alternatives were so clear, O'Mahoney refused to be discouraged about Roosevelt's attitude toward an amendment. Throughout the month following his White House visit, O'Mahoney continued to promote his amendment both inside and outside the halls of Congress. Though he conjured up several drafts, the sum and substance of the joint resolution that he introduced in the Senate remained static. Basically, O'Mahoney's resolution advocated that no law of the nation or state could be held unconstitutional by an inferior court or by the Supreme Court unless two thirds of the judges, "shall specifically and by separate opinion find so beyond a reasonable doubt."[39]

Consistently, O'Mahoney contended that his amendment was no more nor less than what the Courts had reiterated time and again, that there was a "presumption of constitutionality" that enveloped every legislative act.[40] A corollary with this decision was the statement that no law should be declared invalid unless the judge found it so beyond "a reasonable doubt." As justification for his stand, O'Mahoney then proceeded to embrace wholesale the identical argument espoused by the detractors of the Court bill. "It has seemed to me that when a question is so close that four justices of the Supreme Court believe that a law is constitutional and so indicate by their votes, that action by itself raises the reasonable doubt which should protect the statute involved."[41] That this declaration did not boomerang on O'Mahoney in the coming weeks is an enigma to say the least. Time and again in the Judiciary Committee hearings he would corner a witness into admitting that there was obviously some doubt about the constitutionality of an act when a substantial number of judges cast their votes *against* the legislation.[42] If this Janus-

39. "Draft of the Supreme Court Resolution," O'Mahoney Papers.

40. O'Mahoney to John F. McNamee, 26 March 1937, O'Mahoney Papers.

41. Ibid.

42. U.S. Congress, Senate, "Reorganization of the Federal Judiciary," *Hearings before the Committee on the Judiciary and S. 1392—75th* Cong., 1st sess., pp. 15, 253, 299, 450.

like switch within the space of two months bothered O'Mahoney, he did not admit it.

Regardless of the din in Congress, Roosevelt continued to scorn the myriad of amendments that welled up on Capitol Hill. Along with his advisors, the president had long since decided that an amendment was not a feasible solution. Eight days after giving his Court bill to Congress, Roosevelt responded to a letter from C. C. Burlingham, a friend from the days of his youth. "Strictly between ourselves," the president wrote, "there are two main difficulties with any amendment method, at this time."[43] First, no two people could agree on the same amendment, either in language or in concept. To obtain a two-thirds vote in legislatures in the next two years for any amendment would be impossible, a fact Roosevelt claimed his derogators well knew. As an exercise in conjecture, suppose a consensus was reached on an amendment and it was passed. Then the president forecast that the various forces who supported the amendment in Congress would become chameleons and fight the ratification in the states. Roosevelt offered Burlingham a get-rich-quick scheme, "If you were not as scrupulous and ethical as you happen to be, you could make five million dollars as easy as rolling off a log by undertaking a campaign to prevent ratification by one house of the legislature or even summoning of a constitutional convention in thirteen states for the next four years. Easy money!"[44] Dismissing conjecture and levity, the president issued a call to arms, "Therefore, my good friend, by the process of reductio ad absurdum, or any other better sounding name, you must join me in confining ourselves to the legislative means of saving the United States."[45]

Old school ties did not prevent Burlingham from joining the "imperial" opposition, breaking with both Roosevelt and Felix Frankfurter. O'Mahoney and his Senate cohorts

43. Franklin D. Roosevelt to Charles C. Burlingham, 23 February 1937. Franklin D. Roosevelt–M. Dewson File, Franklin D. Roosevelt Library, Hyde Park.
44. Ibid.
45. Ibid.

continued to flay the administration with the merits of an amendment to no avail. At last in the middle of April, Joe O'Mahoney decided that the amendment tactic was doomed. He had resisted strong pressure from his friends to make public his disenchantment with the administration. That he had clung to the amendment approach as a practicable compromise as long as he did is eloquent testimony to his extreme reluctance to break with Roosevelt.

On 28 April, O'Mahoney joined Senators Hatch and Mc-Carran in announcing what he had fought so hard to avoid, his unalterable opposition to the Court bill.[46] The statement created little sensation. For over a fortnight most of Capitol Hill knew of the Old Testament wrestling of O'Mahoney with his conscience. The president's contacts with Congress had long since listed the senator from Wyoming in the enemy camp.

What at last brought O'Mahoney to make this rupture with the administration? In the space of less than two years he had undertaken a partial, if not total, reversal of positions. We have proposed several interpretations that evolved in the Wyoming senator's mind as the Court issue developed. Among immediate catalytic influences that pressed on him in the spring of 1937 were: one, there is no question that O'Mahoney had an intense admiration for the Supreme Court as an institution. Less acknowledged is that O'Mahoney also had a strong desire for a Supreme Court seat. Long after the Court fight, newspapers mentioned O'Mahoney's name whenever a vacancy occurred on the Court. Jim Farley on at least two occasions mentioned his former associate as a possible nominee. Two, O'Mahoney had a basic reverence for the principle of checks and balances. In a very real way, O'Mahoney foresaw the attack on the judiciary as also a broadside against the legislative branch. O'Mahoney shared in the common opinion that, if the president got away with this maneuver, what or who would be the next victim? Three, while O'Mahoney made no pretense of fetish over the sanctity of judicial review, he did view the Court as a protector of minorities. One of the many intriguing points to come out of the

46. *New York Times*, 29 April 1937, pp. 1, 10.

Court fight was the unanimity of Roman Catholic senators in their opposition to Roosevelt's proposal. As a fellow adherent, O'Mahoney could not have helped but be influenced by the position of his cobelievers. Four, O'Mahoney, along with an earthly host of others, plainly felt that the Court plan was political suicide. What made it all the more poignant for O'Mahoney was that he feared it wrecked his chances for the passage of his pet project, the federal incorporation bill. Five, O'Mahoney had a strong conviction that the Court would soon change its position on New Deal legislation. Never an admirer of Homer Cummings, O'Mahoney believed that much of the problem of constitutionality arose simply because the legislation was poorly drafted. The justice department, in his opinion, had not performed its homework. Six, finally, inescapable but omnipresent is O'Mahoney's ambiguity, which permeated his entire approach to the Court issue.

In actuality, from the first announcement of the Court plan, O'Mahoney subconsciously realized that he would eventually repudiate the administration. What commentators on this period have missed was the intensity of O'Mahoney's vacillation, which only his immensely strong attachment to western progressivism, radical-environmental philosophy overcame. Most assuredly, O'Mahoney joined with the host of Roosevelt critics in deploring the tactics of the executive—the formulative secrecy, the transparency of the age issue, the raw display of power in patronage arm twisting, the fact that the Court bill did not represent a solution[47]—but all of this was superficial to his fundamental revulsion.

Far more substantively, O'Mahoney, as hard as he might try, could not escape the conviction that the president was slashing at the moral foundations of his political creed. Above all else, O'Mahoney fought against economic monopoly and political centralization. To Herbert Bayard Swope he wrote, "It is a mistake to assume, however, that because the people of the United States were opposed to big business . . . that

47. The most succinct summary of O'Mahoney's procedural objections is in a radio address transcript with the unconfusing title, "The Judiciary Bill Should Not Pass," 5 May 1937, O'Mahoney Papers.

they are in favor of having all of their affairs run by big government."[48]

All through the long, drawn-out and often boring hearings on Senate bill 1392, O'Mahoney drummed at the theme of economic concentration and unharassed government power. When Dorothy Thompson appeared before the Judiciary Committee to give her impressions of European totalitarianism, O'Mahoney questioned her, "In other words, the totalitarian state is a result of the concentration of economic powers." Miss Thompson, "Yes, yes; it is." O'Mahoney pressed on, "And wherever it happens in the world, wherever this concentration happens, is it likely that the totalitarian state will follow?" Miss Thompson, "Wherever that concentration happens, it is easy to get a totalitarian state."[49]

Several days later in the hearings O'Mahoney again seized the opportunity of spouting his radical-environmental tenets, summarizing the testimony of a professor of government from the University of Texas, "In other words, the expansion of federal power in Washington, the growth of the National government has been the result, has it not, of the fact that commercially and economically there has been proceeding a steady concentration of economic power in the hands of a rather small group in New York City, to be quite exact?"[50] The rhetoric of Mary Lease, Jerry Simpson, or Ignatius Donnelly could not have expressed it better! The O'Mahoney statement sounded like a blend of Populist oratory and Progressive thought.

There is a far closer philosophic bridge than has been commonly realized between the one O'Mahoney—in the role of a vigorous opponent of the Court bill—and the other O'Mahoney—tenacious chairman of the Temporary National Economic Committee. The senator from Wyoming could rationalize the opportunism of the president's Court plan,

48. O'Mahoney to Herbert Bayard Swope, 3 August 1937, O'Mahoney Papers.

49. U.S. Congress, Senate, "Statement of Miss Dorothy Thompson, Reorganization of the Federal Judiciary," *Hearings before the Committee on the Judiciary on S. 1392*—75th Cong., 1st sess., pp. 877–78.

50. "Testimony of Dr. C. P. Patterson," ibid., p. 1357.

but he could not subvert his Progressive dogma. Bigness was wrong; unlicensed power, either in business or government, was evil. He had firmly held to these ideas since his youth as an editorial writer on the Boulder, Colorado, *Daily Herald*.[51] O'Mahoney was not about to toss aside these beliefs in the spring of 1937, as much as he coveted a way out.

While the ideology of progressivism was engrained in O'Mahoney's thought, he did not yield as many of the critics did, to molding Roosevelt in the image of a malevolent dictator.[52] O'Mahoney was as uneasy as his good friennd Amos Pinchot concerning the unbalance of power between the tripartite branches of government.[53] But he adamantly refused to single out Roosevelt as a demon incarnate. In the debate over the Wheeler amendment on the executive reorganization plan of 1938, O'Mahoney gossiped to his good friend in Wyoming, Dr. T. K. Cassidy, "Had I chosen to align myself with Wheeler in his demand that all executive orders reorganizing the government should first have the approval of Congress before becoming effective, the administration would have suffered another defeat." O'Mahoney went on to give his enthymeme, "The controversy, therefore, arising from the Wheeler amendment was between the President and the bureaucrats. I was quite willing to go along with the

51. Joseph C. O'Mahoney Transcript 32, Oral History Research Office, Columbia University.

52. O'Mahoney, though, did suggest that while he would not personally impugn Roosevelt's motives, what of the future? Raymond Moley, who by this time had exited through the back door of the New Deal, was inclined to be less generous. "As I indicated in the editorial, I think we all ought to avoid fighting FDR on any issue where we can possibly give him the benefit of the doubt. But eternal vigilance is going to be the order of things if we are to prevent a mixture of FDR's itch for power and the strange unAmerican party purposes of some of his followers" (Raymond Moley to O'Mahoney, 26 July 1937, O'Mahoney Papers).

53. Amos Pinchot drafted an "open" letter to Roosevelt in which he railed at the Supreme Court bill, the executive reorganization bill, and the Black-Connery bill, insisting that these bills would "throw the country into fascism in a fortnight"; Pinchot wearily regurgitated all the old Progressive dogma (Amos Pinchot to Franklin D. Roosevelt, 26 July 1937, O'Mahoney Papers).

President."[54] One suspects that this is the political pragmatist speaking. In early 1939, O'Mahoney was searching for an issue to exercise his legislative leadership. The Temporary National Economic Committee would soon provide him with that platform; therefore, he saw little gain in continuing to antagonize the president.[55]

As the muggy summer started settling down on Washington, the hearings on Senate bill 1392 slowly, ever so slowly, began to grind to a close. Yet, one more attempt at compromise between O'Mahoney and Roosevelt would be attempted. On 9 June Ralph Immel, former Wyoming native and now Wisconsin's adjutant general, returned to Washington from Cheyenne, where he had conferred with O'Mahoney's intimate friend and Wyoming newspaper-chain owner, Tracy McCracken. Immel immediately sent off a memo to James Roosevelt, who had been an active participant in the legislative-executive relations on the Court issue. Immel commented, "We discussed the court proposal of the President, off and on over a period of three days." Finally on the last day of his visit, "McCraken suggested that he thought the difference of opinion might be worked out, saying of course, that the Senator would have to be given the oppor-

54. O'Mahoney to T. K. Cassidy, 18 March 1938, O'Mahoney Papers.

55. In his memoir, O'Mahoney described how he seized the initiative from Roosevelt. "I had fallen out, to some extent, with the Roosevelt Administration over the Court fight, but I was all for this investigation of the concentration of economic power. . . . So I went to Senator Borah. He and I were in agreement on this Court fight. I asked him to join me in introducing a resolution to establish this economic committee, but to make Congress a part of it. Roosevelt was in a great hurry to go off on a week-end trip, so he sent this message up to Congress at the end of the week, without a bill. By Monday morning when he came back, I had introduced a bill which made Congress a part of the investigation. Of course they couldn't take away from Congress, since they were asking Congress to pass the bill."

One of the chief disappointments in the O'Mahoney interview is the almost total absence of any reference to the Court fight. O'Mahoney was neither asked, nor did he volunteer, his recollections from 1937. Joseph C. O'Mahoney Transcript 36, Oral History Research Office, Columbia University.

tunity to 'save face.' "[56] General Immel immediately grasped the suggestion and proposed a meeting between Roosevelt, O'Mahoney, McCraken, and Gov. Leslie Miller of Wyoming, to which meeting McCracken assented.

Unaccountably, thirteen days elapsed before Immel's suggestion was implemented. Then Marvin McIntyre wrote McCraken, that "a mutual friend of yours passed along certain helpful suggestions. Would McCraken the next time he came East be willing to offer his 'comments firsthand' to the President."[57]

Fate intervened again, as McCraken explained in his answer of 21 July, "When I tell you I have just returned from a month in the Middle West, that yours of June 22 was delivered at my home address . . . and that the maid thoughtlessly put it in the pile of vacation accumulations . . . you will understand why I have not previously answered your letter."[58] Though McCraken refrained from saying so, it was obviously a little late to talk of compromise.

The very next day McCraken dictated his letter to the Judiciary Committee gathered together once again in their committee room at ten o'clock in the morning. Vice-President Garner met with them to inform the committee of what they already knew—the Court bill was dead. For the three days previous, the vice-president had been huddling with congressional leaders. In one of these tête-à-têtes, Garner exasperatedly told Ashurst that all the administration wanted him to do was serve as undertaker. The nervous, giggling Ashurst replied that he would be happy to perform any ceremony that was desired.[59] A motion was requested and made to recommit the Court bill to the Judiciary Committee. O'Mahoney hastily scribbled down the terms, "The Supreme Court out of it, no roving judges, no Supreme Court proctor."[60] These

56. Ralph M. Immel to James Roosevelt, 9 June 1937, Franklin D. Roosevelt—M. Dewson File, Franklin D. Roosevelt Library, Hyde Park.

57. M. H. McIntyre to T. S. McCraken, 22 June 1937, ibid.

58. T. S. McCraken to M. H. McIntyre, 21 July 1937, ibid.

59. Alsop and Catledge, *The 168 Days*, p. 286.

60. A photo of this memo, on five-by-seven scratch paper, went out over wire services. Today the original is in the O'Mahoney Papers.

notes he quickly handed over to Senator Logan, who then drafted the motion. The Court fight had ended, not with pyrotechnics, only sighs of relief.

Even the 22 July meeting was anticlimactic. The administration and its congressional adversaries for weeks had known the obvious, that Senate bill 1392 was doomed to defeat. The only serious question remaining was, who would pronounce the benediction? In reality, ever since Chief Justice Hughes had delivered that "paralyzing blow" of his rebuttal letter in May, Washington pundits refused to give odds on the president.

Then in June came the devastating majority report of the Judiciary Committee. O'Mahoney, given the task of drafting the report, in cold clear logic, almost brutally stated, carved away at the entire Roosevelt case for judicial reform, leaving it in shreds. In fact, he drew the lines so hard between the administration and Congress that compromise, from the day the report was issued, became for all intents and purposes, only a matter for academic debate. A stubborn president of Dutch aristocratic background had met an equally stubborn senator of humble Irish origins.[61]

As soon as the president's "Runnymede," to use O'Mahoney's phrase,[62] became known, the senator from Wyoming received a "rice" shower of congratulatory telegrams. All through the Court fight his mail ran heavily in favor of his stand; now the encomiums were overwhelming. Joseph Tumulty, the old Wilsonian, cheered O'Mahoney from the opening salvo with a requiem of praise, which reached a crescendo by midsummer. On 7 May Tumulty intoned, "as one who realizes the Gethesmane through which you passed, I reach out my hand to congratulate you. I do it not only as an American, but as one who yearns to see men of our faith

61. O'Mahoney never reflected the same sensitivity to his Irish background that some others have exhibited in recent years; for instance see: Paul Fay, *The Pleasure of His Company* (New York, 1966), and U.S., Cong. "Nomination of Francis X. Morrissey," *Subcommittee on the Judiciary United States Senate*, 89th Cong., 1st sess.

62. O'Mahoney to Robert H. Anderson, 15 May 1937, O'Mahoney Papers.

stand firm against the crowd and be willing to gain immortality by making a noble sacrifice."[63] A little over a month later, the majority report of the committee sent Tumulty into another rhapsody. "I read every line of the report with a great thrill and a deep sense of emotion. It was a grand national symphony. Were I a great musician I would love to carry its rhythm into music." The final outcome appeared all too much for Tumulty to bear; in sunset prose he gushed, "You know you have joined the heavenly hosts of our great leaders —you, my dear Joe, have saved America!"

As Joe O'Mahoney sat in his office at the end of July, he did not feel ready for the wings Tumulty so eagerly bestowed, but as he mused about his future he may have dreamed of a political reincarnation. All the tumult, all the praise from his "fellow Americans" sounded to O'Mahoney more like the "last Hurrah!" Regardless of the political capital he made out of his stand, and he certainly was never stronger in Wyoming, he still had to consider that his future in Washington was dimmed for having crossed one of the most popular leaders of his age.

From one vista, a morality play had been enacted in Washington in 1937, although few of the participants realized their character roles. Indeed, had the actors in the Court fight donned masks in a Japanese No theatre, they could not have dramatized their parts more. As so frequently happens when politics translates into dogma, the contestants interpreted their stands in righteous juxtapositions. The Court bill caught Senator O'Mahoney off balance; suddenly he found himself maneuvered into the cruel spot of either adhering to the Progressive, radical-environmental tradition, or surrendering to expediency. Either solution appeared unpalatable, yet he had made the choice years before. Now he had only to reaffirm that faith—he did, after feeling considerable empathy for Job.

63. Joseph P. Tumulty to O'Mahoney, 7 May 1937, O'Mahoney Papers. This article, now reedited, was presented first in the *Pacific Historical Review* 40 (May 1971):183–202. My gratitude to the editor of the *Pacific Historical Review* for permission to incorporate the essay here.

Mr. Thurman Arnold,
Antitrust,
and the
Progressive Heritage

In many respects the impact of statutory public policy on business hinges on the way that it is implemented, and in no area is this more true than in antitrust policy. Here, generalized statutes give administrators an opportunity to select certain kinds of problems for emphasis, reserving decisions as to whether specific applications of the law are justified to the courts. In this entire process there is a large element of pragmatism, and opportunities exist for experimentation, innovation, and interpretation, as well as reliance on stare decisis. Consequently, the tenor of the times and the personalities of public officials have an effect on the vigor and effectiveness with which the antitrust statutes are enforced and the uses to which they are put. For this reason there are always many different perceptions of the objectives, value, and justice of antitrust actions.

At no time in our history, perhaps, more than during the New Deal were these facets of antitrust policy better revealed. And certainly no protagonist of the antitrust approach generated more controversy than Thurman Arnold, chief of the Antitrust Division of the Justice Department from 1938 to 1942. This man and his times serve as a specific example of the general propositions advanced above.

The enforcement of antitrust legislation since the Sherman Act of 1890 has been vacillating and sporadic in approach—confused in policy.[1] This was especially true during

1. Hans B. Thorelli, *The Federal Antitrust Policy* (Baltimore, 1955), provides the best analysis of the origins of antitrust legislation. See also

the thirty years after 1900. From the well-publicized trust-busting of the insurgency period, through the antimonopolistic views propounded by Wilson, to the business-oriented trade-association movement of the 1920s, there was little to suggest that a uniform philosophy of antitrust enforcement had been developed in the United States.

Franklin D. Roosevelt's "New Deal," arriving on the political wave that followed the traumatic shock of the crash of the stock market, did little initially to alleviate the confusion surrounding antitrust enforcement. The first comprehensive legislation to remedy industrial dislocation was the National Industrial Recovery Act (NIRA), which negated the antitrust laws in some areas of industry.

So widespread was the belief that antitrust prosecution would be suspended entirely that Att. Gen. Homer Cummings issued a statement on 6 July 1933 to counteract the multitude of rumors. Cummings emphatically asserted:

> There seems to be an impression in some quarters that the antitrust laws have been repealed or suspended in whole or in part. This is an entirely erroneous impression. Industrial and other groups must abide by the terms and conditions of the antitrust laws unless and until they obtain actual exemption from certain of the requirements thereof by formulating a code under the National Recovery Act, and obtaining its approval by the President.
>
> A large number of industrial activities and arrangements which are prohibited by the antitrust laws, do not come in any sense whatever within the purview of the exemptions contemplated by the National Recovery Act.[2]

Cummings, as shown later in the revelations of the Temporary National Economic Committee, was whispering in a

---

the impressive work of Earl Kinter, specifically, *An International Antitrust Primer* (New York, 1974); S. R. Reid, *The New Industrial Order* (New York, 1976).

2. Statement to the Press, Homer Cummings, 6 July 1933, Franklin D. Roosevelt Papers, Franklin Delano Roosevelt Library, Hyde Park, New York.

cave of the winds.[3] A significant element of the business community during the short and unhappy life of the NRA regarded antitrust legislation as nonenforceable. Some large industrial firms exploited the relaxation of the antitrust laws to increase their share of the market at the expense of smaller concerns.[4]

After the 1935 Schecter case nullifying the NIRA, antitrust enforcement reflected the ambivalence of the Roosevelt administration. The president wavered between the trade association-NRA arguments of Henry Wallace, Adolph Berle, Jerome Frank, and Donald Richberg and the increasingly vocal antimonopolistic position voiced by Felix Frankfurter, Robert Jackson, and Homer Cummings.[5] The Justice Department kept up an unceasing barrage of memoranda that decried the market power of large corporations in the American economy—a situation equated in the public mind with "monopoly."

Slowly the antimonopoly partisans succeeded in gaining the president's favor. The recession of 1937 greatly assisted their case. Roosevelt's political antennae sensed the general discontent in the country. Why not spotlight the monopoly issue? Public uneasiness at the economic conditions in the

3. Harry M. Stephens, assistant attorney general in charge of the Antitrust Division, vigorously protested against the approval of a marketing agreement by the petroleum administrator of several Pacific Coast oil companies, led by Standard Oil Company of California. Stephens claimed that the agreement constituted a cartel, the same agreement for which the companies had already been defendants under an antitrust decree of 1930. Harry M. Stephens to Franklin D. Roosevelt, 24 February 1934, Roosevelt Papers.

4. A graphic description of oil marketing in the Rockies during the NRA period is given in the testimony of Pierre LaFleiche and W. H. Ferguson before the TNEC committee (U.S., Congress, Senate, *Investigation of the Concentration of Economic Power*, 76th Cong., 2d sess., S. Rept. 35, pt. 20:9376–98, 10897–916).

5. For the impact of the trade-association movement on Roosevelt, note Daniel R. Fusfeld, *The Economic Thought of Franklin D. Roosevelt and the Origins of the New Deal* (New York, 1956), pp. 56–57, 101. For a different interpretation see Frank Freidel, *Franklin D. Roosevelt: The Ordeal* (Boston, 1954), pp. 138–59.

country had been increased by a segment of the intellectuals who were producing a spate of tomes on economic concentration in the United States.[6] Politically, it appeared to be an opportune time to launch an investigation.[7]

A most effective pressure on the president for renewed emphasis on antitrust policy came from Congress, where the Progressive bloc, albeit disorganized, was in open revolt. Senators O'Mahoney, Nye, Borah, and La Follette had all contested presidential leadership on a variety of issues. Borah and O'Mahoney especially were attempting to gain political advantage over the Chief Executive on the monopoly issue by again proposing the old idea of a federal licensing bill for all interstate corporations. Indeed, O'Mahoney seemingly never gave up his hope that a licensing act would be passed. Well along into the Temporary National Economic Committee (TNEC) hearings, O'Mahoney wrote the president:

> Nothing has transpired since I had the honor of talking with you a day or so after the NRA decision of the Supreme Court to change my belief that the answer to the economic problem lies in a simple recognition of the fact that the corporations which carry on interstate and foreign commerce should be required to take their charters from the federal government. This solution has been feared by many business leaders because they have seen in it only another effort to strengthen discretionary government control over business. . . .
>
> It can, however, be demonstrated that the result of a wise system of federal charters would be to set business free from

6. Western senators recognized the political implications of the monopoly issue, but were divided as to what legislative measures should be taken. Joseph C. O'Mahoney to Burton K. Wheeler, 9 September 1937, Joseph C. O'Mahoney Papers, Western History Research Center, University of Wyoming, Laramie.

7. Among the more influential volumes were: Adolph Berle and Gardner C. Means, *The Modern Corporation and Private Property* (New York, 1933); Edward Chamberlin, *The Theory of Monopolistic Competition* (Cambridge, 1938); Harold G. Mouton, *The Formation of Capital* (Washington, 1935); John Maynard Keynes, *General Theory of Employment, Interest, and Money* (New York, 1936).

government domination and to set the people free from both the danger of monopoly on the one hand and of the total-itarian state upon the other.[8]

Roosevelt, with his usual political adeptness, had no desire to surrender the initiative on the monopoly issue to Congress; just the opposite, he determined to steal the thunder of the Progressive bloc.[9]

It was against this background of dissent that two events occurred that signaled a radical departure from the NRA philosophy. On 22 October 1937, Roosevelt wrote Att. Gen. Robert Jackson:

> One of the problems that continues to require attention is the inadequacies and defects in our anti-monopoly laws, which I have often reviewed informally with you and others. I want to ask you to undertake, with the help of such others in government service as you wish from time to time to time to enlist, to assemble for me the following:
>
> 1. The important facts bearing upon the success or failure of our present anti-monopoly laws, their economic and social results, and the necessity for revision or amendment.
>
> 2. The different proposals or alternatives worthy of prac-tical consideration, with the advantages and disadvantages of each.[10]

This letter marked a significant step, which finally resulted in Roosevelt's famous antimonopoly speech of 29 April 1938,[11] and the subsequent TNEC investigation.

Six months after the letter to Jackson, Roosevelt appointed

8. Joseph C. O'Mahoney to Franklin D. Roosevelt, 19 June 1939, Roosevelt Papers.

9. In a brilliant essay on the New Deal, Frank Freidel has written, "There are some indications, however, that the antimonopoly program that he launched in the Department of Justice through the urbane Thur-man Arnold was intended less to bust trusts than to forestall too drastic legislation in the Congress" (Frank Freidel, *The New Deal in Historical Perspective* [Washington, 1959], pp. 18–19).

10. Franklin D. Roosevelt to Robert Jackson, 22 October 1937, Roosevelt Papers.

11. The text of Roosevelt's address is in Samuel I. Rosenman, ed., *The Public Papers and Addresses of Franklin D. Roosevelt: The Continuing Struggle for Liberalism, 1938* (New York, 1941), pp. 305–20.

Thurman Arnold as assistant attorney general in charge of the Antitrust Division. Arnold had previously been a Wyoming lawyer and professor at the University of Wyoming Law School, dean of the University of West Virginia Law School, and most recently a professor in the Yale Law School. Arnold did not arrive in Washington as a neophyte in the New Deal scene. He had already served as special counsel to the Agricultural Adjustment Administration and as trial examiner with the Securities and Exchange Commission. Further, he was confidant of many New Dealers such as Robert Jackson, Benjamin Cohen, and Thomas Corcoran. The general public knew him as the highly successful author of two disturbing works, *The Folklore of Capitalism* and *The Symbols of Government*.[12]

A main thesis of this essay is that soon after Thurman Arnold arrived in Washington, a folklore developed around his public image—a folklore that clouded Arnold's aims as interpreted by his contemporaries and has yet to be dispelled by historians.[13] In sum, there has been a failure to understand what Arnold was attempting to accomplish in the field of antitrust enforcement. While many of his objectives have been treated superficially, it is the distortion of his aims that requires explanation.

First of all, there was the unusual Arnold personality. Alsop and Kinter, in one of the more memorable sketches of Arnold, describe him thus:

Thurman Wesley Arnold is a large, somewhat paunchy, middle-aged man with a yellowish face and overflowing human gusto, who looks like a small-town storekeeper and talks like a native Rabelais. He enjoys the distinction of being the only

12. Thurman W. Arnold, *The Folklore of Capitalism* (New Haven, 1937); *The Symbols of Government* (New Haven, 1935).

13. Considering the historical complexity of the New Deal period, it is readily understandable why historians have yet to investigate intensively Arnold's role. Professor Freidel noted in a 1961 bibliographical article, "There is a surprising lack of scholarly monographs of the history of the New Deal agencies." Frank Freidel, "The New Deal, 1929–1941," in *Interpreting and Teaching American History* (Washington, 1961), p. 275. Monographic studies are numerous on the broad topic of monopoly.

New Dealer who is also an Elk, and very likely the only Elk who is also an iconoclast.[14]

Arnold was always good for journalistic copy, whether he was lecturing to his Yale classes or expounding a witticism at one of Washington's innumerable social affairs. That Arnold was eminently quotable, as well as an excellent subject for anecdotes, did little to ensure accurate assessment of his philosophy and role as a government administrator.

As an author, the Yale professor was viewed as an iconoclast. Iconoclasts and suspicion have a habit of being part of the same syllogism. Sen. William Borah, in the hearing conducted on Arnold's nomination for assistant attorney general, announced that he was convinced, after reading *The Folklore of Capitalism* that Arnold did not have "any faith in the antitrust laws."[15] While admittedly this may have been more a reflection on Borah than Arnold, the senator from Idaho was not alone in misreading Arnold's books. Arnold's early works, interwoven with a plethora of allegories and analogies, frequently puzzled readers.[16] Reviewers were prone to find a variety of theses, many of which were seemingly never intended by the author.

If Arnold's literary work led to confusion, certainly his enforcement of the antitrust laws did not clarify his public image. Just when big business was convinced of his un-

14. Joseph Alsop and Robert D. Kinter, "Trust Buster—The Folklore of Thurman Arnold," *Saturday Evening Post* 212 (12 August 1939):5.

15. U.S., Congress, Senate, *The Nomination of Thurman Arnold to be Assistant Attorney General, March 11, 1938: Hearings before a Subcommittee of the Committee on the Judiciary, U.S. Senate*, 75th Cong., 3d sess.

16. Shelby Cullom Davis related the reaction of the Republican nominee for president in 1940 to Arnold's most quoted work: "Several years ago Wendell Willkie was introducing Thurman Arnold to a dinner audience of industrialists and financiers in New York City. 'I have read this man's book, *The Folklore of Capitalism*, three times,' he began. The distinguished diners look surprised. The happy author was ablaze with satisfaction. Then the deluge, 'But I have yet to understand what Mr. Arnold is driving at' " ("The Bottlenecks of Business," *Atlantic Monthly* 166 [November 1940]:560).

quenchable hostility,[17] Arnold launched a massive suit against labor unions with the same intensity that he demonstrated in his direction of the proceedings against the petroleum industry. In spite of Arnold's repeated assurances—that he was not opposing big business because of size per se but only attacking monopolistic tendencies[18]—business leaders in general remained aloof, skeptical, and uncomprehending.[19]

17. Arnold thought that there were three reasons why antitrust laws were disregarded by the business community: (1) they were ignorant of the laws; (2) the laws were obsolete; (3) in a competitive situation if one turns buccaneer, all must fight fire with fire. To have competition without adequate antitrust enforcement was like having a boxing match without a referee, said Arnold ("The Enforcement of the Sherman Act," Address before the Missouri Bar Association, St. Louis) 1 October 1938, manuscript in the Arnold Papers, Western History Research Center.

18. Arnold was perpetually perturbed about the lack of communication with businessmen. In a strongly phrased speech before the National Petroleum Association at Atlantic City, he said: "No one should interpret the application of these principles as an attack on business. They are the opposite of an attack. They are defense of business. Our complaints come from business men. We represent almost exclusively the interest of competitive business. America today needs competitive prices as a balance wheel, in a war market" ("The Antitrust Laws as the First Line of Defense Against War Profiteering," manuscript, Arnold Papers). Arnold voiced these same sentiments many times, see, "The Policy of Government Toward Big Business," *Proceedings of the Academy of Political Science* 18 (January 1939):180–87; *Folklore of Capitalism*, pp. 104, 207.

19. For instance, Frances Perkins, in her remarkable memoir of the New Deal years, described an unforgettable scene between the president of the American Federation of Labor and a group of steel executives whom she had brought together for a conference in her office, "When the heads of the big steel companies—Eugene Grace, Myron Taylor, William Irwin, Ernest Weir, Thomas Girdler—and the executives of smaller steel companies came into my office, Green was sitting there. I started the introductions.

"Most of them did not permit themselves to be introduced to Mr. Green. They backed away into a corner, like frightened boys. It was the most embarrassing social experience of my life. . . . I still could not see why anybody would be afraid of William Green mildest and most polite of men. The steel executives explained to me privately that if it were known that they had sat down in the same room with Wil-

Another element that obscured the true proportions of the antitrust picture for outside observers was the divided counsels in the administration. In response to press queries, Arnold made several pronouncements that the administration was unified in its antitrust approach.[20] Nevertheless, seeds of dissent sown by a few remnants of the old believers in NRA, still played upon Roosevelt's latent faith in the trade-association philosophy. In April 1938, Donald Richberg, during one of the moments he was in temporary favor, wrote Roosevelt:

> The philosophy of the NRA was wholly consistent with the New Deal. The philosophy of the fanatic trust busters, their hostility to all large enterprise, their assumption that cooperation is always a cloak for monopolistic conspiracy, this philosophy is wholly inconsistent with the New Deal.[21]

Three months after Richberg wrote Roosevelt that the antitrust program was the antithesis of the NRA, the *United States News* carried a column refining the position outlined by Richberg. The antitrust philosophy was not diametrically opposed to the NRA, according to the *News*, it was the NRA in reverse:

> President Roosevelt, reversing the tactics of earlier years, now is turning loose the Department of Justice in a quest for industrial recovery.
> The Department's quest consists of searching for what it determines to be criminal practices on the part of business

liam Green and talked with him, it would ruin their long-time position against labor organization to their industry" (Frances Perkins, *The Roosevelt I Knew* [New York, 1946], pp. 221–22).

20. The rumor that there was a conflict between Frankfurter, Cohen, Corcoran, Jackson, and Arnold on one hand and Berle, Henderson, Frank, and Wallace on the other hand was fallacious, stated Arnold. "In view of the attitudes in the past it is natural enough to suppose such a conflict exists. Actually, however, there is no conflict between these two groups nor is there any reason for such a conflict" ("What is Monopoly?" Address before the Advertising Federation of America, Detroit, 15 June 1938, manuscript, Arnold Papers).

21. Donald R. Richberg to Franklin D. Roosevelt, 23 April 1938, Roosevelt Papers.

men. The attack on these practices—the White House is convinced—will improve the chance for achieving prosperity through the program of spending that is about to be started.

All of this is in sharp contrast to the procedure followed in 1933. At that time business men were engaged to forget the nation's 45-year-old antitrust laws and to get together to plan their operations through consultation.[22]

Besides the opposition Arnold inevitably met within the government bureaucracy,[23] his definition of the role he should play as an enforcer of antitrust laws confused even some of his close associates. They were apparently imbued with the belief that he proposed to remake the structure of American industry in conformity with some economist's competitive model. Arnold, however, insisted both in *The Folklore of Capitalism* and in public utterances that he was a diagnostician of institutional decay and not an economic practitioner. Arnold had an innate skepticism of "preachers" with manufactured economic panaceas.[24]

22. *United States News*, 6 June 1938; Professor Freidel concludes that the antitrust program was more of a negative NRA than it was in direct disagreement (*America in the Twentieth Century* [New York, 1960], pp. 348–49).

23. Two years after Richberg wrote to Roosevelt, he sent a cordial note to Arnold, which has more than casual interest in the light of his previous comments to the president. "You are certainly a persuasive cuss! I have just been reading your address to the American Farm Bureau Federation, and I agree with so much of your purpose and efforts that I wish I could be enthusiastic about the whole program. What holds me back is a feeling that a distinction must be made between cooperation in gauging the public and cooperation which is actually in the public interest. The plain need is for the setting of standards and creation of administrative machinery for their enforcement. In a way you are trying to act as lawmaker, administrator and prosecutor, which is not only a tough assignment, but one which should not be entrusted to that abstract individual, a 'public official,' who, in the concrete, may be as smart and well-meaning as you or as dumb and devious as - - - - - - - (you fill in any name that occurs to you)" (Donald Richberg to Thurman Arnold, 14 December 1940, Arnold Papers).

24. On "preachers" Arnold wrote, "The chief difficulty is that there are too many people who believe that economic distress can be cured by preaching and too few who are willing to take practical measures industry by industry" (*The Bottlenecks of Business* [New York, 1940], p. 282).

While Arnold was more than a legal and economic technician he definitely was against using his influence in a legislative capacity. His function, as he saw it, was to enforce and recommend corrective measures. Whether his immediate success in antitrust suits would have been greater had he followed more of a policymaking role is a moot question; that his influence on New Deal economic policy might have been greater is another matter.

While associates, fellow bureaucrats, and the general public may have been hazy on the specific outlines of the Arnold antitrust policy, the assistant attorney general had a well-defined conceptual framework of what he desired to accomplish. Writing to Charles Seymour, president of Yale, on 4 July 1939, Arnold stated that he was not interested in "trust busting for the sake of trust busting"; quite the contrary, he intended to give the Antitrust Division a constructive purpose. The creation of a positive antitrust program had three facets, according to Arnold: (1) a statement of a uniform well-publicized policy was essential; (2) the building up of an effective antitrust organization; and (3) "the elimination of partisan politics from the Division was desired." "I have refused to make a single political speech during my term of office, or to become identified with any exclusively New Deal group."[25]

During his first year in office Arnold made amazing progress in maneuvering to accomplish these goals. He quickly admitted to one and all that the Sherman Act was an imperfect tool at best,[26] but that he was convinced that the "sole weakness of the enforcement of the Sherman Act in the past has been the lack of an enforcement organization."[27] Revision of the law was not the answer, Arnold maintained, but more funds for personnel in the Antitrust Division were essential.[28]

25. Arnold to Charles Seymour, 4 July 1939, Arnold Papers.
26. An excellent summary of the legal evolution of the Sherman Act is in Milton Handler, *Antitrust in Perspective: The Complementary Roles of Rule and Discretion* (New York, 1957).
27. "Free Trade Within the Borders of the United States" Address before the South Carolina Bar Association, Columbia, 11 April 1940, manuscript, Arnold Papers.
28. In the *"Annual Report* of the assistant attorney general" it was

In the first two years, his sizable budget requests received generous congressional support.

In effect, admitting the inadequacy of his organizational analysis of the enforcement problem, Arnold also blamed the general climate of opinion that historically had regarded the antitrust laws as a moral and emotional problem rather than one deserving of economic significance.[29] It was this ignorance of the economic ramifications of the antitrust laws that particularly piqued the head of the Antitrust Division.[30]

The social aspects of the antitrust policy, the remnants of the Progressive attitude toward trusts incorporating moralistic and ethical considerations, annoyed the Arnold of 1937. He believed that these were attitudes outmoded by the complex industrial system of the twentieth century; the United States could no longer afford to be a nation of economic illiterates. Arnold's good friend, H. L. Mencken, perhaps in silent sympathy with Arnold's reasoning, thought this analysis far too sophisticated. For Mencken the solution to the antitrust problem was characteristically simple and clear: the men who wrote the Sherman Act made just one mistake—they forgot to provide for capital punishment.[31]

Accepting the Sherman Act as a workable one, Arnold formulated a procedure for handling antitrust cases. Utilizing the machinery that had long been available for enforcement he undertook two courses. First, he revived use of the consent decree that involved the dropping of indictments in return for the adoption of basic remedial practices by the industry

---

noted that the work of the Antitrust Division was usually regarded as devoted to three major acts: the Sherman Act, the Clayton Act, and the Federal Trade Commission Act. Less appreciated was the fact that the division was responsible for the enforcement of thirty-one other acts (Attorney General, *Annual Report* [Washington, 1940], pp. 54–55).

29. "Fair and Effective Use of our Present Antitrust Procedure," Address before the Trade and Commerce Bar Association of New York, New York City, 28 April 1938, manuscript, Arnold Papers.

30. William L. Baldwin, "Changing Concepts of the Large Firm and Antitrust Enforcement" (Ph.D. dissertation, Princeton University, 1958).

31. H. L. Mencken to Arnold, 24 August 1938, Arnold Papers.

in question, and second, he stepped up criminal prosecution. Arnold contended that the consent decree as employed in previous years was nothing more than a subterfuge.[32] Historically, the government had used the consent decree to accomplish the objective of litigation without going through a lengthy court proceeding. Having secured evidence of an antitrust violation, the government would give the potential defendant an opportunity to make a private compact, whereby, in return for the government's dropping a criminal indictment, the subject of the action would promise not to commit specific violations in the future. Arnold deemed this use of the consent decree "absurd."[33] Instead, Arnold developed a new approach to the consent decree more properly termed a *civil decree*. In the future no prosecution would be dismissed categorically on the basis of announced good intentions. Instead, Arnold proposed that the defendant would present, as formerly, a plan to the court, but this scheme now must incorporate not only sufficient redress of the indictment but, more importantly, offer genuine reorganization on a company or industry-wide basis that would be more beneficial to the general public than would the results of a criminal prosecution.[34]

A crucial technique in this application of a civil decree was that all proceedings must be public, thereby providing the consumers, public commissioners, or competitors an opportunity to object.[35] As Arnold wrote, this utilization of the civil

32. An excellent description of the use and abuse of the consent decree is in Arnold, *Bottlenecks of Business*, pp. 144–62.

33. "How Far Should Government Control Business," Address before the Economic Club of New York, 2 February 1939, manuscript, Arnold Papers.

34. Ibid.

35. In etching the borders of the consent decree Arnold said: "I have not changed the consent decree (I don't like the word 'consent' decree; I prefer 'civil' decree) I have not changed the civil decree policy of the Department in any other way, I think, except to bring it out in the open so that business men can openly come in with their problems instead of in a *subrosa* manner as they have been doing since 1890" ("Business and the Antitrust Laws," Address before the American Trade Association Executives, Washington, D.C., 1 May 1939, manuscript, Arnold Papers).

decree offered in substance, "a reward to the businessmen who really desire to clean up their industry and to prevent a situation arising in the future which would lead to a violation of the law."[36] Modified consent decrees of this type were successfully used in the gas, automobile, typewriter, and container industries.

Although the consent decree, as conceived by Arnold, was a novel contribution to the over-all flexibility of the antitrust laws, it was in the regular enforcement of the antitrust laws that Arnold devised his most concrete and permanent contribution to antitrust enforcement. In the preceding forty years, the Justice Department had launched mercurial attacks on industrial giants, with some degree of success but without accomplishing the eradication of violations in the entire industry.[37] Arnold saw the crux of the monopolizing power in the system of distribution. Speaking to the Advertising Federation of America in Detroit, Arnold noted the adverse effects of the power of producers over distribution. "Incredible as it may seem, in order to keep prices up, industry is choking off its own avenues of distribution, decreasing employment and widening the disparity of prices."[38] The solution prescribed was a comprehensive prosecution at the distribution level in an attempt to remove the artificial "roadblocks." Joseph Alsop and Robert Kinter described the Arnold attack on distribution as one of "hit hard, hit everyone and hit them all at once."[39]

There just was no over-all magic potion that could be administered in one massive dose by the Justice Department to the industrial economy. The most rewarding prosecution formula promised to be the case-by-case indictment.[40] Arnold

36. "Statement of Thuman W. Arnold before the Temporary National Economic Committee," Washington, D.C., 7 July 1939, 20.

37. Joseph C. O'Mahoney to Arnold, 9 July 1939, O'Mahoney Papers.

38. "What is Monopoly?" Address before the Advertising Federation of America, Detroit, 15 June 1938, manuscript, Arnold Papers.

39. Alsop and Kinter, "Trust Buster—The Folklore of Thurman Arnold," p. 7.

40. Regarding the merits of the case-by-case approach, Arnold wrote the editor of the *Saturday Evening Post*: "I contend that the case by case method of handling present problems when they arise and not be-

logically contended that restraints of trade in the movie industry would have little relevance to restraints in the steel industry, while artificial "tolls" in the milk industry in Detroit would differ often from the abuses in the same industry in Chicago. The basic requirement was a pliable policy molded to the necessities of the individual prosecution. Arnold's imaginative ability at selecting prototype cases and administering the antitrust laws in a kaleidoscopic fashion, instead of being bound by inflexible precedents, was one of his most brilliant achievements.

A practical task of undertaking a case-by-case approach necessitated a huge legal staff. Arnold was able during the first two years to obtain sufficient appropriations to increase the number of lawyers in the Antitrust Division from 48 to over 300. Congressional approval of the antitrust program was in large measure due to the tremendous publicity resulting from the indictments—in addition to Arnold's unabashed demonstration that for every dollar appropriated to his division, two or three dollars flowed into the treasury in fines received from indicted defendants.

The widespread publicity buttressed Arnold's program in a variety of ways, not only by stimulating consumer pressure on congressional delegations for increased appropriations, but as a powerful catharsis on industry in general. Arnold saw nothing surprising about the fact that often a successful suit in one sector of business resulted in lower prices in other sectors. In an article in the *New Republic*, he wrote:

> We do not think there is anything mysterious about our results. An antitrust proceeding suddenly confronts the members of an industry with an appraisal of the industry's performance from the point of view of the public interest. It is

---

fore is the essence of a free economy. Instances where the antitrust laws are inadequate I contend we had better legislate case by case rather than attempt to pass sweeping generalities that only end in confusion." Actually, Arnold never did achieve a legal staff of the size sufficient to prosecute on a "case by case" approach. However, he did amass a sizable enough legal force to initiate prototype cases aimed specifically at the distribution level in the economic structure (Arnold to Wesley Stout, 25 August 1939, Arnold Papers).

sharp enough to shock, to induce self-questioning; and there is no reason for surprise that business men with public spirit and imagination sometimes alter their pricing policies as a result of such examination.[41]

The very scope of the Justice Department's suits was justification enough for such business reactions.

Within three years the Antitrust Division had sought indictments in the movie, construction, tire, fertilizer, newspaper, tobacco, shoe, and petroleum industries, not to mention suits against trade unions, the American Medical Association, and various agricultural marketing agencies.[42] In all, Arnold and his colleagues instigated 215 investigations and brought 93 suits.

Concurrently with the antitrust campaign, a broad congressional inquiry had been launched concerning the character and extent of economic concentration in America. The idea for the Temporary National Economic Committee germinated in the recession of 1937 but originated directly from President Roosevelt's famous message to Congress on monopoly of 29 April 1938.[43] The president's message ended

41. "National Defense and Restraints of Trade," manuscript draft of an article in *New Republic* 104 (19 May 1941), Arnold Papers.

42. The Antitrust Division during Arnold's regime was primarily interested in monopoly in business. However, Arnold was not unmindful of the problems in agriculture. In a letter to Colonel Knox, Arnold stated: "At the outset I wish to emphasize that in my opinion there is no basic inconsistency between this special agricultural legislation and the antitrust laws. Whatever privileges may be conferred upon farmers by this legislation, the Department of Justice stands ready to prevent those privileges from being abused in the special interest of a small and aggressive group. Far from being inconsistent with this legislation the antitrust laws are absolutely necessary if the privileges conferred are not to be pushed far beyond their proper limitation and the real purpose of Congress defeated" (Thurman W. Arnold to Frank Knox, 19 December 1939, Arnold Papers).

43. The pressure for the TNEC proceedings issued from diverse sources. Emmanuel Cellar, Congressman from New York, wrote Roosevelt on 31 March 1938, advocating a revision of antitrust laws (Emmanuel Cellar to Franklin D. Roosevelt, 31 March 1938, Roosevelt Papers). The president of the American Federation of Labor wrote Roosevelt a year to the day before the monopoly message endorsing the attorney general's recommendations for an overhauling of the leg-

with the frequently quoted phrase, "idle factories and idle workers profit no man." This expression set the tone of the TNEC probe; the committee was assigned the implied task of uncovering the causes of the depression. Leon Henderson, on the staff of the TNEC, offered a more precise definition of the committee's goals in a memorandum to Roosevelt on 3 September 1939. "The committee plans to outline, in detail, the facts about control in finance, insurance, industry, natural resources—the methods and devices of control—instances of abuses, and to recommend proper legislation."[44]

The TNEC hearings began on 1 December 1938, and lasted until 11 March 1941.[45] The testimony of 552 witnesses filled thirty-seven impressive volumes; the various economic studies by the TNEC staff were collected in another forty-three volumes. As in other investigations of this type, the recommendations were feeble indeed in relation to the comprehensiveness of the inquiry. The main prescription, which had been pointed to from the beginning of the hearings, was the necessity of a vigorous and militant enforcement of the antitrust laws. This was an anticlimactic conclusion for over two years of questioning and cross-examination. Yet there was a significant by-product of the hearings in that American economic strengths and weaknesses were widely publicized. As David Lynch has pointed out, at least the committee brought our knowledge of competitive practices up to date.

Arnold's relationship to the TNEC investigation provides a revealing insight into his conception of antitrust enforcement. As a member of the committee, Arnold was deeply involved in the hearings, provided his division's assistance for specialized studies, and presented memoranda to the attorney general and the president concerning the direction that the

islation on antitrust (William Green to Franklin D. Roosevelt, 29 April 1937, Roosevelt Papers).

44. Leon Henderson to Franklin D. Roosevelt, 3 September 1939, Roosevelt Papers.

45. David Lynch presents an adequate account of the history of the Temporary National Economic Committee in *The Concentration of Economic Power* (New York, 1946).

investigation should take,[46] and testified on antitrust procedures and practices before the committee. Nevertheless, while Arnold sympathized with the TNEC objectives, there was a dichotomy between his personal relationship to the committee and that of the Antitrust Division.[47]

Arnold, understandably, gave most of his time and energy to the task of antitrust enforcement. The TNEC probe, on the other hand, was a committee appointed by Congress and aimed at revision of the antitrust laws. Arnold, of course, desired a more effective statutory basis for antitrust, yet officially he restricted his primary attention to the enforcement, not the development of this legislative structure. While he could have taken a more active role in the TNEC query at the policymaking level, it is difficult to see how he could have chosen any other interpretation of his duties as assistant attorney general.[48]

46. In response to a request from the president for data to incorporate in his monopoly message, Arnold drew up a memorandum suggesting changes in the antitrust legislation. This memorandum was forwarded by the attorney general with the accompanying remarks, "In connection with the proposed message to Congress dealing with the Antitrust situation, I enclose you herewith a memorandum drafted by Mr. Arnold. I am sending it to you in its complete form but have taken the liberty of indicating, by pencilled marks on the margin those portions of the document which I would regard as hardly suitable for a message." Cummings's disagreement was with Arnold's expression rather than substance (Homer Cummings to Franklin D. Roosevelt, 21 April 1938, Roosevelt Papers).

47. "The Policies of the Antitrust Division," Address before the Independent Bankers Association, St. Paul, 3 September 1938, manuscript, Arnold Papers.

48. Arnold, in an article in the *New York Times Magazine*, presented his position most cogently. "The Antitrust Division is attempting to outline a consistent policy for the use of the tools which Congress has given it. Whether this policy is liked by business or not, it will at least be understood. This is the first step toward a sensible amendment. The other step toward the amendment is to survey the whole problem of various laws, many of them express inconsistent policies and philosophies. The effect of this total mass of legislation, decision and practices must be studied. That is the function of the Temporary National Economic Committee set up by President Roosevelt to study the entire

A more practical consideration that limited his relationship with the TNEC hearings was simply the lack of time. The rapid expansion of the Antitrust Division plus Arnold's numerous speechmaking forays, designed to outline his antitrust views in detail across the country, left few hours for any other enterprise, including TNEC.

Just as Arnold's program was producing dramatic results, he was effectively undermined. Support was withdrawn by the administration for his increased budget requests of 1941 and again in 1942. In three short years the Antitrust Division had been remarkably successful, in fact, too successful perhaps for its own perpetuation. One does not have to ferret the subsurface motives for the administration's severely diminished enthusiasm for the antitrust program. The most crucial and obvious explanation was the war in Europe. As early as 6 July 1940, Arnold was cognizant of the political and economic pressures that would utilize the war as a lever to impede antitrust suits. In a letter to a Scripps-Howard columnist, Arnold succinctly stated his position:

> If some combination is imperative to the interest of national defense, it is a reasonable combination which requires no waiver of the law to get this result, fine. However, I fail to see any possibility of the things we are now prosecuting standing the test.[49]

Arnold concluded his letter by noting that the president was in agreement with this statement.

By the fall of 1940, Arnold was not as sanguine regarding the administration's attitude. It became increasingly clear that attack on monopoly was being given a holiday. Atty. Gen. Francis Biddle made a mild protest over the suspension of the antitrust program in the spring of 1942, which was promptly lost in the noise of creating an arsenal to defend democracy.[50] Arnold, for his part, became quite vocal in pro-

monopoly problem" (*New York Times Magazine*, 21 August 1938, p. 15).

49. Arnold to John T. Flynn, 6 July 1940, Arnold Papers.

50. Francis Biddle to Franklin D. Roosevelt, 20 March 1942, Roosevelt Papers.

test of the relaxation of antitrust enforcement. In the Baxter Memorial Lectures delivered at the University of Omaha in 1942, he presented the case for wartime surveillance of monopoly.[51] Because of cartel tendencies inherent in any national emergency, Arnold argued that antitrust prosecution should be increased not abated.

Three years after the war terminated, Arnold was still bitter about being forsaken by the president. Writing on the subject, "Must 1929 Repeat Itself?" Arnold commented:

> F. D. R. recognizing that he could have only one war at a time, was content to declare a truce in the fight against monopoly. He was to have his foreign war; monopoly was to give him patriotic support—on its own terms.
>
> And so more than 90% of all war contracts went to a handfull of giant empires, many of them formerly linked by strong ties with the corporations of the Reich. The big fellows got the contracts, the little fellows were dependent upon subcontracts with the big boys.[52]

The European combat alone would have resulted in a drastic alteration of the antimonopoly attack. Yet there were other cumulative influences that abetted the war psychosis. Arnold in his attempt at an application of the antitrust laws had made numerous enemies.[53] Subjected to unceasing lobbying, the administration, as well as some congressmen, undoubtedly hoped some morning to find Arnold's program mirac-

51. Published as *Democracy and Free Enterprise* (Norman, 1942).

52. Thurman Arnold, "Must 1929 Repeat Itself?" *Harvard Business Review* 26 (January 1948):43.

53. A vivid protest against Arnold's forays was made by Morris Ernst in a letter to the president: "Thurman Arnold is threatening to start a perfectly absurd proceeding against all of the book publishers and retail book dealers. I am involved professionally but my real concern is with the fact that Thurman's fantastic proceedings are being directed against the sole remaining group in the United States which is concerned with the distribution of the printed word and which still have liberal tendencies. I have talked with Bob Jackson about the matter and I would not bother you about it if I did not think it of real significance at this time. I told Bob that I was going to try to see you. I will be in Washington Tuesday and Wednesday of next week. Is there any possibility of getting in for five minutes?" (Morris L. Ernst to Franklin D. Roosevelt, 7 September 1940, Roosevelt Papers).

ulously transformed into a mirage. Aware of these pressures, Arnold considered the best antidote was the one he had utilized many times before—publicity. But this time publicity was not enough to counteract the opposition.

Disillusioned, Arnold resigned and accepted Roosevelt's appointment as judge of the United States Circuit Court of Appeals. *Business Week*, interviewing Arnold in 1949, asked:

> "Judge Arnold, although you are in private law practice now, your ideas haven't changed a great deal since you were in the Dept. of Justice?" Arnold retorted, "Well, I don't know why they should."[54]

Although Arnold's ideas on antitrust policy may have remained stable, certainly his political beliefs during the 1940s underwent a metamorphosis. In the early 1930s, he bridged the philosophies of Justices Holmes and Brandeis. Arnold agreed with Holmes that economic concentration was not intrinsically a curse; however, he deviated from Holmes's doctrine of the totality of countervailing power. Arnold was not convinced that the public interest was adequately safeguarded by competition of industrial giants. On the other hand, he sympathized with Brandeis as to the desirability of humanizing competition with modifications. He wrote the editor of the *Saturday Evening Post* in 1942:

> When our whole thinking is dominated by a search for security, I believe that we have lost the greatest stimulus to industrial activity that exists, and that is the belief . . . the driving force of a society must be based on the preservation of opportunities to succeed or to fail. I am committed to a politics of opportunity versus a politics of security.[55]

Arnold dissented from the Brandeis opinion that big business was an evil to be destroyed and small business a positive good to be preserved.

By the early 1940s Arnold was beginning to sound like a resurrected western Progressive,[56] the tinge of Wilsonianism

54. "Arnold on Conspiracy," *Business Week* (21 May 1949):76.
55. Thurman Arnold to Benjamin Hibbs, 1 October 1942, Arnold Papers.
56. Arnold never arrived at the place the venerable Progressive

was there, but fading. In an amazing letter to William Allen White, he summed up his philosophy:

> I expect you have little realization of how you have caught the imagination of that peculiar brand of liberal who comes from the Middle West and who believes in the simple philosophy that our institutions are fundamentally sound and, therefore, all we need to do is attack entrenched special privileges. The economic planners are always too complicated for me. They were bound to get in power during a period of frustration when people were afraid to face a world in which they had to take a chance of failure on their own efforts. But now, in spite of all the reactionary influences, I begin to feel a new spirit rising in this country. I believe that men like Henry Kaiser, who I got to know very well in my efforts to prosecute the steel companies for preventing him from getting into production on the Pacific Coast, are going to get strong enough through this war that they cannot be stopped. If they do, liberalism in this country is going to change from faith in Government bureaucracy to the sort of thing that you have represented for so many years.[57]

Whether the shift in Arnold's political philosophy was the result of five years of give-and-take in Washington politics, from the estrangement with the administration regarding

---

partisan, Amos Pinchot, did in 1937. Pinchot in a letter to Harry Elmer Barnes asserted, "I am trying to do what seems to be right. I think the President has enough power for all legitimate purposes already, and I really fear we are in great danger of losing our democratic standing—which has been pretty amateur anyhow during the last few years.

"I don't feel that everything that is labeled 'labor' is necessarily in the interest of labor. Nor that things called 'Progressive' or 'Left' necessarily make for progress.

"Also, I do not believe in collectivism. I do believe in the profit system as a means of increasing production and raising the standard of living. I think we ought to have our natural monopolies all owned by the Government, and I don't see any tendency in the present Administration to fight monopoly or privilege or to go much beyond a very surface kind of reform" (Amos R. E. Pinchot to Harry E. Barnes, 1 April 1937, Harry Elmer Barnes Papers, Western History Research Center).

57. Arnold to William Allen White, 9 September 1943, Arnold Papers. The writer is indebted to Robert O'Neil, Indiana University, for bringing to his attention this significant letter.

antitrust programs, or from the fact that he was forced to assume an increasingly defensive position that terminated in an inflexible stand, it is obvious that the Arnold of 1937 was not the Arnold of 1943. By the time he donned judicial robes, Arnold was in favor of sustaining twentieth-century industrialism, at the same time protesting strongly the loss of economic individualism—a stand that a young Hiram Johnson, of three decades past, would have applauded.

In retrospect, it appears that a folklore surrounding Arnold often obscured his antitrust objectives. What then was Arnold's antitrust ideal? The answer is surprisingly simple: his entire antitrust program was oriented toward the benefit of the consumer. In one sentence he summed up his aim: "The idea of antitrust laws is to create a situation in which competition compels the passing on to the consumers the savings of mass distribution and production."[58] It is mystifying that Arnold's goal should have been so largely ignored by so many commentators.[59] Perhaps its very simplicity confused those who were in search of a more sophisticated or complex motivation. On the first page of *The Bottlenecks of Business*, the purpose of the book was outlined as an exploration of how the consumer could benefit from an equitable distribution of goods. In fact, the whole book was an economic and political platform for the consumer.

The question remains: what was Arnold's motivation in raising the consumer placard? Undoubtedly he was aware of the political advantage of casting the consumer in the role of the forgotten man. Roosevelt most certainly was conscious of the political promise of an antitrust crusade. Yet Arnold was enough of a political pragmatist to know, as well as the president, that the amorphous body of consumers was a ca-

58. "The War on Monopoly," Address before the Oregon Bar Association, Gearhart, Oregon, 29 September 1939, manuscript, Arnold Papers.

59. The newspapers were strangely silent in reporting Arnold's emphasis on the consumer. In the extensive clipping file in the Arnold Papers, a search of thirty notebooks revealed only eight clippings devoted to Arnold's interest in the consumer. The above represents a minor revision of an article that was published in *The Business History Review* 38 (Summer 1964), pp. 214–31.

pricious political force at best, its whims frequently shaped by special interest lobbies. Furthermore, it is difficult to accuse Arnold of courting popularity; the wide-ranging indictments against industry and labor alike belie any attempt to be among the political elect. The only clear rationale is that Arnold was sincerely convinced that proper enforcement of the antitrust laws provided the means for economic and social justice.

The political philosophy of Thurman Arnold had evolved into a composite of moralistic individualism, "politics of opportunity," and economic reform—all good tenets of the western Progressive in pre-World War I America.

Index